JJ Lee is Professor of History at University College Cork, and Visiting Glucksman Professor of Irish Studies at Glucksman Ireland House, New York University, 1999-2000.

Author of the prize-wining *Ireland 1912-1985* (Cambridge, 1990), he co-edited, as Distinguished Visiting Professor of World Peace at the University of Texas at Austin, *Europe in Transition: Political, Economic and Security Problems of the 1990s* (Austin, 1992).

He contributes a weekly column to *The Sunday Tribune*.

GW00715495

The Shifting Balance of Power

Exploring the 20th Century

JJ Lee

edited by Gerard Siggins

Sünday Tribune

The chapters and illustrations contained in this book were
first published in *The Sunday Tribune* in 1999

First published in book form in November 2000
by *The Sunday Tribune,*
15 Lower Baggot Street, Dublin 2, Ireland.
Set in 12 point on 15 Stone serif

ISBN 0-9526035-7-8

Designed, edited & produced by: Gerard Siggins
Copy editors: Dr Gary Murphy and Ciaran J Byrne
Illustrations: Jon Berkeley

Once more:

For my wife, Anne,
and our children,
Amhairgín, Caoilfhionn
and Desmond

Introduction

Exploring the history of the 20th century in a series of brief, sharply focused essays, rather than as a sustained narrative, presents particular challenges for the author. Every essay has to make at least one point. Writing has to be pared to the bone. Densely detailed studies are an indispensable basis of historical writing. These essays draw heavily on them, and I include a selection of them in the list of books for further reading. But this volume concentrates on interpretation, and highly personal interpretation at that, rather than detail.

The format compels pungent formulation of propositions. The sharper a formulation, the more potentially controversial it is likely to be – and the more prone to oversimplification, if not downright error. But as one purpose of historical understanding is, or ought to be, precisely to stimulate us to interrogate our own assumptions, and to foster a capacity for independent thinking, arguments that challenge us should help deepen our understanding, even if we reject them. History is an open-ended dialogue, where even apparently definitively closed questions can be reopened either in the light of new evidence or new perspectives.

The text does not aspire to provide a comprehensive survey of the entire century in its manifold variety of theme and place. Instead, it proffers a succession of pointed probes into the use of public power, especially in the international arena. That inevitably means it concentrates on Europe, Russia/USSR, and the USA, with sidelong glances at relevant power relations elsewhere. Even then the focus is mainly on the international implications of internal change rather than on the changes themselves, however intrinsically interesting these may be. Japan's extraordinary rise, the shift in China from Mao's convulsive communism to Deng's state driven capitalism, India's historic wager on democracy in a sub-continent so pervaded by tensions, to say nothing of the tumultuous changes in the Muslim world, the sufferings and achievements of Latin America, the huge challenges confronting Africa, all deserve substantial treatment in their own right. They may loom much larger for historians of international relations in due course if they come to be seen as laying the foundations for future shifts in world power. But as far as the 20th century is concerned, the biggest shifts in power have been the decline of Britain and Germany, the rise and fall of the USSR, and the rise and rise of the USA. It is on these recorded realities that these essays focus. I have, however, appended a select annual chronology of political events around the world.

There is much to be still revealed about the roles and attitudes of the individual personalities discussed here. Many of the relevant archives remain closed. Memoirs and documentaries do indeed proliferate. They can sometimes enhance understanding. But they can also spread vast amounts of misinformation and disinformation, which our education systems do not normally equip readers and viewers to evaluate. It is ironic that at a time when more people are better educated, or at least longer educated, than ever before, they are ever more vulnerable to the deceptions and distortions on the supply side of the information market.

I am particularly concerned with trying to probe the realities of power behind the rationalisations of rhetoric, remembering of course that words themselves, either in the form of ideological slogans, or on the tongues of master communicators like Roosevelt, Hitler, Churchill, de Gaulle, Kennedy, or Reagan, become power realities in their own right. But the two main lessons I would hope readers will take from this book are simple to state, if exceedingly difficult to apply.

The first is how essential it is to overcome the handicap of hindsight and put ourselves back in the minds of decision makers who lived in their time and not in our time. It sounds so easy, but it is one of the hardest things in the world to put ourselves in the position of people who did not know what was going to happen next. It is easy to list the follies of the past. And it gives current commentators a comfortable sense of feeling superior. But nobody sets out to make a stupid decision. The test for the historian, as distinct from the day tripper in the past, or the demented ideologist obsessed with one point of view, is to understand why what now appears foolish appeared sensible at the time. Future generations will pronounce many of our decisions today foolish, even though of course we wouldn't make them if we thought so. Does that mean they will be wiser than us? Not at all – anymore than we are wiser than our parents or grandparents. Those who denounce us for our infantile follies will in turn make mistakes that subsequent generations will correspondingly castigate- unless they have come to learn to think historically. Overcoming hindsight, placing ourselves back in the minds of people who did not share our assumptions, or know what was coming next, requires a major effort of disciplined imagination. That is why good history is so demanding an intellectual and creative challenge, and why none of us can ever do it perfectly.

The second lesson might be titled 'against inevitability'. Time and again in these pages, it will be seen how so much of what we call inevitable in fact hinged on crucial decisions, which could have gone other ways. There were many futures throughout the century, and not simply the future that has become our present. That is why what has come to be called 'virtual history', more modestly known as 'if' history, has a useful role to play, if done properly, in deepening historical understanding. But it too requires discipline and creativity, or it lapses into mere indulgence in wishful thinking.

The essays are published here almost entirely as originally printed as columns in *The Sunday Tribune* during 1999, apart from the clarification of a few cryptic comments, the correction of such factual mistakes as myself or others have detected, the excision of incidental allusions to passing events, and some internal rearrangement of material. They are presented in what I hope is a coherent sequence, but structured in such a way that they can be pondered individually.

The circumstances of composition mean that I have incurred even more debts than usual in finalising this book. Had Helen Callanan not overcome the reluctance of a contributor with a penchant for the irregular to contribute a regular column to *The Sunday Tribune*, I might never have even contemplated it. There can be few editors anywhere who would have shown Matt Cooper's courage or imagination in devoting centre page space in a Sunday newspaper for so long to so challenging a subject. A succession of harassed staff coped with the vagaries of my delivery – including Maureen Gillespie, Claire Grady, Paddy Murray, Martin Wall, Miriam Donohoe, Bea McMunn and Gerard Siggins, and not forgetting Annette Turley, Gaye Rainsford and Maeve Power, who dealt so helpfully with my phone calls.

Jon Berkeley's magnificent illustrations illuminated the page of the newspaper and are again reproduced here.

Ger Siggins, in addition, has not only preserved good humour through the provocations of the publication process, but by keeping his head with such grace under pressure has made the rough smooth. Suffice it to say that but for him this book would not have appeared.

The more I rely on others, the more I realise how fortunate I am in the administrative and secretarial staff on whom I so heavily depend. Ba liosta le lua those who have saved me time, but in the History Department of UCC Norma Buckley, Margaret Clayton, Veronica Fraser – on whom the pressure of this volume bore particularly heavily – Charlotte Holland, Geraldine MacAllister, and Deirdre O'Sullivan have all coped valiantly with the vagaries of my demands, as have Bernadette Bourke, Cheryl Calhoun, Michael Crumsho, Alexis Grausz, Eileen Jamison, Eliza O'Grady, Patricia King, and Caitlin Quinn at various times in Glucksman Ireland House of New York University, and Orlagh Spring at *The Sunday Tribune*.

Historians in UCC have long come to appreciate how heavily they depend on the dedication and resourcefulness of the staff of the Boole Library in compensating for the long decades of underinvestment, while it has been a pleasure to work in the Bobst Library of NYU.

My wife Anne, and our children, Amhairgín, Caoilfhionn and Desmond, have shown such forebearance in spending so much time in the shadow of my deadlines, with Anne putting me even further in her debt by contributing sage observations on the volume itself, that the book is again dedicated to them as inadequate appreciation of their support.

I, of course, remain solely responsible for all errors.

J J Lee
November 2000

Contents

Maps

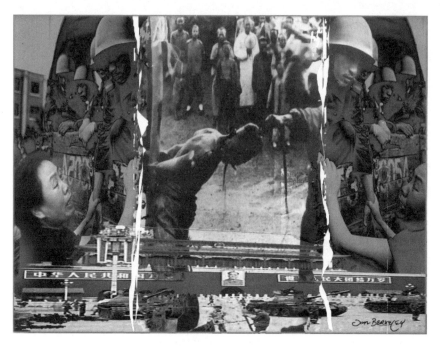

Chapter 1

Century of heavens and hells

People soared into space and were killed in gas chambers in a century of wonders and horrors

AS THE century draws to a close, it is natural for us to want to take stock, to see where we have come from and where we might be going. But it is easier said than done. For how does one begin to characterise the 20th century, the century in which mankind first soared into space and yet plunged deeper into hell than ever before, in this greatest and most terrible of all centuries? How does one apportion responsibility for all these things, good or bad? To what extent are they the result of allegedly inexorable historical forces, like the onward march of science and technology, impelled towards ever expanding new frontiers, or how much is due to the impact of individual thinkers like Keynes, Hayek or Friedman, or media moguls like Walt Disney, Ted Turner or Rupert Murdoch, or political leaders, like Gandhi, Stalin, Hitler, Mao, Thatcher, Gorbachev or Mandela?

However we strike the balance between good and evil, there were vastly' more people on the planet to enjoy or endure the experience. Population grew more quickly than in any previous century, jumping from fewer than two billion people to nearly six billion, an increase which in turn sparked a heated debate about population control, a debate which revealed far more about the ideological values of the protagonists than about likely demographic developments.

The political map of the world this growing population inhabits has itself changed out of recognition during the century. In 1900 that map was coloured red to an extraordinary extent as the British empire, the most extensive the world had ever seen, stretched around the globe, a small state of only 40 million people claiming sovereignty over an empire of 500 million or more, a truly astonishing imperial achievement.

What was left over from the British empire was largely controlled by other European empires, whether overseas, like the French, Dutch, Belgian, German, Italian, Portuguese and Spanish – what was left after the US had relieved it of Cuba and the Philippines in 1898 – or in Europe itself, mainly by Habsburg Austria, Romanov Russia and Ottoman Turkey.

Even nominally independent states could only rarely escape the pressure of informal empire, which stretched far beyond the formal frontiers of imperial supremacy. When the Boxer revolt broke out in China in 1900, the rebels would find themselves rapidly crushed by a consortium of powers, with Britain in the lead, and China put firmly in her inferior place by her strutting superiors. How ironic that the century should end with the boot on the other foot, the pageantry of the withdrawal ceremony from Hong Kong notwithstanding, Britain by that stage having had opportunity to acquire unrivalled experience in the conduct of such ceremonies.

Her experience had begun when Michael Collins took possession of

Dublin Castle in January 1922. We should not of course exaggerate Ireland's role in the events of the century. But neither should we seek to diminish it in a desperate rearguard action to sustain an inferiority complex. That was a symbolic moment in the history not only of the country, but of the century. Ireland had long been a fly in the imperial ointment, the natives having so ungraciously resisted all efforts to raise them, by threat or blandishment, to near imperial level. They could be allowed hive as many of themselves off as it was proving too much of a nuisance to control any longer, to slink off into their bogs, now deprived of the solicitous tutelage of their betters.

But the transfer of Dublin Castle, for all its symbolic significance, still marked only a stage in the education of the imperialist psyche. For there could still be no nonsense about a republic. That would be an intolerable insult to imperial *amour-propre*. Civilisation must be defended by metaphysical monarchists salivating over their ultimate superiority by forcing the oath of fidelity to their king down the throats of the repulsive rebels – at least until Mr de Valera would discover he could swill it around in his mouth and spit it out again without it ever defiling his lips.

But Ireland in 1922 seemed a solitary, if spectacular, exception to normalcy. Trust the Paddies to be contrary. It was still only 25 years since the lesser breeds had flocked to London to pay homage to the Great White Queen, as Victoria's diamond jubilee was celebrated with all the pomp and pride that befitted an empire that girdled the globe.

In 1922, that empire seemed even more in the ascendant, now stuffed with the pickings of German possessions in Africa, Britain having seen off the threat from that quarter in the First World War. She had paid a price for victory in the blood bath of the trenches, but much less than her other two main potential European rivals, France and Russia, which suffered far heavier casualties. To the naked eye, Britain still seemed assured of a resplendent imperial future. General Dyer's timely volleys at Amritsar in 1919, for which a grateful nation would duly reward him, having reminded uppity natives that she knew how to keep them in their place.

In the event, what began as a British century ended as an American one. The shift of power across the Atlantic marks the end not just of the 19th century world, but of the dominant fact of world history for four centuries, European hegemony. That hegemony has now passed to the US. However inevitable it has come to seem in retrospect, many would argue that Europe effectively abdicated by pursuing internecine conflict instead of seeking to unite. For that matter, how many now remember fearing – or hoping – that Khrushchev might be right when he boasted, 40 years ago, that "we will bury you"?

The big question now is whether the new century will continue to be 'the American century'. And if not, whose? Will America decline – or has the cycle of the rise and fall of great powers now come to an end? Or will some form of global government evolve to correspond to the alleged globalisation of everyday life?

One lesson one can draw from looking at the world in 1900, and reviewing the predictions of the time, is that only a fool could be dogmatic about even short term predictions, much less long term ones. Just think of our own case.

Any soothsayer who ventured to predict as late as 1912 the events of the next decade along the lines of what actually happened would have, quite rightly, been deemed fit material for the asylum for the insane. No exercise in 'virtual history' that projected the history of the 10 years from 1912 to 1922 in Ireland as they actually happened, instead of the way contemporaries in 1912 expected them to happen, could have envisaged such an improbable succession of scenarios as real life actually delivered.

There are of course always those who purport to discern the inevitable direction of history. The Soviet experiment, like the Nazi one, turned out to be a monstrous charade based on that proposition. The collapse of the Soviet regime has, ironically, spawned exactly the same type of thinking, but in the opposite direction, about the inevitable triumph of democracy, or liberalism, or pluralism, with the comforting corollary that the good life is here to stay. The good life is defined highly subjectively, for the manipulation of language has become, as Orwell correctly observed, a frightening trademark of our century, and not least in the struggle for 'human rights'. This is so malleable a concept that it can mean the exact opposite to its various champions, most obviously on the issue of abortion.

This is not to deny that certain trends can be discerned in human affairs, particularly now in science and technology. Medical advances have enormous implications not only for our individual physical wellbeing, but for the organisation of society. Increased life expectancy changed concepts of the role of the elderly in society. The contraceptive pill has transformed thinking about relations between men and women, and about the place of children in society.

Research on genetics, now surging ahead, is likely to tell us much more about ourselves, whether we like it or not. It can be no coincidence that Harvard has announced a massive new research centre on what *The New York Times* calls "the sizzling field of genes and how they work," and that Princeton has announced the appointment of the first director of its Institute of Genomic Analysis.

How far the lessons of this 20th century equip us to cope with the implications of the discoveries to come, no less than with political developments, remains to be seen. Although it will be impossible to deal with all these factors in detail within the confines of this volume, we will try to keep them in mind in striking our own balance in the course of this series of reflections on the extraordinary experience of mankind during this century, so full of wonders and horrors, of triumphs and tragedies.

Chapter 2

Cancer at the heart of civilisation

Racist superiority has been central to the development of the West's power structure

TO FULLY understand the world of a century ago, we have to grasp just how deeply western civilisation was anchored in the assumption of the superiority of the white race over all other races. Of course not every European, American or Australian was a full throated racist, but racism was central to the western power structure. There could be variations on the theme among Europeans themselves. Germans looked down on Slavs, northern Europeans tended to look down on swarthier southern

Europeans. The British tended to look down on everybody. These stereotypes weren't necessarily all vicious. But they paved the way for more sinister ones.

Anti-semitism was widespread throughout Europe and America. The rehabilitation of Captain Dreyfus in 1906, 12 years after he fell victim to charges of treachery fuelled by anti-semitic impulses, rectified an individual injustice, but did little to diminish the scale of anti-semitism, at either elite or popular level. One reason why Hitler's anti-semitism originally attracted little particular attention in other European countries was precisely because it belonged to the mainstream of western civilisation.

The German case was by no means the most extreme. If one were to have predicted in 1900 where anti-semitism was likely to become most active, Germany would have ranked behind France, Austria, Poland and Russia. It was not until the murders and burnings on Kristallnacht, 9 November 1938, that the intensity of Nazi anti-semitism began to attract particular attention among the bulk of foreign observers. Even then they were quite clear that this was not sufficient cause for taking any serious anti-German measures.

The full horror of Auschwitz would not become publicly known until 1945. It came as a godsend to many a fighter 'against fascism', who had gone to war simply to defend his country, and whose only complaint about Hitler was not that he was racist, but that he was anti-British or anti-French. Many Americans were of course genuinely revolted by the evidence of the concentration camps. But many Americans too, above all whites from the South, could hardly credibly claim they were fighting to make the world safe for racial equality.

America went to 'fight fascism' in December 1941, after nearly two-and-a-half years of neutrality, not to deliver the world from racism, but simply because Hitler had given her no choice by declaring war on her. As well as genuinely sickening large numbers, the concentration camps allowed even the most dyed-in-the-wool racists of the Deep South to conveniently posture as defenders of democracy and decency, before returning to continue untroubled with their own form of racial discrimination – fully legally, for the Supreme Court decision of 1896 that sanctioned the euphemism of 'separate but equal' racial relations, wouldn't be reversed until 1958, and then only after some blacks had shown they could no longer be herded into corrals of the white man's design.

Ireland – Catholic or Protestant, nationalist or unionist – was not immune to anti-semitism either, even if its expression was relatively muted here. But for all the exhortation of our intellectuals – genuine and fake – for us to abandon our axiomatic insularity and become 'European', as elusive a concept then as now, we were sufficiently part of the main-stream of European civilisation to have already sipped, if not drunk deep, from this poisoned spring.

If racism could flourish within the West, it was no wonder it reached its full flowering in dealings with non-Europeans. For the very essence of overseas empire was racism, the right of the stronger races to conquer and control the weaker, and crush them if they dared revolt, by right of God-given racial superiority.

Or if not God-given, at least nature-given. For the principles of Social Darwinism, the Darwinian 'survival of the fittest', translated into human relations, served to justify any measures necessary to impose imperialist power on weaker peoples. Those fastidious souls, never very numerous, who imagined that empire was really the white man's burden rather than the black man's, succeeded in persuading themselves that empire was simply a temporary responsibility which they held in sacred trust until such time as the natives would be fit to be entrusted to their own care. But even those who thought in those terms tended to see their mission as a very long term programme indeed. Empire was often visualised as a thou-sand-year project. It was no coincidence that Hitler would speak of a thou-sand-year Reich, or that Churchill would bring his second most famous peroration, "if the British Empire and its Commonwealth last for a thou-sand years, men will still say 'this was their finest hour'". He was right about the hour – but wrong about the years.

Neither was it coincidence that the Social Darwinism, so fashionable among imperialists, should have found its most elaborate expression in Hitler's *Mein Kampf* in 1925, where the argument about a hierarchy of races, and about how it is a law of nature that the strong kill the weak, is drawn directly from animal analogy. As Britain had vetoed an attempt by China and Japan to include a denunciation of racism among the principles of the League of Nations established with such fanfare in 1920, it was scarcely in a position to protest against the eager endorsement of the principle by the greatest racist of them all.

There was a cruel irony in Japan picking up the banner of anti-racism, given her behaviour towards China in the 1930s in the horrific treatment of Shanghai, and in the 'Rape of Nanking'. But it is revealing of western concepts of racism that scarcely a thought has been spared for the Asian victims of Japanese racism, compared with the cruelties inflicted on white prisoners of war which, for all their brutality, claimed a far smaller number of victims. Only now are Asian sufferings beginning to penetrate western consciousness. Just as, indeed, full realisation of the racist horrors perpetrated on American Indians has only recently begun to penetrate the aura of glamour in which Hollywood shrouded one of the most callous and cynical campaigns in recorded history.

Yet Japan's contribution to changing the course of world history has been an extraordinary one, at whatever price to her victims and herself. For it was Japan's victory over Russia in 1905 which sounded the shot heard around the colonial world, the victory of little yellow chaps who scarcely counted as human beings at all in racist western eyes. True, the Ethiopians had inflicted a severe defeat on the Italians at Adowa in 1896. But for old imperialist hands the Italians scarcely counted as more than honorary whites, Africa being assumed to begin south of Rome. Even the Russian defeats could be shrugged off by really superior breeds further west. The Russians were not quite the full European shilling, Asia beginning somewhere after Moscow, if not before.

But that did not diminish the symbolic significance of the Japanese victory. And symbolism was crucial to empire. Indeed much of empire revolved around the symbolism of supremacy. That was where the psychic income, so important for imperial peoples, derived from. Most imperial powers did not gain greatly in physical terms from their possessions. Their economies did not depend on their empires, contrary to popular impression. But the psychic gain was immense for the hordes who seemed to need a sense of superiority over others to feel satisfied with their own identity. And this went – and goes – well beyond certifiable control freaks, or thugs or bullies of blatant vintage. It was no accident, but fully consistent with this psychology, that Lloyd George would threaten to resume conflict in Ireland in 1921 if the Sinn Féin negotiators on the Treaty, and the Dáil, would not accept the oath of fidelity to the King.

It was further Japanese hammer blows, this time to the greatest imperial power of them all, the British, above all at Singapore in 1942, where General Percival's white flag symbolised the end of an epoch, that ensured the second world war, in contrast to the first, would not be followed by even more imperialist expansion. However belligerently Churchill might rage that he had not become prime minister to preside over the liquidation of the British Empire, within a few years of his 'thousand years' tribute he had to watch the ritual of retreat gather irresistible pace.

Empire was based ultimately on command of superior power, both physical and psychological. When empire could no longer sustain that power after 1945, its days were numbered. But that had by no means been predictable in 1900. Indeed, one of the great ambitions of some imperialists was to convince the conquered that they were inferior, and that their only hope was to be recreated, however slowly, in the image of their immortal imperial makers. That struggle for the minds of millions has been a key to the unfolding of the 20th century.

Chapter 3

Could the empire have struck back?

Imperialism is dead; long live nationalism.
But this wasn't an inevitability

THE 20th century began as the century of imperialism. It ended as the century of nationalism. This has probably been the greatest historical transformation in terms of the sense of identity of the majority of human beings during the century. How and why did it happen?

Any number of commentators have been busy pronouncing the death of nationalism. And maybe a century hence nationalism will have gone the way of imperialism, perhaps to be succeeded by some form of global political institutions. Who knows? But the decline of the European empires was far from predictable in 1900. It might even be argued that the type of imperialism that had the world at its feet, sometimes literally, was itself simply the most extreme form of aggressive nationalism, and that therefore all that has happened is that a generally less imperialistic form of nationalism has superseded another.

There would be some truth in this claim. World history is, of course, littered with empires that owed nothing to overarching nationalist ambitions. The lust to control, to rule, to strut, to dominate, to humiliate, to feel the flesh beneath the heel, or the stiletto, is an integral part of human nature, normally curbed only by fear of retaliation. Few like to admit, at least in more recent times, to such motives or instincts, or may even believe themselves impelled by other, more benign, motives, of the white man's burden vintage. But a huge part of the psychic income of empire derives from savouring the sense of superiority.

By 1900, however, the imperialism of the main European overseas empires, the British and the French, dynastically driven though they had once been, now derived popular support from distinctly nationalist sentiment. Of course not everyone supported imperialist expansion, not even all nationalists. The Gladstonian-style nationalism that cherished nationality as the right to be different, and as the source of distinctive contribution to a transnational world civilisation, still enjoyed strong support – but not strong enough to resist the more elemental impulses of conquest, now largely based on a sense of racial superiority, and on the right of the stronger to rule the weaker. Even moderate imperialists, like Sir Edward Grey, British Foreign Secretary in 1914, bearer of one of the proudest Liberal names in England, assumed that Britain would, in due course, turn to swallowing the weaker European empires. He assumed that would start with the Portuguese, to be repaid for its loyalty as England's oldest ally by being relieved of the burden of its empire.

One of the tricks of the imperialist spindoctors was to deny that English nationalism was nationalism at all. Nationalism was the disease that affected lesser breeds. England was above all that. This enabled it to pretend that nationalist demands in the colonies for equality of treatment with English nationalism were irrational and unjustifiable, because there was no such thing. The same capacity for self-deception lingers on among those English nationalist propagandists who react with horror to Scottish nationalism today, on the grounds that it will provoke the emergence of an English nationalism – as if what Scottish nationalists resent is not already that sense of the overweening arrogance that constitutes the core of English nationalism.

In retrospect, the imperialist assumption that the 'natives' could be induced to desire permanent incorporation into the empire appears a forlorn hope. Nevertheless, and however much later generations may scoff at the possibility, it came very close to fruition. But for the world wars it might well have achieved success, at least for a much longer period. There was nothing inevitable about either the decline of empire, or about the timing, pace and extent of it. And but for the emergence of a number of remarkable national leaders – or leaders who chose nationalism over rival ideologies – it might not have happened at all.

For nationalism is the great creative ideology of the century. By creative I do not mean that it does not, or cannot, have destructive consequences. It can and does. And it can spill over into other ideologies, from imperialism to fascism to racism, in which the lust for control over other human beings is central. But none of these ideologies is the inevitable consequence of nationalism. Most nationalisms have initially emerged in resistance to imperialist nationalism, even if there is often a danger of them succumbing to the same temptations themselves.

There is no guarantee that nationalism will triumph over imperialism or even racism. Given that the European empires, so apparently invincible a century ago, have collapsed, and that Hitler lost, we have come to assume the inevitability of these outcomes. But collaboration with the conquerors was a widespread reaction everywhere, partly from fear, partly from calculation. Appropriate ideologies of collaboration could be devised for those who took this path. The psychology of collaboration, from 'Castle Catholic' to Indian Prince, from Nazi to Soviet collaborator, is a fascinating subject. It is a far more widespread human reaction to superior force than resistance. And conquerors can be adept at using carrot as well as stick, seduction as well as terror.

The classic case was India. If Britain was incomparably the greatest imperial power, India was incomparably the brightest star in the imperial crown, with more than three quarters of the entire population of the empire. In the Indian case, the appearance of Gandhi on the scene added an almost extraterrestrial dimension to the mobilisation of minds and bodies. For Gandhi must surely have strong claims to be considered the most extraordinary personality to appear – almost as an apparition – on the public stage of the entire century, even if it be true that the majority in the West, perhaps even in India, reject his vision today. The gospel of self-denial can have little appeal in the age of Narcissus.

It is true, of course, that non-violence is a fashionable doctrine, exhortations to that effect tripping constantly off the tongues of our leaders – or rather of the leaders whose countries or causes have already got what they want, often by violence, and now hope to enjoy the fruits of their victories by denying to others the means by which they ascended the ladder. But even if their appeals owe nothing to Gandhian inspiration, and few are genuine pacifists, that does not diminish his fascination. He will certainly have to feature on our final short list of people of the century.

When Gandhi began his first great campaign in India in 1917, he was not of course operating in a vacuum. He was addressing an India already roused by World War I. Nearly 1.5 million Indians were recruited for the glory of killing and dying for their Emperor-King. As Lord Birkenhead, the Secretary of State for India, put it coyly, but with a rough honesty, when unveiling the war memorial to the Indian dead at Neuve Chapelle in 1927, "It would be an insincerity to pretend that ... the objects with which this war was waged could have been known ... to the majority of the Indian army. Many a humble soldier, one suspects, must have thought of his far-away village, sun-swept, unmenaced, and wondered what inscrutable purpose of whatever deity he worshipped had projected him into this sinister and bloody maelstrom."

But Indians were not so stupid that they could not do some thinking for themselves, and deduce that it was no Indian deity that had so designated them as cannon fodder, but their imperial masters. England could not have ruled India without the acquiescence, and frequently the support, of Indian opinion. That opinion had greeted the war enthusiastically. But as it dragged on, minds began to think again. England began to be hooked, as closer to home, on the petard of its own rhetoric.

Birkenhead might claim the Indian soldier could not understand the objectives for which he killed and died. But there were Indians who began to ask if this was a war for the freedom of small nations, why shouldn't India count as a small nation for this purpose? Some even took to wondering how the wanton slaughter testified to the oft proclaimed superiority of western civilisation over 'backward' peoples like themselves.

Without entering here into the intricacies of internal Indian politics, suffice it to say that the fragmented Congress party underwent a transformation in 1915 and 1916, and that even Hindus and Muslims reached agreement on a more ambitious home rule programme.

Although India was certainly not ripe for rebellion, it was sufficiently agitated for Gandhi to sense the time was ripe to launch his first *satyagraha* campaign, or non-violent resistance to injustice. Initially directed less against imperial institutions than against the land system, it soon spilled over into anti-imperialism. It would still take until 1947, after another world war, before India achieved independence, reflecting the resilience of imperial power even in the face of growing pressure.

In the meantime, it will be clear that Ireland wasn't the only country under foreign rule where World War I shifted the trajectory of historical development. If this happened in the course of a war which Britain won, what might have happened if Britain lost? The results if the Germans had won – which appeared quite possible until the entry of America, or even the failure of the Ludendorff offensive in 1918 – are incalculable. Indeed, we often forget that Germany did win on the eastern front, and the result was the Russian Revolution. But why didn't Germany win the war in the west, and turn the history of the 20th century upside down?

Chapter 4

The big 'if' of the First World War

One of the huge ifs of history is 'what if Germany's Schlieffen Plan had worked?'

THE Great War, as the First World War was known until the next round 20 years later obliged a rechristening, remains in many respects the most frightening exhibition of mass slaughter in history. The horrors of the Second World War could be explained by invoking the sheer evil of 'war criminals', who could not be comprehended within the criteria of normal humanity, and whose behaviour allegedly justified retaliatory measures of mass impersonal extermination from the air.

There were of course attempts, especially in Britain, to portray the Kaiser as the incarnation of evil, the 'cause' of the war. But no serious student thinks in these primitive terms. And that is the frightening thing in a way. Had the multiple horrors of the war been the result of evil, they could be rationalised. It is because the belligerents did not scale the peaks of evil, but were normal representatives of the human race, that the war still stands as a warning of the potential for destruction in the heart of man.

One might well wonder how any civilisation, much less one that preened itself on having surpassed all previous civilisations, could have arranged its affairs in such a way as to cause so much suffering and death, leaving millions of widows, orphans and maimed, in addition to the millions of combatants killed, dwarfing the numbers of any earlier war.

The saving grace for the human race is that nobody planned it that way. Had the generals and politicians – and what about all those laughing faces in the trains in August 1914 taking the soldiers towards the front, as if they were daytrippers to a sporting event – known what they were doing, they would indeed be guilty men. Stupidity, or at least myopia, is the justification for the sustained mass slaughter.

Nor, it can reasonably be claimed, that it was even stupidity, at least on the German side, at the start. One of the huge ifs of history is what if the Schlieffen Plan, the German plan to win a war if one broke out, had worked. This is by no means an unhistorical hypothesis, because it came so close to working. Schlieffen himself was now dead, and his successors tinkered with the Plan in a way that arguably reduced its prospects of succeeding. And yet, it came very close to doing so in August 1914.

The Plan was the German solution to the problem of how to fight a two front war against a combined enemy of France and Russia, with vastly superior potential resources, by taking the risk of committing virtually all one's troops to the Western Front, in the hope of a quick and decisive kill in sufficient time to then scurry across to the other frontier and destroy the Russians before they had done too much damage to Germany. Speed was the essence of the whole thing. If one got held up in the West, then one was trapped into a two front war, which even the most optimistic German planner regarded with immense foreboding.

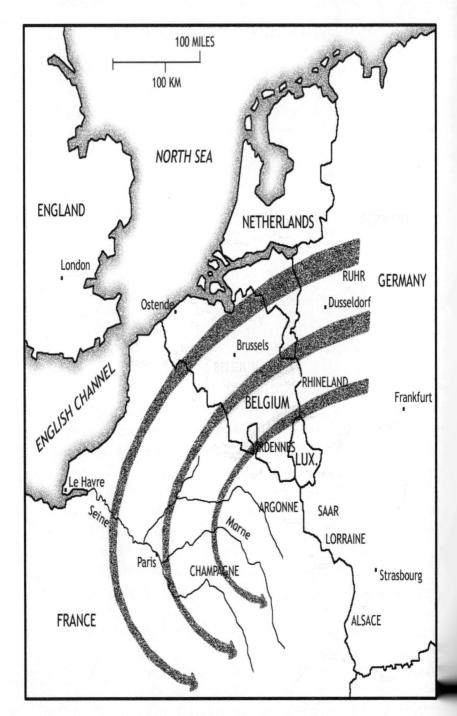

Map 1 The original Schlieffen Plan

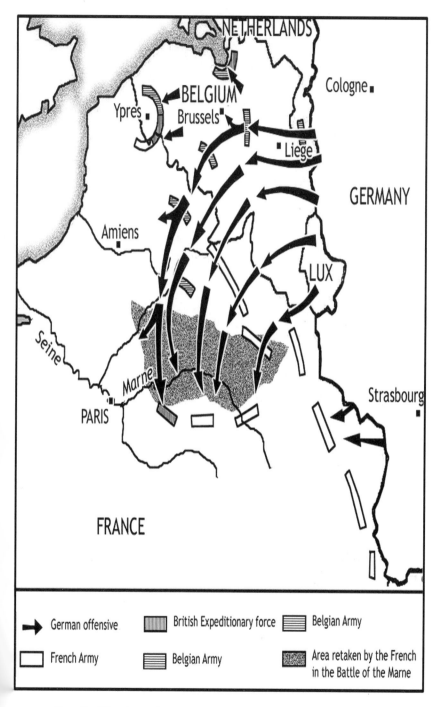

NETHERLANDS

Cologne

BELGIUM

Ypres

Brussels

Liège

GERMANY

Amiens

LUX

Seine

Marne

Strasbourg

PARIS

FRANCE

→ German offensive	
British Expeditionary force	
Belgian Army	
French Army	
Belgian Army	
Area retaken by the French in the Battle of the Marne	

Map 2   The Actual Western Front, August - September 1914

Despite the tinkering with the Plan, the Germans still got to within 40 miles of Paris in a month until they were stopped by 'the miracle of the Marne'. If it required a miracle to stop it, this is hardly much of a tribute to the quality of those French decision makers, civilian and military, who were so enthusiastic for war a month earlier.

This wasn't the only time the Germans might have achieved massive military victory in the west. As late as Ludendorff's offensive in March 1918 they came so close to a breakthrough that Pétain, the incarnation of French resistance at Verdun in 1916, was nearly tempted to fall back on Paris.

By that stage substantial numbers of American troops had begun to arrive in France, a year after America entered the war in April 1917 in response to unrestricted German submarine warfare, after President Woodrow Wilson had won re-election in 1916 partly on a platform of keeping America out of the war. Although America would withdraw from European political affairs after the war until Hitler's declaration of war on her in December 1941 once again brought her out of her neutrality, the entry of America onto the European stage marked a moment of immense symbolical as well as practical significance in the beginning of the dwarfing of Europe that was to constitute one of the central themes of 20th century history.

But that lay far in the future in September 1914, when everything seemed to hinge on whether the German advance could be stopped in the west. And even though it was, the advance still determined in large measure the location of the war. For the war in the west was fought in France and Belgium until the very end, thanks to the momentum of even the failed Schlieffen Plan. What if it had succeeded?

'If' history by definition envelops us in conjecture. But as virtually every statement we make about the importance of anything in life is based on assumptions about alternatives, we are doomed to live in an 'if' world. All that thinking out loud does is to force us to articulate our own silent assumptions. Above all it obliges us to recognise that the alternative to the mess that actually happened is not likely to be some idyllic scenario, with all living happily ever after, but usually an alternative mess.

As a good deal of this book depends on assumptions about alternatives, it is as well for us to be clear about how dominated we can be by silent assumptions from the outset. Just think of the assumptions inherent in judgements about the course of Irish history. If only the Spaniards had landed in Ulster instead of in Kinsale, or the Irish hadn't blundered fatally at Kinsale itself, if the French had landed at Bantry Bay in 1796, if the 1798 rebellion had never happened, or if only it had succeeded, if the Act of Union of 1800 hadn't happened, or had succeeded, or if the Parnell Split hadn't happened, or if Home Rule had been implemented in 1914, or if the UVF bluff – but was it bluff? – had been called in 1914, or if the Easter Rising hadn't occurred, or if Michael Collins hadn't signed the Treaty in 1921, or if de Valera had accepted it, or if we had gone to war in 1939, or whenever Britain chose to go to war, or if Sunningdale hadn't failed, etc, etc.

All our judgements on these matters are inevitably based on 'if' history. The question is how intelligently we think in those terms. Can we control the temptation to find a happy ending?

Had the Schlieffen Plan worked in the sense of driving France out of the war, allowing the Germans to turn their full forces on Russia, the odds are that several million of the lives lost in the following four years would have been saved. But at what price? Probably substantial German annexations in the west, and even more substantial in the east. Who knows what would have happened after that?

Would Tsarism have collapsed in Russia, to be followed by a liberal regime, but with no Bolshevik Revolution, if only because the Germans wouldn't allow it? Would Hitler have ever emerged in Germany, or Stalin in Russia? In a benign scenario, no Auschwitz, no gulag?

Would Britain have remained in the war without any continental ally? Would Germany have sought a *modus vivendi* with Britain, or sought instead to pursue world power through an accelerated naval race, leading to global conflict, with America then deciding to become involved? What would have happened the French and British empires, once the spell of invincibility, which allowed so few to rule so many, had been broken? Would the Germans have insisted on Irish independence as part of any peace deal – not out of any love of Ireland, but to weaken Britain? And would Britain have accepted, given that the Germans did not have the naval power to invade herself at that time? How rapidly would air power, and other technologies have developed in the event of continuing hostilities?

Would the German military, drunk with victory, have sought to restrict the growth of parliamentary power in Germany by instituting a more militaristic regime in Germany itself, out of fear of the growth of the socialists – who had become the biggest single party before the war, and whose rise was feared by the generals – as much as the perceived threat from Russian military expansion? For that matter, why should a parliamentary German regime be any more peace-loving than any other imperialist parliamentary powers?

Some of these scenarios are more improbable than others. But none is impossible. I sketch them to jolt us into remembering how much can hang on the turn of military events. Historians devote far too little attention to military affairs, tending to take the outcome of wars as inevitable, and skipping from the causes to the consequences, as if the in-between can be taken for granted. If there is any war for which that was not the case it is the First World War, at least before American entry – and even that was too late to save the Tsarist regime in Russia.

It is this combination of American entry and the Bolshevik Revolution that make 1917 so important a year in the history of the century.

Chapter 5

The USA enters the war

*America ignores the warning of George Washington's
Farewell Address and becomes embroiled in war*

P ROPHETIC 19th century voices anticipated that the central
theme of 20th century history would be the struggle for
world supremacy between the two peripheral powers, the
USA and Russia. For much of the century they would be
proved right. But the route to that rivalry turned out to be
more twisted than anyone could have anticipated.

The prediction was not itself a particularly startling one. By 1900

Russia had by far the biggest population – and the most rapidly growing – of any of the five major European powers. She had over 120 million people, compared with about half that for Germany, and about a third for Britain, France and Austria-Hungary. Her army was more than double the size of Germany's. Of course we know that she collapsed in the War, and with the eternal wisdom of hindsight we wonder why contemporaries didn't have perfect foresight. Contemporaries were no more lacking in foresight in their circumstances than we are in ours. And yet, despite her defeat by the Japanese in 1904-1905, her First World War collapse astounded nearly everyone.

If the Russians themselves could have anticipated it, they would hardly have forced the pace in July 1914. It was their mobilisation in support of Serbia that turned the local Balkan row between Austria and Serbia into a potential European conflict. And if the Germans hadn't been frightened that time was on Russia's side, so that by 1917 her massive army expansion would dwarf the size of German forces, they wouldn't have been so anxious to make what they saw as a pre-emptive strike. The psychological instability caused by Russia as the great incalculable was a central factor in the assumptions behind the decision that led to the outbreak of war in 1914.

This fear of Russia now seems ludicrous. But it wasn't stupid. In the event it was not so much the Russian army that failed the country, as the Tsarist regime that failed the army. When the soldiers refused to fight any longer in 1917, they were passing a vote of no confidence in a regime that had failed to keep them supplied with food and ammunition. There was incompetence on the military front, but it was as nothing to the incompetence on the home front. But who could have foreseen that, given that so few foresaw how the war would drag on, and become a war of economic organisation and attrition?

And who could have foreseen that Tsar Nicholas II would prove so utterly incompetent at the top of the whole rotten pile? True, nobody thought of Nicholas as the finest brain in the world, but it beggared imagination that he could prove himself so unfit for government during the war itself. It is a sad irony that the Russians, potentially so great a people, should have finished the century as they began it, falling so far below their potential, playing burlesque to the baton of a buffoon.

It would all seem so different across the Atlantic, with one of America's most dominant presidents, Woodrow Wilson, presiding over national affairs since his election on the Democratic ticket in 1912. True, he had failed to reform Princeton to his liking as president of the famous university, but running a country was a simple matter compared with running a university.

Wilson was determined to keep America out of the war in 1914, seeing little moral difference between the belligerents. Rapidly though America was growing – her population of 76 million in 1900 would reach 100 million by 1920 – she was intent on keeping herself to herself, or at least out of Europe. She still clung to the parting wisdom of George Washington's Farewell Address, warning against the danger of entangling alliances with the old European powers.

The First World War – or what turned into the First World War, contrary to anyone's intentions – began as an old fashioned power struggle. Nothing much was needed to justify it to the traditional constituencies, any more than in numerous previous wars. But the traditional constituencies were shrinking. There was now something approaching mass literacy. Having been taught to read, but often not to think, the masses were perfect cannon fodder for the new mass popular press. Because of Britain's peculiar position – not directly threatened by invasion like the rest of the European powers – and with the cabinet split, it was necessary for the war party to incite opinion by appeals for gallant little Belgium, suitably garnished by stories of German atrocities, etc.

The propaganda was brilliantly orchestrated. The imperial power with the biggest single number of subjects under its control proclaimed itself with marvellous insouciance to be fighting for the freedom of small nations. The age of chivalry was magically restored. It was so much simpler to present the war as a crusade for civilisation against the Boche/Hun savages than in terms of simple national interest. The German ruling elite, too, uncertain of the loyalty of the German working class, supposedly indoctrinated against war by socialist doctrine, presented the war as a response to a barbaric Russian threat, to rouse workers to defend the socially progressive Fatherland, with the most advanced welfare state in the world, against the savage hordes from the east.

Nevertheless, a degree of saving scepticism about their own propaganda persisted among more professional players of the power game. The more conventional concept of great power conflict as simply a power struggle left them aware of the danger of stoking passion among publics prone to demonise the enemy.

America's entry in April 1917 shifted the perspective decisively. American public opinion only very slowly allowed itself to be persuaded of the need to enter. How could one be a city on a hill if one descended into the European sewer? But America was not unfamiliar with *realpolitik*, having increasingly flexed her muscles in shouldering British aspirations aside in Venezuela and Panama, as well as capturing Cuba and the Philippines from Spain. Isolationism was not to be confused with pacifism.

Nevertheless, involvement in Europe was different. Public opinion had therefore to be given a compelling reason for abandoning the inherited doctrine. This was so imprinted on their psyches that Woodrow Wilson was re-elected in 1916 as 'the man who kept us out of the war'. Although America was supplying Britain with essential resources, making a handsome profit on the trade, it seems doubtful that she could have entered the war as early as April 1917 but for the blunder of Ludendorff, now virtual dictator of Germany, in launching unrestricted submarine warfare in early 1917. The effort to starve Britain out of the war, which inevitably led to the sinking of American ships, provoked the American declaration of war.

Americans were entitled to be outraged by German action. But once committed, they were psychologically compelled to fight the war as a crusade, partly to overcome the continuing reluctance, partly because the only justification for reneging on the moral foreign policy of a century and more was in the cause of an even higher morality. War now became the pursuit of morality by other means. The high moral ground was the first territory to be captured.

The self-righteousness of public opinion went into overdrive, anticipating its treatment of Japanese-Americans after Pearl Harbour in 1941, for which the government is only belatedly apologising, by a vicious campaign against German-Americans. More immigrants had come to the USA from Germany than from any other country, more even than from Ireland. They had proved good citizens. Now they were subjected to widespread harassment. The assault on their language induced many to switch fully to English, closing down their own schools and newspapers, striving to be more American than the Americans themselves. It was very far from being America's finest hour, a frightening portent of how innocents could become victimised when nationalist passions were unleashed in the service of a sense of moral righteousness.

Wilson himself, and his entourage, began to use phrases that, even when well intentioned, became hostages to fickle fortune. This was to be the war to end all wars, with peace to be ensured by a League of Nations that would resolve disputes by moral criteria. The war would make the world safe for democracy and for self-determination. Wilson's 14 points, proclaimed in January 1918, amounting to a renunciation of the entire old style of European diplomacy, were intended to assert American moral superiority over friend as well as foe in Europe. America would still be sole custodian of the city on a hill. Wilson would soon find out how cold the winds could be up there when he sought to fashion in the Treaty of Versailles the peace to end all wars.

But this lay shrouded in the future in December 1918, as Wilson descended on Paris to a rapturous public reception, garbed in the mantle of righteousness, to preside over the founding of a new heaven on a new earth, the world at his feet. It would not be long before the ground shifted beneath him. America's first venture onto the world stage, so apparently pregnant with possibilities for a new world order of perpetual peace, would end in disaster for Wilson. There would be a terrible price to pay.

Chapter 6

Wilson's new world order

Was it only a question of finding out which way the new era would collapse after the Great War?

WE SO take it for granted nowadays that American Presidents will trundle through Europe regularly that it is hard to recapture the sense of expectation that surrounded Woodrow Wilson's arrival in Paris in December 1918. Was he not, after all, the first American president to have ever visited Europe while in office? Would not the representative of the last, best hope of mankind now inaugurate the era of perpetual peace? Had not his 14 points for a new international order lifted the eyes of millions sunk in the slime of war to the bright uplands beyond. Had not the new world truly come into existence to redress the balance of the old?

Whether Versailles could have bestowed the elixir of eternal peace, or whether it was doomed in any event, and it was only a question of finding out which way it would collapse, must remain one of the great 'ifs' of history. There is no difficulty cataloguing the blunders, or apparent blunders, in retrospect. Was not Germany left seething for vengeance, economically wrecked by a monstrous level of reparations, leading inexorably to the rise of Hitler? Nor was this even the wisdom of hindsight. Did not the most luminous mind in England, the economist John Maynard Keynes, rail against the inanity of the reparations clauses at the time, in his celebrated book, *The Economic Consequences of the Peace?*

How could one expect an enduring settlement when the two most potentially powerful European states, Germany and Russia, were excluded from the peace making process, or indeed left deeply hostile to it – Germany because it was a dictat, Russia because the victors of Versailles sought to overthrow the Bolsheviks by supporting the counter-revolutionary Whites in a savage civil war, which has conveniently passed from western memory, in 1919 and 1920.

Statesmen cannot be blamed for failing to foresee the unforeseeable. But they can be blamed for failing to foresee the foreseeable, particularly the foreseeable arising from their own actions.

It was not because the makers of Versailles were particularly inept that their handiwork crumbled so quickly and so disastrously. Wilson was one of the intellectually ablest of all American presidents. Lloyd George was perhaps the wiliest of all British prime ministers, and by no means the most malign, despite his demonisation for decades in Ireland because of his role in the Anglo-Irish Treaty negotiations. Clemenceau ranks among the more distinguished personalities in the whole admittedly uninspiring pantheon of French Third Republican leaders between 1871 and 1940.

They had genuine concerns about a revanchist Germany. Their scope for manoeuvre was restricted by media campaigns baying for the blood of the Kaiser and of German 'war criminals', their thirst for revenge slaked by stories of German atrocities compared with the unsullied behaviour of their own boys. The French flagellated themselves into a frenzy about an inherent German propensity for aggression. After all, was not 1914 all of a pattern? Had not the Hun ravished innocent Marianne, demurely keeping herself to herself, not only in 1914, but in 1870 as well – conveniently forgetting that in 1870 it had been popular French war hysteria that had forced a reluctant Napoleon III to declare war on Prussia.

Could not the hardliners claim, however, that Hitler's performance vindicated them, justified all their suspicions, that Versailles failed because it was too lenient rather than too harsh? It remains the big unanswered question whether the new German democracy could have in fact flourished peacefully if only it had been treated decently from the outset.

For it was an inherent contradiction that a Treaty designed to make the world safe for democracy refused to treat the new Weimar Republic as worthy of inclusion in the peace-making. The Germany that emerged when the Kaiser fled to Holland, and when the German Revolution of November 1918 led to the highly democratic constitution of the Weimar Republic, was treated as an outcast, its leaders humiliatingly forced to sign on the dotted line with a gun at their head – almost literally, given the brutal ultimatum to them to sign, on pain of resumption of war against them. It didn't take a Hitler to identify the contradiction between the Wilsonian rhetoric of democracy and the treatment of the nascent German democracy.

The irony was that many of the actual terms of the treaty were by no means unreasonable. The reparations issue was botched, it is true, but reparations had become part of European peacemaking. What really galled – and rightly galled – was the insistence on Germany's unique war guilt. It was the sense of moral superiority, a sense cultivated by propagandists during the war to persuade young men to the slaughter, and reinforced by Wilson's brand of morality, that really twisted the knife in the wound, particularly as the Weimar Republic sought to repudiate the militarist imperial ethos.

Nor did it need a Hitler to point to two other glaring contradictions in the way the peacemakers went about their work. Wilson loudly trumpeted the principle of national self-determination as the basis for boundaries in the new world order. But suddenly this didn't apply to Germans. The most glaring example was when the parliament of the new Austrian Republic demanded unification with Germany. The victors said no.

In the bad old days, this could have been explained in the simple terms of "to the victors belong the spoils." But the new world order was to be a new moral order. Now it could be justified on no moral principle, and simply stank as hypocrisy. Elsewhere plebiscites could be arranged – but only if it was felt the result would be 'right' – ie, favour the victors. It was the principle applied closer to home in delimiting the boundary of Northern Ireland. The hand with the biggest gun got to make the decisions – and then called it democracy! No wonder 'democracy' rang hollow as a moral order over so much of Europe – and not just Germany – after the statesmen of Versailles had imposed their version of it.

This applied with even starker force in the world beyond Europe. The 14 points denounced colonialism. In practice it transpired this was only the colonialism of the losers. German colonialism was bad. British and French colonialism was good – so good that not only would it not lose any territory, but it would gain German territory, the hypocrisy further compounded by this being nominally under a League of Nations Mandate rather than as simple grab. But who determined the mandate? The winners.

Indeed the carve up of the middle east, following the collapse of Turkish rule, was a classic piece of imperial manoeuvre, on the best Mafia principles of the bosses sharing out the territorial spoils among the various families. Ironically it was the Italian 'family' that got least, no small factor in the spectacular rise of Mussolini within a few years.

It was ironic too that Lloyd George, for so long the nimble survivor in British politics, should finally lose office over his role in a Greek-Turkish conflict in 1922. But Lloyd George, it should be stressed again for Irish readers, was not an insatiably ravenous imperial wolf. He was just a normally rapacious one, as cynical but even as hypocritical as much of the company he kept.

Wilson was too intelligent not to be aware of these contradictions. But his self-righteousness enabled him to justify them on the grounds of German 'guilt'. Indeed it became necessary for German 'guilt' to loom ever larger in his consciousness as he reneged on so many of his principles.

But it is also true that as practice diverged ever more from principle, Wilson desperately pinned ever more faith in his dream of a permanent League of Nations, which would preside over the new world order, and permit orderly change in boundaries etc, which might in time rectify some of the more glaring anomalies in the Treaty. Wilson was, I think, genuine about this. But he was also unrealistic. For the League was essentially under the control of the victor powers. As they would be the big losers from any revisions, it was a fond hope that the League could pick up the pieces of the Treaty. Wilson was incapacitated by a stroke in September 1919. It is fashionable to assert that his dream was dashed by the refusal of the Senate to sanction the Treaty, and thus allow America join the League, in March 1920. But American membership would have been no panacea for the problems. Lamenting American isolationism as the cause of the League's failure is really to evade the issue that a League purporting to be based on justice was in fact based on a victors' dictat.

Two rival new orders would emerge to challenge Wilson's – Hitler's a little later, but more immediately Lenin's, as the Bolshevik Revolution erupted in Russia, preaching another new heaven on a new earth. Would that fare any better than Wilson's?

Map 3   European frontiers 1919 – 1937

Chapter 7

Lenin's blighted dream

*Bolshevik success was far from preordained;
Lenin was really necessary*

AMERICA'S first foray into reordering the world failed dismally in the Treaty of Versailles and the misnamed League of Nations. It then briefly seemed that a very different concept of international affairs, Lenin's idea of an international socialist order achieved through revolution, might offer a serious alternative both to the Wilsonian ideal and to traditional *realpolitik*.

It was one of the manifold ironies of a Peace Conference rich in ironies that Russia was not represented. It was, after all, she who had raised the stakes in 1914 by deciding to support Serbia against Austria, transforming a local Balkan issue into a potentially European conflict. The morality of Russia's decision is a matter of opinion. Its stupidity is not. The price of getting it wrong would be terrible, and for the Tsar, Nicholas II, literally fatal.

Not that the Tsar should be saddled with the main responsibility. Uncommonly stupid though he was, even by undemanding Tsarist standards, he was not so stupid that he wanted war in 1914. But his advisers did, even to the extent of manoeuvring him into the war. But it was he, further discredited by the behaviour of the egregious empress and the sinister Rasputin, who bore the odium of not only defeat but the colossal slaughter suffered because of the sheer incompetence of the regime. With food so scarce as output declined with 15 million peasants conscripted for the front, and with inflation rampant, it was no wonder that a revolutionary situation existed by 1917.

Given that it was Bolsheviks who killed the Tsar and his family in grisly circumstances at Ekaterinburg in 1918, it is easy to forget that Tsarism was not brought down by the Bolshevik Revolution in October 1917. It collapsed under the weight of its own incompetence in February, eight months earlier. Lenin, the Bolshevik leader, wasn't there. He had been in exile for over 10 years. It didn't need Lenin to bring down the Tsar. The whole rotten edifice simply imploded.

It is tempting to skip over the eight months between the fall of the Tsar and the Bolshevik Revolution as merely an interlude while history waited for real history to begin. But that would be simply unhistorical. For it would imply that no other outcome was possible, that the history of revolutionary Russia was preordained. And that would be simply false, and lead to a fundamental error of understanding. Those whose psyches depend on neat straight lines leading inexorably to the next 'stage' should not do history, or attempt historical thought.

Of course it was fashionable for a long time, given Bolshevik success, given the USSR's rise to superpower status, given the alleged basis of Bolshevism in the allegedly infallible doctrine of Marxism, to assume that the outcome was historically ordained. Did not vast impersonal forces decree the onward march of history according to the Marxist model, from feudalism to capitalism to socialism? Were not events mere details along the preordained route? It seemed somehow indecent, when the USSR bestrode half the world, to wonder if the regime had come into power as much by accident as by manifest historical destiny. Was it not frivolous, nit-picking of the most pedantic kind, to wonder if Lenin were really necessary. But the fall of the USSR has reminded us of how many tricks Clio can have up her sleeve.

Historians are no more resistant to the lure of success than any other specimen of humanity. Regiments of historians lined up to sing the praises of the revolution. Here is Isaac Deutscher, by no means an uncritical observer, writing in an impeccably scholarly publication: "Despite some Bolshevik illusions.... it cannot be doubted that the day of 25 October/7 November 1917 stands like a huge and indestructible landmark in the annals of mankind...."

The shattered illusions of historians now recall, no less than the shattered status of Lenin, nothing so much as the vast and trunkless legs of stone of Ozymandias, King of Kings.

For students of the 'what ifs' of history, 1917 in Russia provides a real feast for speculation. This no longer seems wasted energy. The fact that it is impossible to be sure about alternatives does not mean that alternatives weren't possible.

We can nevertheless dismiss, I think, the assumption that Tsarism would have survived in early 1917. Its fate was sealed. But what would succeed Tsarism was far from certain. There were many to say things cannot go on like this in the Russia of 1916 – but precious few to predict Lenin would be in power a year later.

Look at what actually happened. The fall of the dynasty created a power vacuum that was never really filled. If the successor cabals of Prince Lvov and Alexander Kerensky had the wit to make peace, Bolshevik appeal would have been blunted. Instead they plunged the army into more dreadful and futile carnage. It would take Lenin, after his Bolsheviks came to power in October – although in truth this amounted to almost as abject an abdication as the Tsar's eight months before – to grasp the nettle, and to beg for peace.

The price was huge in territorial terms. It is now easily forgotten that Germany won the war against Russia. The peace of Brest-Litovsk in March 1918 was a dictat. Russia was driven back to virtually her present boundaries – losing the Ukraine, the Baltic lands and Poland, or 46 million people, about one third of her population. Lenin, or Trotsky on his behalf, swallowed it all. Lenin was determined on peace at any price, just as Kerensky had been determined on war at any price.

So far was Bolshevik success from being inevitable that Lenin himself failed with an attempted revolt in July 1917. Having only arrived in April, he fled again until the very eve of the October Revolution. Gaining power in October was actually relatively easy in the power vacuum. The problem was less gaining power than holding it. It was at this that Lenin excelled. He had to create a power centre in a vacuum.

The subsequent struggle would drag on for three years, in a series of savage wars, replete with massacres on both sides, vicious anti-semitism, especially among right-wing Whites, famine and mass destruction. This had nothing to do with the final crisis of capitalism, or with the inexorable march of history. Much of it was old-fashioned warlord stuff.

The Bolsheviks, whose situation often looked desperate against Whites, Cossacks, Ukrainian peasants, invading British, French, American, German, Austro-Hungarian, Romanian, Japanese and Polish forces, and who were driven back on small areas around Petrograd and Moscow, were saved not by vast impersonal historical forces but by the demonic energy of Trotsky – only to be in turn stopped at Warsaw in 1920 when Pilsudski halted the western charge of the 27-year-old Tukhachevsky, who had chased the Poles back from deep in the Ukraine and saw no reason why he shouldn't keep going as far west as he could.

Agile though his adaptation of Marxist theory to changing circumstances had been – according to the theory socialist revolution ought not to break out in Russia at all at this stage – Lenin clung to the belief that it was in the most advanced capitalist centres, and especially Germany, that socialism would triumph. Socialism in one country, especially if that country was Russia, had no prospects. He had been among the few socialists to have the courage of his Marxist convictions at the outbreak of the war. Whereas the socialists of most of Europe supported the war, contrary to the teachings of their socialist faith, Lenin held the defeat of Russia to be necessary for the success of the international socialist revolution.

He got the defeat of Russia alright. But the sequel did not go according to doctrine. The failure of the socialist uprisings in Germany after the war shattered his theory, and the defeat of the Red Army in 1920 at Warsaw effectively ended any hopes of imposing Bolshevism through force of Russian arms.

If the personalities of Lenin and Trotsky were crucial to Bolshevik success, neither was it any inevitable impersonal force of history that brought Stalin to power in the USSR in the deadly power struggle against the more prominent Trotsky following Lenin's death at the age of 54 in 1924. Lenin had warned unavailingly against the menace of the obscure brooding Georgian. Whether Stalin was the true heir of Lenin in his rule by terror, or whether he perverted Lenin's legacy, he decided that foreign adventures made no sense for so weakened a Russia. He would retreat into building socialism in one country, and leave the world order for later.

Ironically the two potentially great 'peripheral' powers, America and Russia, had withdrawn in large measure from European political affairs a few years after Wilson and Lenin had dreamed of imposing their respective world orders. Policy in both cases lurched from internationalism to isolationism. But there was a difference. In America's case the lurch was back to business as usual. In Russia's case it amounted to nothing less than an attempt to build a new civilisation. Stalin decided that before there could be a new world order, there would have to be a new Soviet order. The price would be a fearful one.

Chapter 8

Stalin and state terrorism

*It was under Stalin that state terror scored
more kills than ever seen before in peacetime*

THE RUSSIA of the Tsars was a shambles before its collapse in February 1917. Who knows what might have happened had Lenin not seized power in October 1917, or at least such power as there was to seize? I say Lenin rather than the Bolsheviks. There was nobody else, not even Trotsky, who had Lenin's nose for power. He subordinated everything else to getting and keeping it. An opportunistic idealist, an inspired improviser of policy as well as theory, his single-mindedness about power meant that his tactics in chaotic circumstances had to consist of a series of U-turns, however consistent his strategy remained. Lenin had not only to launch a revolution, but to virtually create a new state. Even with Lenin at the helm, the ship threatened to founder time and again before it navigated its way through so many treacherous currents, beat off the boarding parties – at least 11 – and finally steered into calmer, if blood-reddened, waters.

So absorbed are western Europeans with western Europe, that our vaunted humanitarianism not only frequently fails to carry beyond Europe, but often stops well short within Europe itself, as the last decade of tragedies in former Yugoslavia too eloquently demonstrates. How often do we remember that World War One claimed far more dead on the eastern than on the western front? How many of us pause to ponder the aftermath in Russia? Probably three times as many died from revolution, counter-revolution, and famine in former Tsarist Russia between 1918 and 1923 as died on the western front in the entire war. In the scale of human suffering, western Europe was almost as much of a sideshow in World War One and its aftermath as in World War Two.

Controversy has raged as to whether the USSR might have developed differently if only Lenin had lived – or at least if only Stalin had not eventually won out in the protracted succession struggle after Lenin's death in 1924, his victory consummated by the exiling of Lenin's heir apparent, Trotsky, and the dismissal of Bukharin, in 1929. These rows have less to do with historical reality than with the political, ideological and psychological needs of current combatants, whether politicians, intellectuals or historians clinging to the faded visions of the Utopia that never was and now looks as if it never will be.

If Stalin can be presented as perverting the legacy of Lenin, then the aura of the Bolshevik revolution can be salvaged, as Gorbachev tried to do, and all the blame for everything that went so horribly wrong can be heaped on Stalin for betraying the revolution. For its ideological enemies, on the other hand, if Stalin can be shown to have merely fulfilled the Leninist word, then the Revolution can be denounced as carrying the poison of Stalinism from the outset.

Lenin was as ruthless as Stalin. He expounded a theory of state terror, which he implemented in practice. But there were differences. Even though the differences may have been differences more of personality and circumstance than of doctrine, they did exist.

Ruthlessly though Lenin applied terror against his enemies, he did not decree nearly as wide, almost as universal, a range of targets as enemies as would Stalin. For Lenin the party was supreme. There could be only one true party. Outside the party there was no salvation. But he allowed fairly free speech within the party. Greatly though he was respected, his pronouncements often followed fierce internal exchanges. A genuine intellectual, he relished the cut and thrust of debate, as long as loyalty to the Revolution was not in doubt. Within the parameters of the Revolution, artistic life was relatively free through the 1920s as long as Lenin's principles survived. Remarkably, the Revolution did not devour its own children as long as Lenin lived. It was Stalin, not Lenin, who would murder virtually all his enemies, not to mention many of his supporters.

Stalin had no more fixed tactical principles than Lenin. He began as a moderate against Trotsky in the debate about the speed of implementation of heavy industrialisation, which nearly all Bolsheviks agreed was a practical and ideological prerequisite for true socialism. Then, having outmanoeuvred Trotsky, he switched to Trotsky's policy in the face of the grain crisis of 1928.

It was in the ferocious drive to collectivise agriculture between 1928 and 1932 that the utter indifference to human suffering fully emerged. The horrors of the Lenin years could at least be explained on the grounds that the country was at war, that self-defence dictated savage measures.

It was part of Stalin's political and psychological genius to manage to generate a sense of a USSR at permanent war, firstly against the kulaks, nominally the class enemy of rich peasants, but in reality all peasant opposition, most of which could not be classed as kulak at all, then against traitors within the party, especially after 1934.

Though the figures are disputed, it is possible that Stalin's various forms of terror may have claimed up to 15 million victims, whether through execution, murder, torture, prisoners starved or frozen to death in the secret police slave labour camps, or on the way to them. Long before Jews were crammed into the cattle trucks for the Nazi camps in the war, Stalin's cattle trucks were trundling with their human cargoes through the USSR, to disgorge in the Gulag camps the living and dead for the glory of the coming utopia.

What was it all for? The statistics of industrialisation under the five-year plans that began in 1929 are indeed impressive. Eighteen million new industrial jobs were created between 1929 and 1939, numbers rising from 11 million to 29 million. There was, officially, no unemployment, at a time when much of the capitalist world was sunk in deep slump. However much concealed unemployment there may have been – the constant complaints about loafing workers suggests that the actual proletariat took a somewhat dimmer view of their production targets than the theorists of socialism – the appearance contrasted impressively with the dole queues of capitalism.

True, the agricultural statistics look less impressive. Total output only recovered the 1928 level in 1938, and then only because Stalin relented sufficiently to allow some private plots. But the failure of output to rise did not constitute failure in Stalin's eyes. That would assume that the main purpose of collectivisation was to increase output. It wasn't. It was to simplify the procurement by the state of surplus output for the rapidly growing industrial labour force in the towns. The total collected for the towns rose from 14% in 1928 to nearly 40% a decade later. For Stalin, this was victory.

For the 90 million peasants – a disproportionate number of them women, given the massive losses of men during the wars – the problem was that much of the grain taken from them was not a surplus. There was no surplus of this size to collect. That didn't matter to Stalin. The towns had to have priority over the countryside, in which most Russians actually lived.

Collectivisation was first and foremost a political measure. Stalin knew well that revolution broke out in towns. The Bolshevik Revolution had depended on revolting workers in a few large towns in the first instance. The huge increase in urban population could constitute a political threat, if it faced severe food shortage. It was politically crucial to feed the towns, at whatever cost to the countryside. That was what collectivisation was about. The peasants could survive on what was left over. If they couldn't, that was their problem. The hideous Ukraine famine of 1933-1934, in which probably at least three million starved to death, in scenes only too familiar to any of us who care to recall Irish famine, was merely the most graphic example of the logical consequence of this mind set, where the food must be torn from the starving growers to feed the towns.

In contrast to Lenin, Stalin set out to destroy his enemies from 1934 on, when a movement for putting a more human face on the party sought to elevate Kirov, the Leningrad party boss, to a more prominent role. And he saw enemies everywhere. Kirov was duly assassinated, perhaps with Stalin's complicity, certainly to his advantage. Stalin, purporting to be shocked, used the excuse to exterminate anyone he suspected of even potential disloyalty to himself within the party. Ninety-eight of the 139 members and candidate members of the Central Committee elected at the 1934 Congress were executed by 1939.

The terror was horrific. Although the show-trials of 1936-8 involved only a handful, they were the crowning showpieces of the entire process. They included the big three of the old guard, Zinoviev, Kamanev, and Bukharin, a warning that treachery could infiltrate the highest ranks – and that any disagreement with Stalin could be construed as treachery. Any possible source of alternative attraction to Stalin was purged, including the army high command, with Tukhachevsky, the most prominent soldier, shot in 1937.

Stalin was adept at turning his hired killers on one another. No sooner had he used the secret police chief, Yagoda, to set up the first show trials, than he dismissed him in favour of Yezhov, whom he then used to execute Yagoda in 1938, only for Yezhov to fall victim in turn the next year. It was now that the Revolution truly devoured its children, with the assassination of Trotsky in 1940 in Mexico the symbolic climax of the purification from heresy of the one true communist faith. Never in peacetime had state terror scored so many kills.

How did Stalin do it? How could he sustain tyranny on this scale without provoking any effective resistance? Indeed, how could he earn adulation not only from so many within the USSR, but from so many outside it, including not only genuine communists, but observers of the stature of George Bernard Shaw and Sidney and Beatrice Webb?

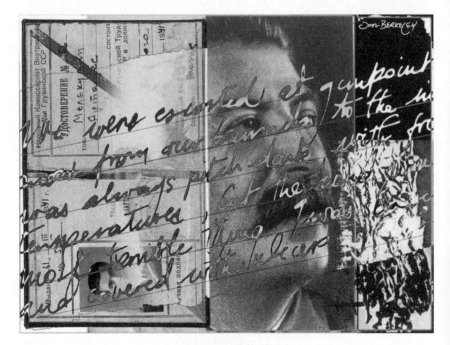

Chapter 9

Stalinist harvest that is still reaped

The tragedy of ordinary Russians in a terrorist regime

TERROR stalked Stalin's Russia. It entered into the marrow of Stalinist society, to such an extent that the very phrase, Stalinist society, is virtually an oxymoron. Fear was fed by the pervasiveness not only of the secret police but of informers willing to accuse friends and neighbours, colleagues, superiors, inferiors, and even relatives, of 'crimes' against the state. The system bred total suspicion. Stalin's Russia was a giant mass laboratory for the creation of a new man – and the results were frightening. New Soviet Man was, first and foremost, an informer.

Trust could take no root in such an atmosphere. Sowing mutual distrust among his subjects is the oldest trick of the tyrant's trade, as Aristotle had observed more than 2,000 years before. Alan Bullock, in his *Hitler and Stalin: Parallel Lives,* observed that there was "no better preparation for writing about Hitler and Stalin than a close study of Thucydides, Tacitus, and those sections of Aristotle's *Politics* that deal with the Greek experience of tyranny". There was nothing new in Stalin's strategy, nor in his determination to apply the other two techniques that Aristotle identified with tyranny, breaking the spirit of his subjects and making them incapable of independent action.

Never in history, however, had any ruler carried those techniques to such nightmarish lengths, Stalin himself giving the lead in his own circle, where no one was safe from his morbid suspiciousness. For the full understanding of Stalin and his system, one might garnish the classics with case studies of the mafia, and just a dash of Marx thrown in. For there were some genuine idealists to be found among all the thugs and opportunists. It was a combustible cocktail, and for the true believers, a tragic one. Many of them would die, after torture, still singing Stalin's praises, so blinded were they to reality.

In this atmosphere it was impossible for a civil society to emerge. Civil society cannot exist, much less flourish, without a certain degree of trust. Indeed by institutionalising the culture of denunciation, and destroying any concept of trust, Stalinism laid the basis for the continuing paralysis of Russian society. The Stalinist harvest is still being reaped, as a potentially great people are reduced to the playthings of mafia gangs – the private enterprise equivalents of Stalin's mafia state. The psychology of suspicion remains so deeply ingrained, suppurating through the collective psyche, as to cripple a later generation, even when the external forms of the terror regime have largely withered away. In any balance sheet of Stalin's achievements, the sinister shadow from the grave must be taken into account.

That is one reason why the assumed magic elixir of 'democracy plus the market', which was supposed to launch Russia into sustained capitalist economic growth, has proved so disappointing. Although the market too

57

is a mechanism for economising on the need for trust, a minimum level of trust in institutions is required – if only trust in the relative fairness of the legal system – for the market to function. And Stalinism, by prostituting the legal system entirely to its own whims, destroyed any faith in law, a prerequisite for any concept of society.

Stalin was a natural thug, who attracted kindred spirits to his court and his service. Thugs, bullies, sadists, paranoids, or similar incarnations of evil, will presumably always be with us. The banality of evil, Hannah Arendt's phrase for Adolf Eichmann, could be applied equally well to Stalin's squads. There is no solution to that, beyond trying to ensure that the conditions conducive to their coming to the surface do not emerge – which is why politics is so important – or that they can be crushed in time if they do surface.

What is in a sense even more frightening is the response of many of the victims, and many witnesses, to the poisoned chalice of Stalinism. Many adjusted to the terror, although the resentment of many of the collec-tivised peasantry frequently surged to the surface, and was more general-ly reflected in their canny attitude towards collective property. It is ironic that what was perhaps the most effective exhibition of *de facto* labour sabotage of capital in history, more effective even than on slave planta-tions, should have been seen in the response of the Soviet agricultural workers to collectivisation.

The current explosion of research into everyday life in Soviet Russia, and into the Stasi regime in East Germany, now that the archives are open-ing, is proving instructive, not only about Stalinism, but particularly about the wider response to totalitarianism. The genuine informer/ collaborationist mentality is far more widespread than our idealised image of normal behaviour presumes. In the Soviet case, the lure of per-sonal advancement was an incentive to hordes of younger cadres. If denunciation of a superior promised promotion, career ambition could overcome putative scruple, giving the informer a stake in the terror regime, blinding one to the possibility that one's own turn was only a mat-ter of time.

More widespread again is the acquiescent mentality. Men and women who may not themselves commit deliberate calculated cruelty, or even inform, will not resist either. Genuine resistance is rare. It is rare because it is rarely feasible. There is every excuse for the indigenous victims of tyranny not to mount effective resistance to it. But there is far less excuse for foreign fellow travellers to blind themselves to the nature of the regime, much less extol tyranny as the road to utopia. One of the saddest stains on western civilisation this century is the queue of leading western 'humanitarians', journalists and intellectuals, including famously George Bernard Shaw and Sidney and Beatrice Webb, who travelled to the USSR and returned warbling its praises, to say nothing of the likes of Sartre and his disciples by the Seine. A new civilisation was indeed being forged. And the route lay through Moscow. But it was the route to hell, and not to heaven. The tourists were of course in many cases part duped. But they were only too willing to be deceived. They chose to see only what they wanted to see.

The pat phrases of 'progressive' thinkers were trotted out by westerners. "I have seen the future and it works," was a standard one. The New York Times correspondent in Moscow, whose reporting ranks among the great case studies in media disinformation, brushed aside protests about the terror with the phrase "you cannot make omelettes without breaking eggs," as if the bodies of millions literally broken, was a trifling consideration.

Sympathetic observers of Stalinism could point to what, on paper, were admirably progressive achievements. The 1936 Soviet constitution positively breathed 'progressive' sentiments. And were they not right to laud the drive to mass literacy, banishing the ignorance and religious superstition of the ages at a stroke as Soviet Man, side by side with liberated Soviet Woman, strode towards the uplands of enlightenment?

They would indeed have been right if literacy had been applied to that purpose. The irony was that literacy was then used for indoctrination. It was another device to suffocate thought. Impressive though some of the technical education could be, by indoctrinating children with the ideology of the state, the system further subverted any concept of a civil society. Russia today, for all her literacy levels, is much more the victim than the beneficiary of the Soviet education system.

Not wishing to see allows the escape route of claiming that one did not know, as so many Germans claimed about the Holocaust. In the Soviet case, even Alexander Solzhenitsyn, one of the genuine literary and moral giants of the century, whose *Gulag Archipelago* exposed the credulity, or worse, of a whole generation of fellow travellers, surmised that even within the USSR "there were many who did not even guess at its presence and many, many others who had heard something vague. And only those who had been there knew the whole truth." This seems all the stranger coming from Solzhenitsyn who estimated that no fewer than 25 million prisoners died in Stalin's prisons and camps between 1934 and 1953. How can anything like that number disappear with so many failing to notice?

And how can one induce the necessary distrust and pervasive suspicion among a population which had only a vague idea of the reality, or couldn't even guess at it? We will return to the question of the role of 'ordinary people' in totalitarian regimes when we come to consider the question of how much 'ordinary' Germans knew about Nazi extermination policies. But the question looms quantitatively much larger in Stalin's Soviet Russia. It is an absolutely crucial question for any verdict on human nature.

It is hardly for us to wax superior. We have been happily spared the experience of finding out how we would react in similar circumstances. And we, too, are adept at seeing only what we want to see. Look at the justification regularly advanced by apologists for terror, not least state terror, still far and away the most common form of terror in the 20th century world.

These issues were already on the agenda of world history before they would arise in further hideous form in Hitler's New Order. How did the corporal of 1918 came to be in a position to launch his own vision of a New Order two decades later?

Chapter 10

The rise
of Hitler

*Never before had a power so crushed in one war
recovered so rapidly to scale such heights in the next one*

STALIN was the greatest mass murderer in recorded history. But Hitler looms larger in western consciousness, partly because of the Holocaust, and even more because he actually went to war against the west. However convenient the horrors of the concentration camps turned out to be for burnishing the self image of the West as the champion of good against evil, Hitler's crime in the real world was to have gone to war against the wrong enemies. Had he only danced to the tune of western diplomacy, and launched his war against Stalin from the outset, leaving the West alone, he could have slaughtered as many Russians as he wanted, soldier and civilian, men and women alike, without the western powers losing a wink over it – as long as he didn't win too quickly, of course, for fear he might turn on them next.

In fact, for long after the war western rhetoric chose to slight the Soviet contribution to victory, and the extent of Soviet suffering during the war. Even today, how many war films deal with the eastern front rather than the western? Who would guess from the barrage of self-indulgent propaganda that at least 10,000,000 civilians died in the USSR compared with 62,000 in Britain. Even allowing for the disparity in population, this was a ratio of about forty to one. This is not for a moment to denigrate the British contribution to victory over Hitler. But it is to put in perspective the relative scales of civilian suffering.

Even then, it was with great reluctance many of the British establishment went to war against Hitler in 1939, and then patently on grounds of national interest rather than morality. America, of course, remaining neutral for over two years, never went to war against him at all until he declared war on it on 11 December 1941. Only days earlier, when America declared war on Japan following the Japanese attack on Pearl Harbour on 7 December, it conspicuously failed to take the opportunity of declaring war on Japan's ally, Germany. However heinous Hitler's behaviour, America was not prepared to go to war against him, aware though the administration already was of the war of extermination in the East.

As is very natural, America's belated entry made her doubly anxious to parade her stainless virtue, so that this too, like Woodrow Wilson's image of the First World War, became a *Crusade in Europe*, the very title of General Eisenhower's memoirs, as if America had donned her armour, mounted her charger and levelled her lance to rescue the damsel in distress, rather than had the whole effort forced on her, after being left with no choice in the matter.

Even today it is striking how many American television programmes and films manage to convey the impression that America voluntarily declared war on Germany from the goodness of her heart, to save mankind from evil incarnate.

Hitler could hardly be faulted for lack of ambition. To manage to go to war against the USSR and the USA, in the space of only seven months, was a unique achievement in the annals of diplomacy; but how did he come to be in a position to do so in the first place? How did a Germany, so badly defeated in 1918, come to rule virtually from the Atlantic to the Volga barely 20 years later?

Never in history had a power so crushed in one war recovered so rapidly to scale such heights in the next one – though the achievement would be quickly emulated by the USSR itself, which went from the nadir of the diktat of Brest-Litovsk in 1918, when it lost more than 40% of its population, to the heart of Berlin in 1945 – despite some disasters on the way. But it was Hitler, not Stalin, whose initiatives led to a new world order after 1945 – although the opposite of the one he sought.

Whatever similarities can be detected between the personalities of Hitler and Stalin, their paths to power were very different. Although a revolutionary from youth, Stalin could never have made the Bolshevik revolution. He was relatively junior in the ranks, and it took him several years to secure his position as undisputed party leader after Lenin's death in 1924. Even then, he owed his success to his position as party secretary that allowed him use the party as the ladder to climb to power, over the backs of his rivals, and to consolidate that power over their corpses.

Hitler, on the contrary, began from scratch in 1918. This unprepossessing Austrian corporal, a war hero, but lying in hospital nerve-gassed at the end of the war, with no apparent prospects at the age of 30, emerged from the murky factional politics of right-wing groups as leader of the small Nazi party in 1921.

It was one thing to become leader of a minuscule party. It was something else to become Chancellor of Germany – and unlike Stalin after Lenin, from outside the system, rather than within it. Hitler had to make his own revolution. He had to be Lenin and Stalin rolled into one.

But didn't conditions favour him? Wasn't the creaky Weimar Republic doomed from the start? Didn't the dictat of Versailles leave the vast majority of Germans seething with indignation, panting to follow any leader who promised to avenge this intolerable insult?

Well, actually no. Of course Germans resented losing some territory.

They had a good case against Allied hypocrisy. And they were regularly reminded of the Treaty through the constant messing over the reparations clauses. But Hitler was blue in the face denouncing Versailles between 1919 and 1933. He was no louder in his denunciation in July 1932, when the Nazis won 37% of the vote, than in May 1928, when they got only 2.6%. His anti-Versailles rhetoric was constant, the Nazi vote very variable. While he certainly mopped up votes from 1930 onwards from several other right wing parties, this still doesn't explain why he was the main, and belated, beneficiary – and even then fell far short of a majority of the popular vote in 1932.

But didn't the inherent instability of the Weimar state help him – over 200 political assassinations between 1918 and 1923, as rabid rightwingers killed their enemies, including two foreign ministers, the Catholic leader, Mathias Erzberger, and the famous industrialist, Walther Rathenau? Didn't the French invasion of the Ruhr in 1923, when they weren't getting their reparations fast enough, provoke a patriotic backlash in Germany that launched Hitler's rise?

Well, actually no. However great the instability, and however intense the indignation, when Hitler attempted his coup in Munich in 1923, it was crushed immediately, with Hitler himself carted off to prison.

But wasn't that just it? Didn't that give him time to write his famous testament, *Mein Kampf* ('My Struggle'), which became a bestseller and converted millions to his cause?

Well, actually no. *Mein Kampf* only became a bestseller after Hitler came to power, for obvious reasons. The first volume, published in 1925, sold only 23,000 copies by 1929, the equivalent for a book in Ireland of about 1,000 copies. The second volume sold even less. Hitler would be still waiting to become Chancellor if he were depending on *Mein Kampf* as election literature.

But surely there was a bedrock anti-semitism among Germans to which Hitler's rabid rhetoric appealed, and which brought 'ordinary Germans' flocking to the swastika?

Well, actually no. There were certainly anti-semitic impulses in German culture, but Germans were by no means the most anti-semitic people in Europe, and anti-semitism was not an election winner in Weimar. Hitler actually had to tone down his anti-semitic propaganda to win votes.

But surely the material suffering caused by the great inflation of 1923, which reputedly reduced the German middle classes to penury by making their savings worthless, created willing voting fodder for the Nazis? Didn't rampant inflation soften up respectable Germans for Hitler? Doesn't that stand as a warning to posterity of the political dangers of inflation, as the rhetoric of conservative finance ministers, and nowadays nominally left wing ones too, regularly reminds us? Well, actually no. Runaway inflation is certainly no way to run a normal economy. But the inflation ended abruptly in 1923 when the government abolished the worthless old currency and brought in a new Mark which gained immediate public confidence. The inflation did nothing for Nazi fortunes over the next six years. Ironically, it was only when deflation became the government's response to the Great Slump in 1929 that the Nazi vote jumped. The panic that the great inflation spread among savers did not send them flocking to Hitler. What we have to explain is how he secured office not in 1923, but in 1933, ten years later. If the psychological consequences of inflation should not be forgotten, neither are they a sufficient explanation of Hitler's later success. Inflation is far too facile an explanation for the rise of Hitler.

Chapter 11

Why Hitler triumphed

There was no sense of inevitability about Hitler's rise, even after he was appointed Chancellor

IF EVER A subject has suffered from the infallibility of hindsight, it is the Rise of Hitler. Even today, those convinced of his 'inevitability', due to some demon lurking in the tormented German soul, are tempted to trawl for his origins deep in the primeval German past, via Bismarck, Frederick the Great and Luther, to duly find Hitler grinning up at them out of the pages of Tacitus 2,000 years ago. But there was nothing inevitable about him.

What was virtually inevitable was that any government holding office when the Great Slump hit in 1929 should have lost office by 1933. Few, if any, freely elected governments in the world survived the slump.

In the USA the Democrat, Franklin Roosevelt, succeeded the Republican Herbert Hoover in 1933. In Britain, the first ever peacetime National Government succeeded a Labour government as early as 1931.

It would have been astonishing if the government in office in Germany in 1929, under the Social Democrat, Hermann Mueller, had survived in the eye of the economic storm. For that storm raged more furiously in Germany than in any other European country. Unemployment reached 40%, more than double the rate in Britain or France. In addition, agriculture, which still employed about 30% of the workforce, suffered a catastrophic fall in prices, leaving both town and country mired in despair.

Dramatic political change was almost bound to result from such a disaster. The real question is why Hitler and the Nazis were the main beneficiaries.

That seemed inconceivable in 1928, when the Nazi vote fell to below a million out of nearly 30 million, less than 3% of the total. Far from Hitler's rise appearing 'inevitable', it seemed in 1928 that Hitler had shot his bolt. It was not only the Slump, but the ineptitude of the response to the slump by the political establishment, that gave him his chance. Without entering here into the convoluted debates about the constraints under which a succession of governments operated during the Slump, the fact is that they hopelessly failed to halt the spiralling unemployment or the collapsing agricultural prices.

It was natural for voters to turn to the opposition, as they did everywhere. The problem was that the only opposition in Germany was the Communists or the Nazis. All the other parties had shared in Weimar coalitions. In effect, the Nazis now gobbled up the other right wing parties. But the Communists split the left, attacking, under Stalin's direction, not the Nazis but the Social Democrats, as their main enemies. Stalin's first priority was always to gain control of 'his' side, whatever the consequences for anyone else. So instead of combining to oppose the Nazis, the German left tore itself apart.

The total votes for right and left remained quite close. But the right was nearly united, the left badly split. Who knows what a united left could have meant? It might not have prevented Hitler's coming into office. But it would certainly have changed the nature of the game.

It was mainly Nazi ability to mobilise economic grievances that sent their vote soaring from 2.6% in 1928 to 18.6% in September 1930, to 37.4 % in July 1932, before it fell back to 33.1% in November 1932.

Of course Hitler was manoeuvred into office on 30 January 1933 by the intrigues of a conservative *camarilla* around the elderly President, Hindenburg, ironically enough after his first reverse at the polls in five years. But the fact remains that Hitler could not have counted if his party had not grown so much, and it was still much the biggest party. The vote for the second biggest, the Social Democrats, had fallen from 30% in 1928 to 20% in 1932. By 'democratic' criteria, Hitler had a strong claim to the Chancellorship.

Those who want to ascribe the rise of Hitler to some flaw in the German character have to explain why a majority of Germans never voted for him. They also overlook the fact that by 1928 the Weimar Republic, which so many in retrospect declared doomed from the start, seemed relatively successful. It had overcome huge challenges to steer into calmer democratic waters. Italy had Mussolini. Spain had General Primo de Rivera. Poland had Marshal Pilsudski, Hungary had Admiral Horthy, Russia had Stalin. France and Austria were racked by instability. Even in Britain, the General Strike of 1926 and the long drawn out miners' strike had brought social tensions to the surface. In comparative context, the Weimar performance was quite respectable.

It is true, of course, that if a majority of Germans never voted directly for Hitler, nevertheless the Nazis got far more votes than any other party. But it seems unhistorical to suggest the vast majority of those were voting for Auschwitz, although how many would have still voted Nazi if they knew what was in store, we cannot know. Some were voting, no doubt, for a restoration of German great power status. But all the right wing parties used similar rhetoric. What distinguished the Nazi programme was that it offered specific policies to beat the Slump.

In response to falling agricultural prices, for instance, the Nazis proposed guaranteed prices. This has since become commonplace. Roosevelt would do something very similar to salvage American farmers. But this was denounced by doctrinaire liberal economists as flouting the 'rationality' of the market, as well as by socialist economists, full of doctrinaire disdain for the primitive peasantry whose only historic mission was to vanish from history. In the long run they were right. But in the short run they would be dead. For the manner in which the peasantry would disappear made all the political difference.

If farmers flocked to Hitler, it was only partly because of the glorification of rural virtues in Nazi rhetoric. This was no more than the standard rhetoric of all right wing parties. His appeal to the rural vote was rooted solidly in a common sense agricultural programme that none of the other parties would emulate.

The same failure of imagination afflicted industrial employment policy. Unemployment fell from more than six million to three million during 1933 and 1934. This is often attributed to Hitler's rearmament policy, which more peacefully inclined parties could hardly have pursued. But it wasn't until 1935 that rearmament became important. The fall in unemployment in 1933 and 1934, which allowed Hitler consolidate his popular support, was due more to 'old-fashioned' public works and building activity. These policies weren't even specifically Nazi ones. They were part of the public debate – but the official mind dithered over them. Hitler did not.

It was a self-serving excuse of conventional free marketeers to suggest that it was some inexplicable gadarene rush of the irrational masses that brought so many voters, predominantly Protestant middle class, but with a fair scattering of Catholic and working class, into the Nazi electoral camp. That sober journal, *The Economist*, which in 1930 had no difficulty attributing the Nazi vote to the Slump, came by 1932 to explain it in terms of 'the wayward emotional element in German political life'. Admitting now that there could be rational economic reasons for voting Nazi would oblige it to question its own conventional economic wisdom.

It is easy to forget how many contemporary commentators did not regard Hitler's rise as inevitable. Following his November setback in 1932 *The Economist* felt that he now faced 'rather poor prospects', concluding that 'this transalpine *duce* is no Mussolini'. Indeed and he wasn't – but for very different reasons than *The Economist* surmised.

When Hitler finally became Chancellor in 1933, but with a coalition cabinet in which the Nazis held only a minority of posts, and with Hindenburg's favourite, von Papen, as Deputy, many wondered how long so patently inferior a creature could last in such exalted company. Surely now he was cornered? As *The Economist* again put it, 'Herr Hitler has been hoist into the saddle. It is now to be seen whether he can keep his seat, with Freiherr von Papen perched on the crupper behind him and digging in his East-Prussian spurs'. As intelligent an observer as Dan Binchy, the great scholar, then the Irish representative in Berlin, expressed the same view, confident that Hitler would prove no match for the experienced upper class statesmen now enveloping him.

We know it didn't turn out that way. But we need to remember there was no sense of inevitability even after he took office. It was his success in outmanoeuvring his allies that changed utterly the political landscape. Even though he still failed to win an absolute majority in the snap election in March, he found ways of 'constitutionally' turning Germany into a one party state by July.

The only force that could oppose him was the army. When the officers made clear they would not brook the ambitions of his old time comrade, Ernst Roehm, boss of the Brownshirts, to supercede the army, Hitler had Roehm slaughtered during the Night of the Long Knives, June 30 1934. The officers thought they had him in their pocket then. But when Hindenburg finally got around to dying in August 1934, Hitler made himself Fuehrer, imposed an oath of personal loyalty to himself on the army, and launched the political manoeuvres that would by 1938 make the officers his servants rather than vice versa.

The despised Austrian corporal proved far too clever for the generals – as he would shortly for the diplomats of Europe, whom he would outmanoeuvre on the international stage as he outmanoeuvred his rivals on the domestic stage. But none of that was preordained either.

Chapter 12

A truly awful decade

*Even before World War II, the 1930s was
a period of violence and mass slaughter*

W E THINK of the Second World War as the greatest charnel house in history. And so it was. But it is easy to forget the victims of violence of the thirties. To the many millions of victims of Stalin's various slaughter systems, we must add the million or more killed, often in the most gruesome manner, graphically recorded in Iris Chang's *Rape of Nanking*, during the Japanese invasions of Manchuria in 1931 and of China in 1937, the

300,000 Ethiopian victims of Mussolini's barbarity in 1936, and the half million or more victims of the murdering hate of both sides in the Spanish Civil War from 1936 to 1939.

The suffering of the 'thirties has been largely forgotten, overshadowed both by the horrors of the following decade, and by the capacity of western civilisation not to think of Russian victims of Stalin, or Chinese victims of Japan, or African victims of Mussolini, as equally human beings as westerners. Had Hitler never lived, the 1930s would rank among the most barbaric decades in recorded history.

And yet it is Hitler who dominates our image of the 1930s, because of what was to come. Could he have been stopped?

It is often claimed that had the French and British resisted his reoccupation of the Rhineland in March 1936, in breach of the Versailles Treaty, that he would have been halted forever, if not indeed toppled. But that is highly unlikely – slowed down, perhaps, but halted, hardly.

We should also be clear why the French did not move against him. French public opinion did not, basically, want to risk war over what appeared so minor a matter. Neither did the British. Why should they? For all Hitler's restlessness, it was difficult for the handful of Cassandras who understood his real objectives to rouse a reluctant public opinion to the danger. He himself mouthed the rhetoric of peace, coupling the Reoccupation with wide-ranging peace proposals, couching his demands in the language of national rights – after all was he looking for anything which the Treaty of Versailles had not sanctified as legitimate for the victors? – simply the right of Germans to live under German rule. What was he doing in Germany but re-establishing respect for law and order? Was he not solving the slump, turning Germany into a full employment economy, so that there was an actual labour shortage in 1936, when France herself had sunk deep into economic crisis?

There were, of course, harsh German laws against Jews. But anti-semitism was widespread in western Europe and America. We know the Holocaust was waiting, even if it was not finalised in its full gruesome Auschwitz/Birkenau-type scientific horror until 1942. But the public did not know that in 1936. Few Jews had been actually killed at that stage. Even by 1939, following the rampage of *Kristallnacht*, fewer Jews had been killed

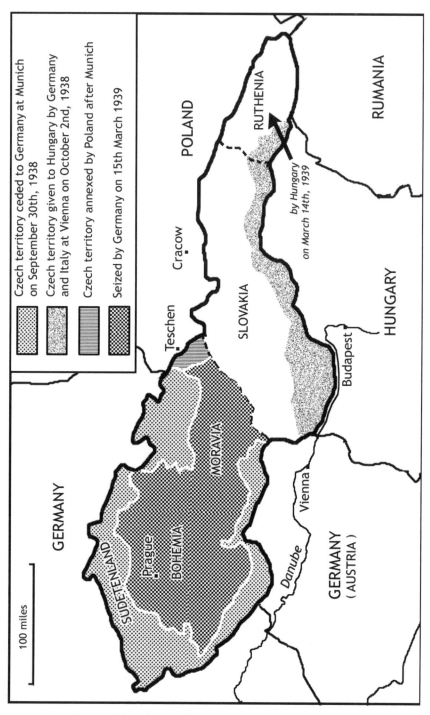

Map 4   The dismemberment of Czechoslovakia 1938

by the Nazis than blacks had been lynched in America since the war by the Ku Klux Klan.

Many western countries imposed severe quotas on the number of Jewish refugees they would take in the late 1930s. The war was not fought to save the Jews. That was a good propaganda ploy. But it was not the reality. There wasn't a solitary reference to the plight of Jews in the statements in the House of Commons in September 1939 leading to the British declaration of war.

Why then should the French have been expected to risk war in 1936, on the basis of what they knew at the time, over a minor matter on which most of the world probably thought Hitler was justified, and on which French opinion itself was, at the very least, deeply divided?

Even if the horror had been anticipated it is by no means clear what steps would have been taken. Every European country pursued what it saw as its self-interest in 1939. Britain and France of course declared war on Hitler when he invaded Poland, ostensibly on the basis of their guarantee to Poland in March when Hitler had broken the Munich Agreement of the previous year by invading the rest of Czechoslovakia, contrary to his promise on Chamberlain's worthless sheet of paper guaranteeing 'peace in our time'.

Hitler did not want war in the west in 1939. Why should he want a two front war? He assumed that the Nazi-Soviet Pact of 23 August, when the two great ideological enemies agreed to partition Poland between them, ensured that Britain and France would find a way of evading their guarantee, on the precedent of their ditching Czechoslovakia the previous year.

What he overlooked was that distrust of himself had become so great that Britain and France, although still with some reluctance, felt their interests were now better served by war than by peace. Britain and France did not go to war to save Poland any more than they went to war to save Jews. They went to war to save themselves. The only way they might do something for Poland was by launching an attack on Germany from the west. They had no intention of doing so. Neither their mindsets nor their military dispositions were determined by concern for Poland. Instead, they sat on their heels during 'the phoney war' for nine months after Hitler's invasion of Poland, waiting for Germany to attack France.

But it was no 'phoney war' period for Poland, the term itself betraying an incurably self-centred western perspective. During that period Poland was being subjected to barbarities such as no European people had ever suffered on so systematic a scale, in an explicit process of nation-killing, through the systematic murder of the educated elite, to leave the Polish people reduced to a mere torso in the Nazi racist model. Inured to horror though we have become from the series of subsequent horror shows, the treatment of Poland from as early as September 1939 ranks among the crimes of the century. The sweet words for Poland in the House of Commons on 3 September turned out in reality to be no more than useless weasel words, designed to flatter British *amour propre*, adding insult to ineffectuality.

Britain and France went to war in their own interest. The question is why did they decide their self-interest was better served by war than neutrality in 1939, when they had reached the opposite conclusion on Czechoslovakia at Munich less than a year before?

Two things had changed. Firstly, the majority could no longer persuade themselves that Hitler's ambitions were limited to reuniting Germans, as he had so long declaimed. His ambitions were now widely feared to threaten fundamental British and French interests.

Hitler had, it is true, unfeigned admiration for the British as a great imperial people, a genuine master race who knew how to keep their inferiors in their place. He often spoke of leaving the British with their empire, as long as they left the continent to him. But who could now trust him? And in any case, this scenario did not hold much comfort for the French. Secondly, the British and French believed themselves militarily better placed to win now than a year before.

The great irony was that it was precisely the military collapse of Britain and France in 1940 that destroyed the reputation of the diplomacy of the 1930s. Chamberlain was justified, as far as anyone could tell at the time, in claiming that the western allies were much better prepared for war in 1939 than in 1914. And yet the western front held for four years in the first war. It collapsed in six weeks in the second. The evacuation of 338,000 troops from Dunkirk, only three weeks into the campaign – for all the legendary heroism of the little boats putting out across the Channel to rescue the stranded army, and for all legitimate British pride in the epic deed – was in cold reality a stunning British defeat.

On paper it was inexplicable. Had Hitler disposed of overwhelming power, there would be a simple explanation. But he didn't. Far from the Germans enjoying irresistible advantage, the British and French had actually more men, more planes, and more tanks. And yet they collapsed. Had they held out, the diplomacy of Chamberlain and Daladier might seem no worse than that of their predecessors before 1914. Civilian reputations often depend on the fortunes of war. If their side wins, the politicians and diplomats involved are hailed as farsighted. If their side loses, they are dismissed as myopic or worse – for exactly the same diplomatic performance. Many a political and diplomatic reputation has depended on the soldiers, being won or lost retrospectively on the battlefield more than in the chancellery or foreign office.

Had Hitler's attack on France stalled – as virtually every reasonable person expected, and indeed reasonably expected, and as it might well have if Guderian's tanks hadn't penetrated faster than the German High Command itself anticipated in the week from 10 May – the entire war would look very different. So then would the diplomacy of the 1930s. But the tendency in recent western thought to take the results of war for granted, as if what happens in war itself is somehow preordained, particularly in the twentieth century when so many assume that war is decided more in the factory than on the battlefield, leads to a gross underestimation of the importance of the military factor. The military history of the Second World War shows how little is in fact predetermined, even in an age of science and technology.

Chapter 13

World turned upside down

As the Panzers swept through France, Germany's victory in World War II seemed very likely

STRANGE though it now seems, Neville Chamberlain felt he had reason for satisfaction after Hitler's invasion of Poland in September 1939. What is more, this was no inexplicable aberration on the part of a Prime Minister who had taken leave of his critical faculties. His view that Hitler was in trouble was quite widely shared at home and abroad, even in fascist Italy, where Mussolini was so alarmed by the turn of events that he refused to declare war on France or Britain until 10 June 1940, when they

77

seemed safely defeated. Hitler found himself going it alone in the west.

It was for that very reason that many German generals contemplated the military prospects gloomily. They remembered the futile carnage of the First World War. Now the French Maginot line, stretching from Switzerland to the Ardennes, loomed more formidably in their imaginations than any trench system. The Ardennes were deemed impassable, leaving the German High Command with no option, as it saw it, but to come through central Belgium, where the French in turn prepared to mass their main forces.

Had Hitler kept to that plan, the outcome would have been highly uncertain. The German High Command was by no means confident of victory. But Hitler changed the plan. Or rather, he opted for an alternative plan in early 1940 when his attention was captured for it.

In several countries small numbers of military thinkers sensed that the real lesson of the Great War was not that the defensive would always win, but that the next war would depend on speed, and on the skill with which the new agent of mobility, the tank, was used. Charles de Gaulle advocated this in France, just as ardently as von Manstein or Guderian in Germany. But more senior officers in both countries dismissed this thinking. The difference was that von Manstein was able to get through to Hitler directly, and that it was Hitler who ultimately determined strategy.

Why should Hitler be prepared to be convinced, almost on the very eve of the campaign? Mainly because he knew he was in a quandary. After all, he hadn't expected to be at war with France and Britain at this stage. It was they who had decided to go to war with him, not vice versa. He didn't just need victory. He needed quick victory. He needed this because he too was thinking of the Great War – but on the Home Front. Convinced that Germany had lost the war because of the collapse of civilian morale due to deprivation, he was determined that civilian living standards should not be reduced – as seemed inevitable in a long war. The German economy was already at full employment. It seemed to have no slack left to take in. Therefore increased military output could only come at civilian expense. So he needed a quick kill. In his mind slow victory was a contradiction in terms.

Von Manstein's plan for a fast tank-led thrust through the Ardennes, left virtually unguarded by the French, which would sweep towards the

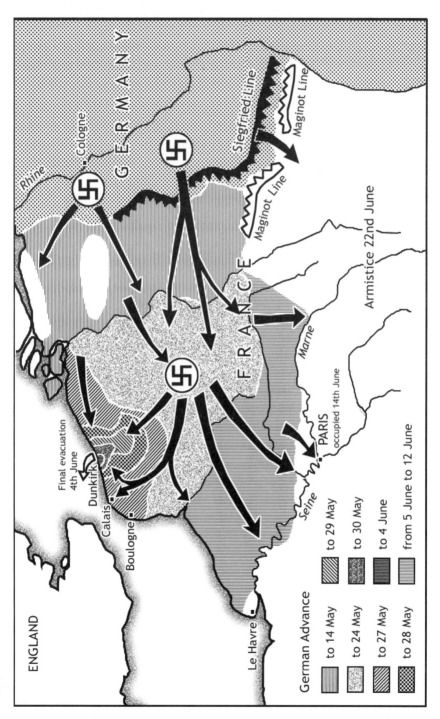

Map 5   The Fall of France 1940

Channel ports, coming round behind the French forces engaged on the Belgian front, trapping them in a pincer movement, perfectly suited Hitler's political thinking. Apart from that, Hitler was psychologically fascinated by the technology of speed. He was one of the first politicians to use aeroplanes for his electoral rallies. He made the Volkswagen into a symbol of German success. For all the Nazi rhetoric of a people rooted in the ancestral soil embodying eternal values, Hitler could be highly receptive to innovative thinking about technology.

But was this strategic shift, and all this elaborate planning, really necessary? Were not the French, British and Belgian forces so inferior in numbers and equipment that they stood no chance anyway against so superior a German war machine? The supreme irony of the Battle of France is that the western powers had not only more men, but more tanks, and better ones, than the Germans. The difference was in the use made of them.

The French used their tanks mainly as adjuncts to their infantry, dispersing them widely, and often slowing them to infantry pace. The Germans concentrated theirs into columns, intended to break through enemy lines, and to keep going, often ranging far ahead of the infantry. In the event, they duly cut through the Ardennes, inducing panic in the French and British forces when they swept up behind them out of nowhere.

The same gulf in tactical thinking occurred in the use of air power. Here the Germans did have an advantage, although in the quality rather than in the number of planes. But the biggest difference of all lay in the tactics. The German airforce worked closely with the army. The French and British did not. The French had no central command at all, with the result that many planes apparently never even took off during the entire campaign.

Whatever the precise details – and in so rapidly shifting a scenario there was bound to be huge confusion - the basic point is that the forces in men, tanks and planes were very evenly balanced. This was what made the scale and speed of Franco-British defeat so astonishing.

So mesmerised were contemporaries by what was happening that Mussolini, who had remained neutral at the outset, nearly missed the boat entirely, only scrambling to get into the war on 10 June, with Hitler already effectively victorious. It was only now that Mussolini could bring himself to suspend disbelief sufficiently to take the plunge, fearful of losing a share of the spoils.

Readers must be tired by now of my obsession with the danger of hindsight. But the fall of France is a classic example of a case where the minute the impossible happens we react as if not only we, but those swirling in the currents of the time, knew about it all along. But so startled were even the German generals, even Hitler himself, by the speed of their success, that they actually stopped from time to time, unable to believe their own eyes about what was happening before them.

Nor were they foolish to be concerned. Spectacularly though their strategy succeeded on the northern French plain, it was a high risk tactic, and several times a close run thing. Tanks, for instance, could get cut off. Two brilliant tank commanders, Guderian and Rommel, narrowly escaped death or capture on 17 and 20 May, within ten days of the invasion.

Seen from this perspective, Hitler's decision, which has been called inexplicable, to halt his tanks between 24 and 27 May, only 10 miles from Dunkirk, from where 338,000 men would be evacuated to England in the course of a week, when it is assumed that the tanks could have gobbled them up if they had kept going, seems far less inexplicable.

Much the most likely explanation is that Hitler was as stunned as virtually everyone else by the speed of success, and thought time was necessary to regroup, for fear of a French counter attack from the south. And he had no idea that the evacuation would be so successful. But then nobody had. How many foresaw the 'Miracle' of Dunkirk, as the 'little boats of England' rallied to the support of the navy to ferry the forces back across the Channel? No wonder Hitler felt the defeated army could be picked off any time, when Churchill himself, who had just succeeded Chamberlain as Prime Minister, didn't expect that more than 45,000 men could be rescued.

When France collapsed, Hitler imposed a peace that left most of the southern half under French rule, the 84-year-old Marshal Pétain setting out his stall in Vichy, a regime which still poses basic questions about the politics and morality of collaboration. Only a handful of French mutineers refused to capitulate, or to recognise the legitimacy of the Vichy regime. Soon to be pre-eminent among them would be the still virtually unknown Charles de Gaulle, now about to begin stamping his truly extraordinary personality on the history of his time, but whose defiant broadcast from London on 18 June, proclaiming that France had lost a battle but had not lost the war, must have sounded the height of absurdity to nearly anyone who may have heard it. It was an insight vouchsafed to few in the chaos of the inexplicable collapse.

To the new French government, de Gaulle was simply an officer disobeying orders. The fool had defied the wise men with the keen long faces, who duly sat in council and sentenced him to death – *in absentia*. After all, he had no mandate for his insubordination. Did he perchance indulge the inconvenient sentiment that the majority had no right to do wrong?

The stakes in the Battle of France were enormous. A continuing conflict on the Western Front, or even a compromise peace, would have raised huge problems at home for Hitler. It would have made his invasion of the USSR the following year impossible. A defeat would have threatened his regime. Even had he hung on to power, he could have done far less damage. Fewer potential victims would have fallen into his grasp.

His victory, on the other hand, made his will unquestionable, endowing him with a public image of invincibility and reinforcing his own belief in his destiny. The fall of France meant that the war turned into something no one on any side – not Chamberlain, not Hitler, not Stalin – had foreseen on 1 September 1939. At a stroke it made almost all the calculations of the diplomacy of the 1930s seem foolish, when many might have looked quite sensible but for so stunning a military denouement.

A more protracted conflict in the west would inevitably have changed calculations on all sides, not only those of Hitler and Churchill, but of Stalin and Roosevelt, and even Tojo in Japan. And yet we have come to take so unpredictable an outcome almost casually for granted, and to pass judgement with the certainty and myopia of hindsight.

Chapter 14

A close run thing: Battle of Britain

If the Germans could have invaded Britain in 1940, they would have rolled over it, but Hitler was more interested in Russia

HITLER had no plans ready for his next step after the capitulation of France on 22 June 1940. How could he have? He had no more expected the collapse than anyone else had. He found himself at a bit of a loss as to what to do next, flailing around for the rest of the year, torn between his impulse to destroy Russia and the danger of leaving Britain defiant behind him.

His first instinct was to offer Britain peace. After private feelers elicited no response, he duly did so, in his victory address to the Reichstag on 19 July. Promising to allow Britain keep "an empire that it was never my intention to destroy or even to harm," he appealed to what he called "reason and common sense in Great Britain... I can see no reason why this war must go on."

This made sense. Who wants an enemy at one's rear? Not that Britain at this stage was much of an enemy. She had effectively no army. Yes, more than 300,000 men had escaped from Dunkirk. But they now had virtually no arms. If the German army invaded, it would roll over Britain. When Churchill proclaimed in his clarion call on 4 June, on the morrow of Dunkirk, that we will fight on the beaches, etc, his listeners, however roused by the rhetoric of resistance, must have wondered what they would fight with.

But Hitler did not want to expend time and resources invading Britain. Hence his peace feelers. They were tempting, and many were tempted. In fact Churchill's fighting speeches were aimed at isolating the possible peace party in Britain no less than at raising public morale, and persuading the Americans, whose support he was desperately soliciting, of Britain's will to resist.

Even if Hitler's offers weren't genuine – and who in their senses could trust him at this stage? (but then there are always those out of their senses waiting to be duped) – would Britain not gain time to re-arm, and build up her defences for the next round? Even if Hitler achieved another stunning victory over Russia in 1941, would it not take him months to mop up? Britain would surely gain nearly two years. And with a bit of luck, she might gain a lot more. Maybe Hitler would not crush the USSR so easily? Having Hitler and Stalin tearing each other to pieces would be ideal from Britain's point of view.

Churchill would have none of it. Critics of his insistence on continuing at all costs – he even envisaged fighting from Canada – point to the relative positions of Germany and England 50 years later, and ask, who won the war? They attribute the decline of Britain and the rise of the USA to Britain's willingness to bleed herself dry against Germany, leaving the USA to pick up the winnings and replace Britain effortlessly as the dominant world power. They surmise that Britain might not have lost her empire in the Far East if she were not so stretched by war against Germany, fondly imagining the empire surviving far longer.

But Churchill had not become prime minister – and as recently as 10 May – to sue for a compromise peace. His appointment had nothing to do with the German invasion of France the same day. Chamberlain fell because of the fiasco of the British attack on Norway, enthusiastically advocated by Churchill, to prevent German access to Swedish iron ore. Chamberlain bore the blame, and was forced to resign.

But there was no guarantee Churchill would succeed him. It was only because Lord Halifax, the foreign secretary and the king's first preference, ruled himself out, that Churchill got it. He was still widely unpopular in his own party, and his first task was to make sure of Tory support. Chamberlain drew more Tory cheers than Churchill on entering the Commons after the appointment, and only his willingness to serve under Churchill steadied the new government.

Churchill's whole image exuded belligerence and bellicosity. His personality thrived on challenge and excitement, to the extent at times of becoming prisoner to the exuberance of his own oratory. To even contemplate a compromise peace now on Hitler's terms, however apparently reasonable, would be to destroy the bulldog image, apart altogether from his genuine hatred and distrust of Hitler.

This left Hitler with little choice but to launch the Luftwaffe, so successful in France, against the Royal Air Force, to clear the way for invasion.

The Battle of Britain has, understandably, acquired such mythological status in the British self-image that it is difficult to remember just how uncertain the outcome was. The small initial German advantage in fighter numbers was probably balanced by the superiority, including better radio equipment, of Spitfires and Hurricanes, over the German ME 109s and 110s, while British output of fighters, more than double the German in the three crucial months of July, August and September, swung the balance of effective fighter numbers in Britain's favour. And the weather favoured the British – not a 'Protestant wind' this time, but plenty of still probably 'Protestant cloud', it being a shade early for 'inclusive, multi-cultural' cloud at this stage.

The British had a clear advantage in leadership, where Hugh Dowding was in a different class from Hermann Goering, who was in addition mis-led by a grossly incompetent air intelligence service, which constantly underrated British aircraft production and exaggerated losses to a ludi-crous extent – claiming that 644 British planes had been destroyed by 20 August, compared with the real figure of 103. Goering could be forgiven for wondering where the British planes kept coming from when the RAF should have had no aircraft left.

After a severe mauling on 15 September, Hitler called off invasion plans on 17 September, the Germans having lost 1,733 aircraft for the loss of 915 British since the attack was launched.

Even then, it was a close run thing. Had Goering appraised the situation correctly, the outcome could have been very different. He failed to concen-trate on knocking out the vulnerable command centres and radar stations, whose importance the Germans failed to appreciate fully, and in early Sep-tember switched bombing attacks from airfields, crucial to the fighting capacity of the RAF, to London, in a futile attempt to break civilian morale, which was irrelevant in the immediate circumstances. Here was yet anoth-er example – and what an example – which inevitably depended on the course of battle itself. It could have gone either way.

Churchill's celebrated encomium, "Never in the history of human con-flict," as he told the Commons on 20 August, "have so many owed to much to so few," was magnificent. But it was also war. Success was by no means certain at that stage. Handsomely deserved though the tribute was, it did not come from a victor surveying the field, but from a leader rallying his troops in the smoke of battle. It almost proved premature.

'The few' were becoming fewer, and came close to breaking point in the next fortnight. Pilots could not be produced as quickly as planes, and Dowding had to husband his men more than his machines. With just under 1,500 pilots in early August he was down to less than 1,000 at the end. They deserved their luck, for they resisted long enough to break Hitler's will to break them.

Attacking Russia with Britain undefeated may not actually have made much difference to Hitler's eastern campaign. A year later he almost defeat-ed Russia, even while also engaged in North Africa. The truth was that the Battle of Britain served to mask Britain's military decline. Never again could her intervention determine the fortunes of continental war – the fall of France had proved the end of an era in that respect. Nor would victory enable her hold her empire for much longer, even if defeat might have lost it even faster.

What made the Battle of Britain historic in global terms was that it kept Britain undefeated long enough to become a base for American troops two years later. It was a major event in American history. If Britain had been occupied it is difficult to imagine the consequences for America, or how the war would have developed.

The price of defeat for British society would have been incalculable. In due course, Britain's Jews would have been corralled for slaughter. If Churchill's imperialism, shot through with racist tinges, incarnated the more debased impulses of aggressive nationalism, nevertheless the inspiration for his defiance of Hitler derived from an uncomplicated romantic nationalism.

By no means did all his countrymen share in this inspiration. There were plenty of Hitler's men of 'reason and common sense' to rationalise, out of conviction or calculation, the merits of collaboration. Whatever the ultimate outcome, it would have made an ignominious chapter in the island story.

Had the USSR not defeated Germany, the Battle of Britain might have mattered little. North Africa and Montgomery of course loom large in British imaginations. But a more detached perspective is necessary. Rommel never had more than 5% of the German army in North Africa.

Once Hitler invaded Russia in 1941, there was never less than three-quarters of the German army on the eastern front for the rest of the war. British and American exploits would dominate the postwar film industry. But it was the titanic struggle on the Russian front that decided the war.

Why Hitler chose to take the gamble, and how close he came to success, is the ultimate story of World War II.

Chapter 15

The uncle Joe of all defeats

Stalin's inept leadership helps explain how the Soviet armies performed so poorly during Barbarossa

EVEN at this distance in time, grasping what exactly happened on the eastern front remains a major puzzle of World War II. This is partly because it is only since Gorbachev permitted the opening of the Soviet archives in 1987 that indispensable source material has become available. Even then, given the Byzantine style of Stalin's court, given his own inveterate furtiveness, one is driven to the limits of one's understanding of the human psyche to penetrate the inner recesses of a personality at once a cunning, duplicitous, vicious thug, and a shrewd and perspicacious player of power politics, a cross between Ivan the Terrible, Peter the Great and Al Capone.

The fashionable catalogue of alleged mistakes Hitler made during Operation Barbarossa implies that he would otherwise have captured Moscow, with whose fall the will and ability of the Soviets to resist would have collapsed. Maybe that would have been the case. But if so, it would have been from human failure, not because of inability to resist further. Even if Moscow had fallen, the weather would have held up the advance for several months.

With the Soviet war production machine already churning out huge amounts of equipment from its bases in the Urals, the Soviet army in 1942 was not only bigger, but increasingly better equipped, than the German army. How then did it keep losing until the struggle at Stalingrad finally turned in Russia's favour with the surrender of the German Sixth Army in February 1943? Even when it began to win, it still took Russia more than two years, despite its massive superiority in numbers and equipment, to drive the Germans back to Berlin.

It is too easy to be dazzled by the Russian economic miracle in transferring so much equipment eastwards to the Urals into assuming the inevitability of Soviet victory. It was certainly a remarkable production performance. But to get it in perspective it is important to appreciate how many cards Stalin had in his hands in June 1941, in order to realise just how badly he played them, and how close his blundering came to squandering his assets.

We know that Stalin was taken completely by surprise by the German invasion, despite all the warnings he received. There is therefore a natural tendency to assume that it was only from then on that the USSR switched to a serious war footing, and that she had to make up for lost ground compared with Germany.

In fact, almost the exact opposite was the case. Hitler conducted Blitzkrieg to allow life go on as normal. The moment the Polish and French campaigns were over, Hitler instantly ordered reductions in war output. Even the increase in the production of weapons deemed necessary for the invasion of Russia occurred at a very modest level – and then Hitler ordered reductions in October 1941 when he was convinced of certain victory.

The USSR, on the other hand, was already on a much more sustained war footing since at least 1937, which makes Stalin's misreading of Hitler's intentions in June 1941 all the more bewildering. The tyrant who would trust nobody in Russia apparently trusted Hitler! It is still inexplicable, unless we are missing some silent calculation behind the Stalin facade, which I suspect we are, but Stalin will hardly have deposited a nice note of explanation in the archives about it!

This lack of Russian preparedness naturally facilitated the speed of the German advance. But the USSR was not militarily greatly inferior to Germany in 1941. The real question is not why Barbarossa failed, but why it enjoyed so much success. Stalin's critics would respond in a word: Stalin. The last word has hardly been heard on the matter. After Stalin's idolators, himself in the lead, claimed Stalin as the father of all victories, his later critics are inclined to castigate him as the father of all defeats. One could take the easy way out by saying the truth lies somewhere in between. But that is really no answer.

For the question is, where in between? As of now, the balance has tilted heavily against Stalin. This is not mainly because of his undoubted responsibility for the surprise element in the German invasion. For, even fully prepared, Soviet forces would hardly have put up much better resistance. They continued to play into German hands well into 1942, mainly in obedience to Stalin's directives. For Stalin insisted on controlling strategy, and even in large measure tactics. And he was a disaster.

Stalin always thought of Stalin first. He must maintain control over the military, or they might threaten his position. He therefore insisted on parallel command in the army, with the military shadowed by political commissars and agents reporting directly to Stalin himself, or to Beria, his chief of the secret police. Stalin believed in the offensive as fanatically as Hitler. He wasn't bothered about casualties. Soviet soldiers were as expendable during the war as the kulaks before it. So little did the human cost of victory matter to him that Russia lost three to four times as many men as the Germans. In fact, if collectivisation was a war against the kulaks a decade earlier, Stalin's conduct of the war could be deemed a war against the surviving peasants, whose only choice lay between the horrors of Hitler and the horrors of Stalin.

Stalin began by fighting two parallel wars – the war against Hitler, and the war against his own military. It was only when he belatedly grasped that his waging of the internal war could lose him the war against Hitler that he pulled back and gave the military a much looser rein from late 1942. Time and again Stalin overruled military advice during 1941 and 1942. And not only overruled, but often threatened with death officers venturing contrary advice. Nor were these threats necessarily idle ones. Several generals were shot after the invasion. Soviet prisoners of war, who must count among the saddest victims of the entire war, worked to death as millions were by the Germans, were denounced as traitors, their families often at risk of further harassment.

The result was exactly the same in the army as in civil society during the 1930s. There was an almost total failure of trust. The officers gave the advice they knew Stalin wanted to hear. Stalin in trauma, as he was for a week after the invasion, and again in October 1941, with the Germans at the gates of Moscow, may actually have inflicted less damage on his own armies than Stalin compos mentis, given the mentis he was compos.

The ineptitude of Stalin's leadership helps explain how the Soviet armies performed so poorly during Barbarossa. It was not from lack of numbers. The size of the army rose from 1.1 million men in January 1937 to 4.2 million by January 1941 – and by another 1.2 million by June. If the transfer of Soviet armaments production ahead of the German armies to the Urals was a war miracle, the Urals already accounted for 20% of total armaments production by June 1941.

It was in 1940, not after the invasion, that the huge Stalingrad and Chelyabinsk tractor plants changed to tank production. Tank output rose so rapidly from 1939 that by June 1941 the Soviet army had nearly 24,000 tanks, more than all other armies in the world combined. Even in the chaos of the second half of 1941 Russia produced more tanks than the German economy in the whole year.

Of course most of the Soviet tanks were inferior models. But the army already had 1861 T34s and KVs in June 1941, fewer in number but in many respects superior in quality to the 3,600 tanks with which Hitler launched Barbarossa. The problem was greatly compounded by the Soviet misuse of their tanks, very similar to the French a year earlier, spread out as an adjunct to the infantry, rather than concentrated like the German.

The irony was that Soviet military doctrine had evolved far more dynamically than French during the 1930s, with the young Marshal Tukhachevsky inspiring a great deal of creative thinking. The Soviet strategists had certainly not solved all their problems before the purges. But with Stalin's decimation of the officer class – apart from the killing of Tukhachevsky, it is estimated that up to 40,000 officers were killed or imprisoned in 1937-8, and another 40,000 in 1939-41, the killing continuing even after the invasion began – virtually all creative thinking stopped.

The Soviet army was bereft of an experienced officer corps, with an utterly inadequate NCO cadre, badly equipped communication wise, crucial for co-ordinating tank and infantry activity, frozen at Stalin's insistence in a misguided strategy, and virtually forbidden to use local initiative by the presence of political commissars. Because of all this the army failed to offer effective resistance until Stalin grasped that self-preservation required a reversal of attitude.

Not until June 1942, with the demotion of Lev Makhlis, his main 'political' agent in the military, following the disasters in the south, did Stalin hint at a change of direction. The abolition of the war commissars in October signalled a more definite shift, now reinforced by the propaganda of 'The Great Patriotic War' as Stalin belatedly summoned the national heroes and symbols of Russia, not least religion, to inspire further popular sacrifice. By a quirk of fate, he who claimed 'scientifically' to have the key to the future found himself resurrecting the past to survive the present.

But that done, now surely victory was inevitable? How could Germany possibly resist such overwhelming power as the USSR on its own, much less with her Anglo-American allies, could bring to bear? But there would be many a twist in the tale yet.

Chapter 16

How Hitler misread Russia

It was hatred of communism that drove Hitler to invade Russia. The gamble brought down his '1000 year Reich'

THERE IS no great mystery attaching to Hitler's invasion of the USSR on 22 June 1941, even if some historians have worked hard to find one. Once again, they succumb to the temptations of hindsight. We know the invasion failed disastrously in the end, and brought the 'Thousand Year Reich' crashing about Hitler's head until he had no way out but the cyanide and the bullet in the Berlin bunker as Soviet troops prowled overhead on 30 April 1945. But it is his expectations at the time that require reconstruction to understand why Hitler thought as he did. Debates about his motives and objectives continue to rage among historians. But hatred of communism, and of what he saw as its Jewish carriers, had been Hitler's driving demon since he first formulated a political creed in the trauma of the German defeat in the First World War.

As the partition of Poland with Stalin in the Nazi-Soviet Pact in August 1939 gave him a long common frontier with the USSR for the first time, the likeliest bet as to his next move if he had not miscalculated the Anglo-French reaction to his invasion of Poland in September 1939, would have been an invasion of the Soviet Union in 1940.

If so, the Anglo-French declaration of war gained Stalin over a year's respite, at the expense of France, Belgium, Luxembourg, the Netherlands, Denmark, and Norway. Hitler hadn't intended invading any of these at the time. Even in 1940 his invasion of the smaller states might be dismissed as simply the 'collateral damage' of Anglo-French policy.

Hitler's disdain for Russia could only have been reinforced by the perception of Soviet weakness due to Stalin's murderous purges of the general staff. Even if the purges did not necessarily damage the quality of military leadership to the extent that was long assumed – although Stalin killed more Soviet generals before the war than fell in combat during the war – it was the German perception that was important, a perception reinforced by the dismal display of the Soviets in the Winter War against Finland in 1939-1940.

That conflict is one of the most extraordinary wars in all history. Stalin took advantage of the breakdown in the international order to impose territorial demands on Finland to enhance Soviet security. But the hopelessly outnumbered Finns fiercely resisted the vastly superior Soviet forces. If 25,000 Finns died in three months, they inflicted massive casualties on the Red Army before the weight of numbers finally told and the Finns succumbed to Stalin's demands.

It was natural for Hitler's mind to turn east even while he toyed with the idea of invading Britain following the British rejection of peace overtures. As early as 21 July 1940 Hitler gave orders to explore possibilities for an invasion of Russia, even apparently dallying with the idea of invading in October, which would seem madness, even without hindsight, given the imminence of winter. The speed of victory in the west fostered wild expectations of virtually instant triumph.

It is common to refer to Hitler's gamble in invading Russia. But Hitler didn't think his Operation Barbarossa was much of a gamble. To his mind, there was far less of a gamble involved than with the invasion of France. He didn't dare put a timescale on his French campaign. But he confidently expected Russia to fall in a matter of months. What is more, he declared it had fallen in little more than three months after returning to Berlin from the front, in his famous October victory speech in the Berlin Sportspalast.

Nor was this simply a burst of Hitlerian hubris. Even the more sceptical generals were swept along in the euphoria of the speed of the early breakthrough, as if this were another France. The cerebral Halder felt the campaign was already won by 3 July, less than a fortnight after the invasion.

For many, perhaps most, commentators, the turning point in the entire war came in the second week of December 1941. The German drive that brought the army within sight of the Kremlin towers on 5 December was then repelled by Zhukov's counter-attack. The bombing of Pearl Harbour on 7 December provoked an American declaration of war on Japan, and then to cap it all Hitler, as if in a frenzied *Götterdämmerung* production, himself declared war on America on 11 December, even after Roosevelt had taken care not to declare war on Germany at the same time as on Japan in response to Pearl Harbour. Wasn't it now all over bar the shouting? It could surely be only a matter of time before the overwhelming industrial power of America decided the outcome?

There are two responses to these prevalent assumptions. Firstly, the war on the eastern front had to be won and lost on the eastern front. It would in all likelihood be won and lost before American involvement in the war could make a decisive difference, either through direct invasion of western or southern Europe, or through bombing of Germany.

Secondly, even if one were to accept that it was only a matter of time, the issue of precisely how much time was crucial for the fate of millions of victims of both Hitler and Stalin. During the war itself, at a genocidal level, the extermination camps had not yet begun to operate systematically in December 1941. At a more general level, millions would die simply by virtue of being deemed enemies by Hitler and/or Stalin. And after the war, of course, it mattered hugely for the fate of a hundred million survivors in eastern and central Europe, whose lives would be largely determined by where the Soviet and western armies would find themselves at the end of the war.

The widespread assumption that the outcome of the war was essentially predetermined from December 1941 has led to assumptions that Hitler, too, assumed this. It has even been suggested he somehow 'knew', on the basis of fleeting diary entries by Halder and Goebbels on 18 November and 18 August respectively – yes 18 August – the war was lost well before 5 December.

This has in turn led to all sorts of criticisms about his conduct of the invasion. How did Hitler ever think that his three million men could roll over nearly twice that number of Stalin's? And why did the Germans – Hitler himself can hardly be blamed for this – continue to underrate the number of men Stalin could mobilise? When they had routed the armies they knew about by mid-August, they found another 160 divisions materialising apparently from nowhere. When these in turn were decimated by October – three million Russians had been killed or captured already – yet another massive force emerged from the steppes.

Why didn't Hitler listen to the advice of the military professionals, Brauchitsch and Halder, who wanted to concentrate the attack on Moscow, on the assumption that they would destroy the main Soviet armies en route, who would feel obliged to stand and fight, instead of dispersing his forces by sending von Leeb north to Leningrad and von Rundstedt south into the Ukraine?

Why was Guderian, whose tanks had achieved as spectacular success in Russia as in France, obliged to swing south to help von Rundstedt in the Ukraine, when he had made such a breakthrough in the centre, reaching Smolensk as early as 16 July?

Why again did the Germans not allow for the state of the Russian roads – or rather for the lack of roads? One need not fully share Liddell-Hart's certainty that "if her road system had been developed comparably to that of the West, she would have been overrun almost as quickly as France" to wonder why more cognisance had not been taken of this factor.

What, indeed, if Hitler had responded to Stalin's peace feelers in Octo-

Map 6   The Eastern Front 1941 – 1945

ber, when Stalin thought – and who could blame him – that he was losing the war, he not having the benefit of the searing scholarly insight that Hitler thought he was losing it!

And what, above all, if only the Germans had not treated the Ukrainians even worse than Stalin? Their initial reception had often been enthusiastic. The Ukraine, the richest agricultural area of the Soviet Union, had suffered savagely from the war against the kulaks during the collectivisation campaign – which Stalin would go so far as to tell Churchill was tougher than the war against the Germans. It was only seven or eight years since at least three million Ukrainians had starved, or been starved, to death in the Great Ukrainian Famine. It was beyond the Ukrainian imagination to conceive of a yet more ferocious savage than Stalin – until the Germans began applying racist doctrine to themselves, and drove most of them back into Stalin's arms. Race war brought even more vicious, or at least more extensive, mass murder than class war.

And yet, for all the blunders attributed to the Germans in general, and Hitler in particular, the bottom line remains that 1941 had been another year of dazzling success for German arms. The balance of probabilities undoubtedly shifted in December. But it did not shift enough to allow confident prediction about the course or even the outcome of the conflict. The German army would drive forward, well beyond its front line of 1941, over southern Russia for most of 1942. Spectacular advances on this scale were a curious way of preparing for 'inevitable' defeat. The most reasonable conclusion is that it was still all to play for at the end of 1941, and that, despite the colossal economic and technological potential of America, the human factor still remained crucial.

Chapter 17

How Hitler misread Germany

Having appointed Albert Speer economic supremo, the Führer then tied his hands

THE conflict on the eastern front between 1941 and 1945 transcended all previous experience of war in scale and savagery. Although all estimates are liable to revision, it seems that at least 12,000,000 soldiers were killed in combat – about nine million on the Soviet side, and three million on the German. That compares with probably fewer than 10 million in the entire First World War on every front. One must allow in addition for the five million Soviet prisoners who died – or in reality were murdered, whether directly or from being worked to death on starvation rations – and about half a million German prisoners who would die in Soviet captivity. Then at least another 20 million Soviet civilians – some estimates go closer to 40,000,000 – were killed, usually deliberately and brutally.

And finally, about 13 million Germans, their families settled in eastern Europe for generations for the most part, fled ahead of the rampaging Red Army, no doubt wisely, given the passion for revenge unleashed by German behaviour, to become refugees in Germany itself. Never in history had so many been slaughtered, bereaved or uprooted by a single war.

And it might have been more. For even if one believes that Germany was bound to lose in the end, decisions taken by Hitler, right from the outset, brought that end appreciably closer than might have been the case. Those decisions were all in one sense political – but they related to the economic, diplomatic, military, and scientific dimensions of the war.

The colossal Soviet production effort that yielded such massive increases in armament output is now widely credited with marking the decisive power shift in the struggle in the east. The conclusion appears obvious – however spectacular the early Blitzkrieg victories in the west, and even in the early days of Barbarossa itself, wasn't size bound to count in the end?

Maybe it was, even if it would matter greatly when, where and how that end actually came. But the USSR only got the chance to stay in the war because Hitler failed to bring the full potential power of Germany to bear on the invasion. His tactic of using Blitzkrieg to square the circle between running a war while sustaining civilian consumption levels, although initially spectacularly successful, meant leaving the German economy far from fully mobilised for total war when he invaded the USSR. It wouldn't be until spring 1942 that the German economy shifted onto a total war footing. Of course the German economy had been preparing for war for several years before 1939. It was the extra shift Hitler was loath to risk.

The sharp rise in German military output for the next two and a half years, until nearly the end of 1944, revealed how undercommitted to total war the economy had been. This increase is often ascribed to the impact of Albert Speer, the 36-year-old architect whom Hitler appointed to take charge of the war economy in early 1942. No doubt much of the credit must go to Speer. But he was appointed only because his predecessor, Fritz Todt, was killed in an air crash in January, shortly after Hitler had already taken the crucial decision to shift to a much higher production gear – the decision that both symbolically and substantively marks the end of the Blitzkrieg mindset. Whoever was in charge – and Todt was an able man – was likely to have produced improved results. Policy didn't change because Speer took charge. Speer took charge after policy had changed. Making all due allowance for his self-promotional skills – he was so consummate a propagandist in his own cause that nothing he says can be taken fully on trust – he implemented the new policy with impressive efficiency.

But was it already too late? Neville Chamberlain, in a phrase which came back to haunt him after Dunkirk, claimed early in the war that Hitler had missed the bus by not going to war in 1938. That is highly contentious. Whatever about that, it can be argued that he really missed the bus not once but twice after going to war. The first time was during the so-called 'phoney war' period between the fall of Poland in September 1939 and the invasion of France in May 1940. The second was in what one can call a second 'phoney war' period between the fall of France in June 1940 and the invasion of Yugoslavia and Greece in April 1941, blending into Barbarossa in June. This is not normally called a phoney war, but only for the simple reason that Britain suffered bombing, and because the British engaged in a land war in North Africa and Greece. From Hitler's point of view, however, these were hardly wars at all, registering virtually zero on the Richter scale of war production, and consuming only a tiny proportion of German resources in material and manpower.

The real issue was Russia. And yet he thought he could defeat Russia while running the German economy on virtually a business-as-usual basis (and before saying what stupidity, nearly all foreign observers thought so too – and in reality he very nearly did). The figures have to be seen to be believed – even if one should never take figures at total face value. There are certainly qualifications to be made to these figures. But the implications are nonetheless crystal clear. There was substantial slack to be taken in, once the German economy went on to a full war footing. Look at the figures for aircraft, tanks and heavy artillery.

German aircraft production only crept up from 9,000 in 1939 to 10,000 in 1940, to nearly 12,000 in 1941. Compare this with her output of nearly 25,000 planes in 1943 and 40,000 in 1944, despite the massive bombing she suffered.

At first sight, the increase in tank production seems more impressive. Total output rose from about 1300 in 1939 to 2200 in 1940 and 5200 in 1941. But compare this with the rise to 9200 in 1942, 17,300 in 1943 and 22,100 in 1944. Hitler actually invaded the USSR with only a small increase in the number of tanks used in the French campaign. Despite Hitler's own fascination with the motor car, despite the way Volkswagen had entered the vocabulary as a household word, despite the rhetoric of the autobahn, despite the vaunted efficiency of German technology, despite the central role of mechanical engineering in German industrialisation, the backbone of the German supply system in Russia was not motorised vehicles but horses – 650,000 of them at the outset.

The figures for medium and heavy calibre artillery pieces are likewise striking. German output rose from 2000 in 1939 to 7000 in 1941. This may seem impressive – until one notes a rise to 41,000 in 1944.

Of course American and Russian production rose massively after 1941 also. But it was Hitler who was planning invasion, after all. He had the advantage of knowing what he had in mind – but got his calculations wrong, if not by much. If the German war economy had been organised during 1939-41 to deliver anything like its performance of 1942-4, instead of cruising along during the two phoney war periods, one would certainly be entitled to wonder whether the USSR could have resisted effectively, given that she was brought to the brink of defeat by forces relying on a grossly undermobilised German economy in 1941.

The great irony is that even when Germany shifted to a full war footing, her output still fell well below her potential. Once again, in the economy as well as on the battlefield, the use made of resources mattered hugely. Germany produced vastly more steel and coal than the USSR until 1944. But look at the use they each made of their resources. One staggering statistic is that in 1943 the USSR managed to get 24,000 tanks and 48,000 heavy artillery pieces from eight million tons of steel and 90,000,000 tons of coal. Germany in the same year got only 17,000 tanks and 27,000 heavy pieces from no less than 30,000,000 tons of steel and 340,000,000 tons of coal.

Germany's greater resources produced significantly less output. If available 'resources' in any crude sense, as distinct from the use made of resources, had determined the conflict in the east, the odds would have been heavily in Germany's favour. How can the discrepancy between material resources and output be explained?

Speer had no doubts about the matter. Even allowing for bias, he clearly had grounds for complaint. Despite the huge increase in output under his direction, he was as conscious of frustration and failure as of success. His main enemies were not the Russians, or even the bombers. His enemies were the German military themselves, and Nazi ideology.

In contrast to the Soviets, who quickly reduced the types of tanks and planes to a bare minimum number of models, which could then be mass produced by relatively primitive techniques, Speer found himself, over two years into the war, inheriting the opposite extreme. There was no centralised mechanism for military ordering. Procurement officers submitted widely varying specifications, invariably demanding the highest standards of workmanship and highest quality materials, whatever the needs of the overall war effort.

Although the military strongly resisted Speer's programme of rationalisation, by 1944 he had whittled down 42 aircraft designs to 5, 151 types of lorries to 23, 12 anti-tank weapons to one. This contributed to roughly a trebling of weapons output and a doubling of output per worker over two-and-a-half years. But it was a constant struggle against the insistent clamour of the procurement perfectionists.

The struggle was exacerbated by the intrusion of both Nazi ideology and Nazi organisation. Labour was self-evidently a key factor in armaments production. But Speer had no control over labour supply. That was the province of Fritz Sauckel, a fanatical Nazi. Where Speer wanted the millions of prisoners of war and conscripted civilians, up to 7,000,000 at one stage, to be properly fed, if only on the functionally rational grounds that well fed workers could produce more, Sauckel, consumed with master race ideology, insisted on working many to death. Where Speer soon recognised that Sauckel's tactic of conscripting civilians from occupied countries, often through simple press-ganging, and dragging them to Germany, was depressing their productivity, he only partly succeeded with his alternative of bringing the work to the workers as far as possible, rather than vice versa.

Women workers were another example of tug of war between ideologues and functionalists. Where Stalin had no compunction about flinging Russian women into factory work in conditions just as primitive as those endured by men, not that they were used to anything better anyway, Hitler long refused to hear of introducing women workers into heavy industrial production, partly because of the ideology of female domesticity, partly because of the presumed negative impact on the standard of living and on civilian morale.

While Hitler trusted Speer as much as he trusted anyone, he realised that a war commissar, with control over all aspects of war production, would accumulate enormous power into his own hands. Hitler hesitated to rationalise the structure of command, even to prosecute the war more effectively, for fear of creating a possible rival to himself. He had appointed Speer in the first place within half an hour of the news of his predecessor Fritz Todt's untimely death, at least partly to forestall Hermann Goering's grab for the post of armaments minister. As Goering was already in charge of the Luftwaffe, this would have expanded his empire too greatly for Hitler's liking.

Speer gradually increased his authority simply because he got things done, but much of his time was spent manoeuvring to find ways of doing them by circumventing the formal authority structure. The results are all the more impressive, even allowing for the extra resources acquired through conquest, when account is taken of the damage done by American and British bombing, which probably reduced output by a third and slowed down delivery time by destroying so much of the transport system.

Hitler had of course brought the American bombing on himself. For it was he who chose wantonly to declare war on the USA on 11 December 1941, four days after Japan bombed Pearl Harbour and three days after Roosevelt, in declaring war on Japan, had very carefully not declared war on Germany. Nobody really knows why Hitler acted as he did.

Chapter 18

How Hitler misread America

In declaring war on the USA, Hitler hopelessly underrated the astonishing mobilisation power of American industry

IT IS customary to think of America's entry to the war after Pearl Harbour on 7 December 1941 and Hitler's declaration of war on the USA four days later as marking the point of no return in the Second World War. Wasn't Germany doomed once America's industrial might was mobilised? Maybe she was – assuming that she did not drive the USSR out of the war before then. But how long would that be? The general assumption was at least two to three years. In fact the only rational argument one can advance for Hitler's declaration of war is that he shared this assumption, and felt the war would have been decided in Europe before America could become fully engaged.

This was to hopelessly underrate the astonishing mobilisation power of American industry. It was an understandable error on the basis of the evidence available, but that evidence overlooked the fact that America was still in slump in 1941, with massive reserve capacity. It is easy to forget the traumatic impact of the Great Slump on the USA. It was psychologically probably even worse there than anywhere, because it so savagely exposed the Horatio Alger myth that everyone could make it in America. In practice this was simply not true for the majority of blacks, or for many poor whites. But for the bulk of white Americans, there was enough visible evidence of individuals making it for the self-image to be sustained and burnished. The organs of public opinion, the mainstream rhetoric, of America, invested ceaselessly in polishing the myth, never more so than during the Jazz Age of the 'Roaring Twenties', when the bright young things did their thing, and prosperity was here forever. It wasn't therefore just the pockets, but the entire value system, the raison d'etre of national and personal existence, the very sense of personal identity, virtually of virility, that the Slump threatened to destroy.

The shock of slump to the national nervous system was probably even worse in America than in Weimar Germany. The difference in the political response was that Americans could turn to an alternative mainstream party, the Democrats, given that the Republicans had been in the White House since 1920. In Germany every single constitutional party had been in coalition in recent memory during the twenties. All were tainted by the stench of ignominious failure, opening the door to anti-system parties of Right and Left, nazis and communists. The Democrats were not anti-system. Indeed, by happy chance, they threw up a candidate for the Presidency in 1932 in Franklin Delano Roosevelt, who knew how to work the system like none other, turning out to be the most formidable American political personality of the century.

Roosevelt's landslide victory in 1932, after 12 years of Republican rule, was much more a vote against the Republicans – who didn't even produce a new face but ran Herbert Hoover for re-election – than for himself personally. It reflected the depth of despair in an America ravaged by slump –

it is easy to forget now the riots, and confrontations with police, as desperate men sought food in a culture convinced that poverty must be the fault of the individual when it was clear to all but the wilfully blind that the mass unemployment was the fault of a broken down system and not of individual inadequacy.

Roosevelt had no magic elixir to solve the slump. His New Deal, involving the state in far more economic activity, for all its gusto, did not recreate full employment. Critics of the New Deal might scoff that it amounted to little more than a song and a prayer and whatever you're having yourself. Roosevelt might even have agreed privately. But he would have been quick to point out, and rightly so, that whereas the critics had nothing to offer, what they overlooked was that the New Deal mobilised the most important factor of production of all in the circumstances – hope.

Roosevelt was a master of psychology. When he claimed that the only thing we have to fear is fear itself, he went straight for the nerve centre of the impact on personality rather than relying on what he saw as the slide rules of the economists. It was just as well. Had the Slump lasted much longer, or had the hopes roused by FDR failed, who knows what depths of social conflict might have ravaged the USA?

Roosevelt had an extraordinary ability to inspire trust through sheer power of personality. It is no coincidence that virtually every President since has sought to lay claim to his legacy, including the Republican, Ronald Reagan. Roosevelt was the original 'Great Communicator' among 20th century presidents. Kennedy's speechwriters could polish sharper phrases, Reagan and even Clinton could convey a more ingratiating folksiness. But none were in Roosevelt's class as a communicator. He had the good fortune to arrive with the age of radio. Television has so superseded radio as a communicator of political spectacle that we forget how for a generation radio was the communication wonder of the century. The tricks of TV performance – make up, good looks, body language – were meaningless. It was the instrument of the voice. And Roosevelt used his voice, as only Churchill among his contemporaries in the democracies could use his, to win hearts as well as heads. The fireside chats, made possible only by the radio, in which this patrician could speak directly to millions of Americans as if he were talking to them alone, and could appear to enter into their problems as if they were the only ones who counted at that moment, were wonders of the art of communication.

But even his communication and leadership skills could not shake Americans out of their renewed commitment to neutrality during the 1930s. The experience of the First World War had left a very sour taste in American mouths. From their perspective they had violated the most solemn teaching of the founding fathers, George Washington's injunction to America to avoid entangling alliances, the conviction that America could no longer be the city on the hill, so cherished in the self-image, if she came down to dirty her toes in the foetid waters of the old world.

And all for what? What had so many thousand American boys died for on the fields of France? To be manipulated by the cynical players of old world politics for their selfish purposes, to buttress their colonial empires and sustain their ill-gotten gains? We are so habituated to America's global power that we find it virtually impossible to visualise a world, so recent in time, in which America played so restricted a political role. But the mindset behind it is understandable enough. As far as European affairs were concerned, it was as simple as once bitten, twice shy. Unless America's own security was seen to be directly threatened, American public opinion remained resolutely opposed to further adventures in Europe. In 1937, Congress actually strengthened the neutrality laws.

Such degree of distaste for Hitler's policies, and for the murders of Jews during *Kristallnacht*, as existed, did not suffice to shake public commitment to neutrality. Roosevelt, who detested Nazism himself, went as far as he felt he could in educating public opinion as to the potential threat to America of a Nazi conquest of Europe. He secured support for programmes of aid to Britain, though with a sharp eye to a good bargain for the USA, picking up British bases in the western hemisphere, knowing that Britain had little bargaining power, and that Churchill was pinning all his hopes on bringing America into the war. From an Irish perspective it is rather a pity that America didn't have some territorial claims against Britain. It would have been intriguing to see how that would have played out in the real world compared with the cloud-cuckoo land of the British 'offer' of Irish unity in June 1940.

Roosevelt, like Churchill and Hitler, had of course much more than voice. Voice was not enough. But without voice it is doubtful if he could have roused the response he did. Voice could not solve slump, although the hope it inspired was probably a significant psychological factor in restoring the faith of men and women in themselves.

The manner of entry into the war was so satisfactory from FDR's perspective that there were even those to suggest he suppressed foreknowledge of Pearl Harbour to ensure maximum public outrage. There is no plausible evidence on that score, but what is true is that general American policy was likely to force Japan to a crucial choice between reversing her expansionist policy since 1931 or else opting for all out war against the USA. FDR must have known war was a distinct possibility, even if he could not anticipate the precise manner of the outbreak.

Even the most rabid conspiracy theorists have difficulty in suggesting that Hitler had no choice but to go to war against America in December 1941. The decision was Hitler's, and Hitler's alone. It would prove to be his greatest blunder.

There is usually a plausible rationale for even Hitler's more dubious war decisions, but this one baffles analysis. It is true that there was an alliance of sorts under the Tripartite Agreement of 1940 between Japan, Germany and Italy – but it was a defensive alliance only, the signatories promising to support one another in the event of their being attacked by another power. This did not require him to go to war against America, anymore than it required Japan to go to war against Russia when Hitler invaded. Hitler may have hoped to persuade her to come in, thus forcing a two-front war on Stalin, but if so, he was deeply disappointed. Japan never did go to war against the USSR.

Hitler may also have reckoned that it was only a matter of time before Roosevelt found some way of declaring war, and as America would in the meantime continue to supply Britain with an increasing flow of resources, he should get his retaliation against American shipping in first. He may have hoped that the war in Europe would then be over before the USA could effectively enter, given that it would take her at least a year to train her first batch of recruits. And he almost certainly underrated the sheer speed with which the USA could turn her economy to massive war production.

It is reasonable to assume that the USA would have entered the war sooner or later against Germany. But it made a huge potential difference to the nature of the post-war world whether it was sooner or later. It has been a central theme of this book that 'inevitability' explains nothing, if only because *when* the 'inevitable' happens changes the consequences of the 'inevitable'. The same thing happening at different times is not necessarily the same thing. Consider the following scenarios for a moment.

Even assuming that Germany was going to lose, suppose that the war in Europe hadn't ended in May 1945, but had lasted a few months longer, as could easily have happened – if, for instance, Speer had been given more authority by Hitler earlier, or if Hitler had not declared war on America so early, if at all. D-Day might well not have happened when it did in June 1944, or it might well not have succeeded against a better equipped enemy. Even assuming Germany was eventually defeated, it would have been in very different circumstances, with a very different balance between Soviet and American forces.

Or assume that the USA had the atomic bomb while war still raged in Europe – she tested it successfully little more than two months after the German surrender. Would President Truman have dropped the bomb on German cities with the same alacrity as on Hiroshima and Nagasaki? Or would these have sufficed as demonstration explosions for the Germans too? Or what?

It can never be stressed too often, given the widespread American assumption today that America declared war on Hitler to 'fight against fascism', that it was Hitler who declared war on the USA, which remained neutral as long as she could, and entered the war on the same grounds of perceived national interest as every other belligerent. But this is not ideologically convenient for many Americans today.

A massive exhibition of American Art in the Twentieth Century opened in the Whitney Museum in New York early in 1999. The caption introducing the Second World War period boldly asserts that, after the Japanese attack on Pearl Harbour 'within a few days, the United States, allied with France and England, declared war on Germany, Japan and Italy'. This is all the more effective because the writer obviously believes every word of it, so there is no attempt at deliberate deception. But just look at the misconceptions.

The biggest, of course, is about America declaring war on Germany. But note also the reference to her ally, France, when the USA actually continued to recognise the collaborationist Vichy regime of Marshall Pétain. It wasn't until 1944, after D-Day that Roosevelt could bring himself to accept de Gaulle as the incarnation of Free France. If the reference to France is misleading, note how there is no reference at all to America's main new ally – the USSR. Even a decade after the effective end of the Cold War, it seems emotionally impossible to conceive of the 'evil empire' as an American ally, so it simply finds itself unconsciously airbrushed out of the alliance.

It would be easy to dismiss all this as merely ignorant folk-belief. But this is no declamation by some parade orator. This is composed by the educated for the educated. It is a particularly arresting exhibition of the manner in which history can be re-imagined to satisfy our present self-images. Not of course that the Irish have to go to the US to discover this. Are we not dab hands at it ourselves?

Chapter 19

Death from the skies

There are modern parallels to the debate over whether the bombing of Germany was either crucial or moral

THERE IS a natural tendency to assume that Hitler's Declaration of War on America on 11 December 1941 made German defeat inevitable. Whatever about that, it certainly can be claimed that without American involvement, Germany might not have been defeated. The Russians, of course, broke the thrust of the German advance at Stalingrad in January and February 1943, while the USA was still only marginally involved in Europe. Nevertheless, while it seems unlikely that the USSR would have defeated Germany even after Stalingrad, it is just as possible that Germany would not have defeated the USSR. They could have fought each other to a draw. After all, it took the Soviets more than two years to get from Stalingrad to Berlin even with American involvement in the west, and despite the destructive bombing campaign over Germany.

How did the British and Americans come to repose such faith in the bomber? It was partly to placate Stalin. He was already charging the British with cowardice for failing to invade Western Europe in 1942 – just think of the cheek of it, given that it was his own pact with Hitler in August 1939 that allowed the Germans to invade Poland. But Stalin was not one to be incommoded by a trifling detail of that sort.

And there was, as usual with Stalin, method in his self-righteousness. He knew full well that Britain and America needed him. He could stoke their fear that he would patch up a separate peace with Hitler in the east – he even turned the fact that he had already done a deal with Hitler to his advantage – and let them confront the full weight of German arms in the west. That was improbable, but not impossible, and it was a scenario that the British and Americans had to take seriously. Churchill and Roosevelt took it seriously enough to arrive at two decisions at Casablanca in January 1943 that had far-reaching consequences. The first was to demand the 'unconditional surrender' of Germany. This was partly to reassure Stalin that they would make no separate peace in the west. The irony was that it probably didn't much matter to Stalin. As he trusted nobody anyway, he would simply assume that they would break the pledge as soon as it suited them. But it did mean that no alternative German government was likely to emerge if the only negotiating terms open to it were unconditional surrender. The likelihood of any successful opposition emerging within Germany was very slim in any case. 'Unconditional surrender' made it even less likely.

The second decision was that instead of trying to open a second land front in France, Britain and America would first concentrate on the sky front, by massively intensifying the bombing campaign against Germany.

Bombing remains one of the most contentious issues in 20th century warfare, from both a practical and moral point of view. Emotions roused by bombing – of London and Coventry, of Hamburg and Dresden, culminating in the nuclear horrors of Hiroshima and Nagasaki – have given rise to passionate debates not only about the war, but about the meaning of civilisation in the 20th century.

There is a natural tendency for critics of bombing on moral grounds to also argue that bombing cannot win wars. Critics often claim that bombing simply stiffens the resolve of the victims. Examples are cited of British grit in the face of the Blitz, or of German doggedness in fighting to the end, or of North Vietnamese resilience in the face of the B52s, or indeed, the stiff resistance of the Serbs in the face of Nato bombing. More moderate critics assert that while air power can make a difference, it cannot win wars on its own. Connoisseurs of opinion on bombing had a field-day in 1999 rummaging through the running commentaries on the Serbian conflict. John Keegan, the respected defence correspondent of the *Daily Telegraph*, beat his breast in public, conceding that he was wrong to claim that bombing couldn't do the trick, once he had heard of the Serb 'capitulation'.

Keegan had, in fact, no need to reverse himself. 'Success' depends on the war aims of the bombers. Bombing Serbia to achieve agreement on Kosovo was a very different matter to bombing Germany to achieve 'unconditional surrender'. It all depends on circumstances.

Opinions on the practical results of the bombing of Germany range from the view that it made no difference at all to the view that it virtually won the war on its own. They continue to reflect the clash of opinion during the war itself. These were held so passionately that, years later, the air ministry in Britain attempted to suppress the official history by Sir Charles Webster and Noble Frankland because it failed to follow the Ministry line.

Opinions on the morality of bombing range from the belief that it is immoral in any circumstances to the view that the only morality in war is the defeat of the enemy, garnished in the German case by the gut feeling that they had it coming to them because of their earlier Blitz against British cities.

The practical question is easier to analyse than the moral one. It cannot seriously be doubted that the bombing of Germany made a significant difference to the timing of the end of the war in Europe, although it would be going too far to claim that it definitely changed the outcome. Critics contend that the fact that German armaments output trebled between 1942 and 1944 shows that the bombing must have been ineffective. How could output grow so fast otherwise? But the real question here is whether output would not have increased even faster but for the bombing, and the best estimates available suggest that the bombing reduced the potential war output of the German economy by about one-third.

It did more than that. Although it took until the Spring of 1944 for the Americans and British to secure command of the air over western Europe, by May 1944 they enjoyed virtually unimpeded bombing of fuel depots and railways.

Without this command of the skies, D-Day, for all the superiority of the American production machine, couldn't have happened in June 1944. Total command of the air was a prerequisite for the success of D-Day. Even with that command, the western allies were nearly thrown back into the water.

Had the beachheads not been secured, the invasion could hardly have been mounted again until the following year. D-Day was not exactly an excursion of day-trippers which could have been resumed at the weekend. Defeat would have marked a dramatic reverse. Who knows how Hitler and Stalin might have responded in those circumstances?

It therefore seems very doubtful if the investment in air power could have been used more effectively in other ways. But that still leaves unanswered the moral question, as to whether the blanket bombing of civilians was necessary to break the German will to resist. Bombing seems to have claimed somewhere between 750,000 and one million victims, many burned to death by the fire bombing that most spectacularly incinerated Hamburg and Dresden. This was the direct consequence of policy, not an unfortunate accident of collateral damage.

The Casablanca directive on bombing was quite explicit that the objective was not only to destroy war production directly, but "the undermining of the morale of the German people to a point where their capacity for armed resistance is fatally weakened". This was a euphemism for "killing as many civilians as possible". The civilians were killed alright. Civilian morale was doubtless damaged. But that damage does not seem to have weakened resistance by the armed forces. It is doubtful if the bombing of civilians – mostly women, children and old men – reduced the length of the war by as much as a month, or maybe even a week.

The British and Americans attitude was that the Germans deserved it. Hadn't they begun it, with the bombing of London in early September 1940? The German response was that this bombing of London was provoked by four British attempts, however ineffectual, to bomb Berlin, beginning on 25 August 1940.

This is chronologically correct, although of course Hitler had no hesitation whatever about bombing civilians, as the cases of Warsaw in September 1939 and Rotterdam in May 1940 indicate. But it also seems to be the case that Churchill, and even Roosevelt – Stalin goes without saying – believed in 'extermination' bombing. Terror bombing was the ultimate symbol of total war.

There is a straight line from this mindset to the dropping of the atomic bombs on Hiroshima and Nagasaki. The bomb was initially intended for use against Germany. Some claim that it would never have been dropped on a 'white' country. But the 40,000 incinerated in Hamburg in 1943 and the further 40,000 in Dresden in 1944 – to take the most conservative estimates – were nearly as big an increase on the 800 killed in Rotterdam in 1940 as Hiroshima would be on Dresden. The mindset that could bomb Dresden would scarcely shirk use of the A-bomb.

Ironically it may even be that it was the success of the earlier bombing of industrial targets in Germany, insofar as it may have significantly shortened the war in Europe, that forestalled the A-bomb being first used over Europe rather than Asia.

Chapter 20

The birth of the nuclear age

The morality of using the atomic bomb was not a political issue; only if it hadn't been used would questions have arisen

"ABIES satisfactorily born", the phrase by which Churchill learned from the Americans on 17 July 1945 at the Potsdam Conference of the successful test of an atomic bomb must surely count as one of the most infelicitous phrases ever devised to announce the arrival of a weapon of mass death. Within a month, the 'babies' would slaughter nearly 200,000 victims, mostly human babies, children, women and old men in Hiroshima and Nagasaki. Debate still rages about how justified President Truman was in deciding to drop the bomb. Truman, who would become a notable president despite his utter lack of experience on succeeding Roosevelt in April 1945, described the building of the atomic bomb as "the greatest achievement of organised science in history". And the Manhattan Project, the code name for the massive enterprise, was indeed an epic of both scientific and organisational achievement.

The impact of World War Two on science, and of science on World War Two, deserves a volume in itself. Suffice it here to say that it was made possible by the extraordinary development of international science over the previous half century, through the cumulative work of numerous individuals, including Einstein, Becquerel, Rutherford, Soddy, Eddington, Aston, Chadwick, Szilard, Hahn, Strassmann, Frisch, Meitner, Bohr, Wheeler, Peierls, von Halban, Kowarski, Wigner, Teller, Fermi and Oppenheimer, hailing from France, Britain, Switzerland, Germany, Italy, Hungary, Austria, Denmark and America.

Debate continues as to whether Germany could have produced a bomb earlier if Hitler had given the full green light, and on the role of Werner Heisenberg in contributing to the possible delay on moral grounds. But morality posed few problems for most Manhattan participants. In one sense, the question that might be put was not whether Truman's decision to use the bomb was justified, but why there was no decision to use the bomb – in the sense that the decision was so taken for granted by both Truman and his advisers that a moral issue simply did not arise. The non-use of the bomb would have required a decision. The use of it did not.

Churchill found his own inimitable way of expressing the American and British mood at Potsdam on receipt of the news: "There never was a moment's discussion as to whether the atomic bomb should be used or not. To avert a vast, indefinite butchery, to bring the war to an end, to give peace to the world, to lay healing hands upon its tortured peoples by a manifestation of overwhelming power at the cost of a few explosions, seemed, after all our toils and perils, a miracle of deliverance...."

This was understandable. But "at the cost of a few explosions", which might take 200,000 civilian lives, graphically captures Churchill's concern for human life. That the matter "was never even an issue" Churchill seemed to think was somehow a tribute to the values for which Western rhetoric purported to have fought the war. Indeed, Truman would finish the chapter on the bomb in his memoirs with the observation, without a trace of conscious irony, that now "maybe the teachings of the Sermon on the Mount could be put into effect". Truman did make a feeble attempt to cover the moral problem by claiming that "I wanted to make sure it would be used as a weapon of war in the manner prescribed by the laws of war" by dropping it on a military rather than a civilian target.

This was patent window dressing. The purpose of the bomb was terror. The more civilians killed, the more effective the terror. Indeed, Nagasaki was unfortunate enough to get the second bomb even though it was only second choice – it was intended for Kokura, but after the pilot failed to find a break in the clouds he was diverted to Nagasaki. So much for the pious Churchillian claim that "we agreed to give every chance to the inhabitants". Granted that the Americans had no choice but to build a bomb, given their justifiable fear that Hitler would get there first, on the basis of the rightly-respected creativity of German science, how had Western civilisation nevertheless reached the stage where mass death could be taken for granted?

In only five years Western consciences had leapt from outrage at the bombing of Rotterdam to virtually unquestioned acceptance of mass slaughter from the air on a scale a hundred times greater – and not just acceptance, but in some cases delight, as reflected in the gloating of cartoons on news of Hiroshima. Nor was this a case of the militarist mind unleashed. Truman's advisers included the presidents of Harvard and MIT.

Insofar as Truman's thought process can be reconstructed, almost all his retrospective justifications can be queried. The most compelling one was that American lives would be saved if the Japanese surrendered before the land invasion contemplated for November had to be launched. Truman didn't need statistics to tell him of the willingness of the Japanese army to fight till death. The example of the latest carnage at Okinawa was right before his eyes.

Nevertheless, he offered no plausible estimate of the likely number of

American casualties during an invasion. He mentioned a quarter of a million dead and a half million wounded.

But the figures could have been taken out of a hat. George Marshall mentioned a half million dead. In 1946, the figure of a million total casualties, dead and wounded, was bandied about. Churchill, an ardent advocate of atom bombing, as of all other bombing, decided that a million dead would sound better in his memoirs, and so killed off the wounded to get his nice round figure of one million.

Yet it would have been irresponsible of an American president not to have anticipated a worst-case scenario. Maybe Japanese civilians would not fight as fanatically as soldiers. But 1.9 million Japanese were in arms of some sort in Japan in July 1946. However hastily mobilised many of them were, and however badly armed, no-one with the experience of Okinawa could have been other than pessimistic about the likely death toll.

Two other factors obviously influenced the assumption that the bomb would be automatically used. The first was a burning desire for revenge for Pearl Harbour by giving the Japs a taste of their own medicine. The second was fear of Stalin acquiring a stake in the Far East. The Americans had been madly anxious to get him into the War with Japan, if only to save the lives of their own soldiers, until the moment they had the bomb. Then they became equally anxious to keep him out, for fear of his potential threat to their interests. And the bomb would serve nicely as a warning to him to watch his step not only in Asia but in Europe as well. Therefore, the more devastating the explosion the better.

And from the victims' point of view, it could be argued, what difference did it make whether you were incinerated by one bomb or by many, as had happened in Tokyo and Dresden a few months before. One might even argue that compared with the bombing of Dresden, it could at least be claimed that the A-bomb had a clear objective: the rapid ending of the war.

The justification for the bombing of Dresden was much less plausible. It was not a major centre of war production. Its population, again mainly children, women and old men, was swollen by the influx of refugees flying ahead of the Russian armies. Had the victims – and up to 80,000 may have been slaughtered – been rounded up by ground troops, and forced into buildings which were then set on fire, presumably the conscience of the 'civilised' world would have recoiled in horror. Broiling the victims by bombing has the great advantage of requiring no such conscience recoil. We can continue undisturbed in the tranquillity of our sense of moral superiority.

What is most saddening about the dropping of the A-bombs is not their actual use, but rather the triumph of the mentality in the course of the war that no moral issues were involved in the mass slaughter of any form of human life. The A-bomb was not a new frontier in man's inhumanity, merely the logical terminus of a journey already close to destination.

Chapter 21

Democracy and double standards

For Churchill, small nations had no rights against the big boys

HITLER'S invasion of Poland would not in itself have started the Second World War but for Britain and France having committed themselves to Poland's support in the event of a German invasion. The invasion, of course, turned out to be not only a German one but a Soviet one also. Britain and France honoured their commitments insofar as they declared war, however ineffectually from Poland's point of view, on Germany. But they did not declare war on the

USSR. The reason is clear. They felt that Germany posed a direct threat to themselves. They did not feel that Russia posed such a threat. It was, therefore, the incongruous situation in September 1939 that Poland was being nominally defended against an invasion from one direction, but not from another. Nothing could have made it clearer that the concern of Britain and France was not for Poland, but for themselves.

This was, of course, in accord with decision-making by every state, belligerent or neutral, affected by the war. They all sought to pursue what they felt to be in their own best interest. So it had been since time immemorial. However repelled many British had been by the murders of *Kristallnacht* in November 1938, it wasn't then, but only after Hitler occupied Prague in March 1939, breaking the Munich Agreement, that Chamberlain offered Poland a guarantee. Hitler could kill as many Jews as he liked, as long as he did not threaten Britain or France.

Exactly the same thinking applied to attitudes to the USSR. Stalin had actually tortured and slaughtered incomparably more victims before the war than had Hitler. But he could kill as many as he wanted, as long as his foreign policy did not threaten the perceived interests of Britain and France. Invasion of Poland by the USSR did not threaten their interests, as they saw them. Hence the 'guarantee' to Poland only against a German invasion, not a Soviet one, even if everything they knew at the time suggested that a Soviet occupation would be every bit as brutal as a German one, if not more so.

The same thinking applied to British and French, and indeed American, attitudes to Japanese atrocities – 'the Rape of Nanking' in 1937 is the best known in the West – as long as their own interests were not directly affected.

The horrors of Hitlerism, once the war began, were naturally a godsend from a propaganda point of view. A war entered on grounds of national interest could be presented as a struggle for civilisation, a glorious crusade to make the world safe for freedom, democracy and apple pie.

In all this deluge of propaganda, poor Poland faded into virtual oblivion. There was, to be fair to those among the western allies with a conscience, an element of denial in all this, for the fate of the Poles would turn out to be, apart from that of the Jews, the most horrific of all victims of either Hitler or Stalin. Both Hitler and Stalin, who had far more in common than divided them, set out to destroy Poland as a nation. With remarkably similar methods, they sought to decapitate Polish society. In addition to the three million Polish Jews, the Germans are estimated to have murdered about two-and-a-half million other Poles, beginning immediately in September 1939. Stalin is estimated to have killed or deported to the Gulag between one and one-and-a-half million of the 13 million people in his Soviet occupation area.

Warsaw alone would lose 700,000 citizens, more than the entire military and civilian casualties of Britain and the USA in the war, 200,000 of them in the Warsaw Uprising of August-September 1944 when Stalin's army stood idly by to let the Germans kill as many independent-minded Poles as possible to make it all the easier for Stalin to impose his puppet regime.

Both Hitler and Stalin made particular targets of the creative elements in Polish culture – intellectuals, academics, clergy, officers, doctors, lawyers, business people, and journalists, who were the victims of mass rampages during 1939-41. The Katyn massacre of Polish officers, on Stalin's orders, was merely the tip of the iceberg.

Hitler set out to destroy Polish culture in the area he annexed directly to Germany, above all by destroying the Polish language. Language killing has long proved a favourite tactic of nation killers. There was nothing original about the German assault on the Polish language, merely about the thoroughness with which it was implemented.

What did the British guarantee do for Poland? At the end of the war, Poland found herself shunted west on the map of Europe, with Stalin keeping his spoils under the Nazi-Soviet Pact, shifting as 'compensation' the western border of Poland 125 miles west and expelling over three million Germans.

Well, Stalin would, wouldn't he? What else could you expect from him? Indeed. And no doubt he thought of this stratagem himself. But he didn't need to. For it was suggested to him by none other than Winston Churchill at the Tehran Conference in 1943, at a time when thousands of Polish volunteers were fighting in the British army. Was this just another example of perfidious Albion, or what?

Churchill's proposal to Stalin at the Tehran Conference in 1943, that

Poland should be shifted westwards on the map of Europe, brilliantly illuminates the Churchillian world view. Even more illuminating was Churchill's insouciance in describing the whole affair in his memoirs, as if it were the most natural thing in the world that weak states should yield to the interests of stronger states, as indeed de Valera observed in his response to Churchill's strictures on Irish policy.

It never seems to have crossed Churchill's mind that there could be any other legitimate way of looking at international relations, other than the primacy of the interests of the strong against the weak. Nor was this simply the case when a great power was fighting with its back against the wall for its very existence, as with Britain in 1940. There was no question of that being the case any longer by Tehran. It was simply the normal state of international affairs.

This world view appears at its starkest in Churchill's reply to Stalin's question as to whether they should consult the Poles beforehand about their fate. No, said Churchill. We will decide their borders, and then "go to the Poles … and advise them to accept." This, it is worth reminding ourselves, is not Stalin's account, covering his tracks with his customary smokescreen of mendacity. This is Churchill's own telling, so blithely oblivious was he in his self-righteousness to the possibility that anyone might think there was anything odd about it.

This was the same Churchill who excoriated Neville Chamberlain in coruscating style over the manner in which he had decided with Hitler to change the borders of Czechoslovakia at the Munich Conference in 1938, without consulting the Czechs. He himself now revealed precisely the same mindset about other people's borders. Only more so. For Chamberlain could at least plead, rightly or wrongly, that he was faced with the threat of a disastrous war. Churchill faced no such ultimatum at Tehran. It was he who chose gratuitously to open the issue, behind the backs of the Polish government-in-exile in London.

Why then did Churchill try to turn Tehran into a Polish Munich? The only difference between Hitler at Munich and Churchill at Tehran was that Hitler's behaviour, as Churchill saw it, threatened British interests. His own proposals for rearranging Poland at Germany's expense were meant to buttress British interests by weakening postwar Germany.

Before British interests, in Churchill's mind, there could be no false gods. Nor did he make any bones about this. The best summary of his world view is provided by himself, as he told Ivan Maisky, the Soviet Ambassador in London, in 1938: "Twenty years ago I strove with all the energy in my power against communism, because at that time I considered communism, with its idea of world revolution, the greatest danger to the British empire. Now communism does not present such a danger to the empire. On the contrary, nowadays German Nazism, with its idea of the world hegemony of Berlin, constitutes the greatest danger for the British empire. Therefore, at the present time I strive against Hitler with all the energy in my power..."

It is a full and frank proclamation of priorities. So much for all the propagandistic rhetoric about the 'fight against fascism' for 'freedom' and 'democracy'.

It was for long virtually impossible to criticise Churchill because of his hold on the public imagination, thanks to his leadership of Britain in the darkest hours of 1940. That leadership was indeed magnificent. The manner in which he rallied his country in the face of impending disaster was arguably the greatest single feat of nationalist leadership of the century.

I have little time for a fashionable type of British revisionism that denounces Churchill for failing to respond to Hitler's peace overtures in 1940. I believe that Churchill got Hitler right, in the sense that no peace would be permanent, that with Hitler it was all or nothing, and that he would turn on Britain as soon as opportunity again offered. Whatever criticisms in detail may be made of his leaderships, nothing should be allowed detract from the inspirational quality of Churchill's national leadership at that time.

It can also be strongly argued that Britain's interests in 1940-41 happened to coincide with the wider interests of preserving civilisation against a dire threat. But that was a happy coincidence. The real issue was much more power than values. And in that power play, Poland was simply a pawn.

How the incomparably cuter Stalin must have smirked to himself as he listened to Churchill's grandiose scenarios of the postwar world, of how we three, the USA, the USSR, and Britain "should guide the future of the world," acting as trustees to ensure "the right of all nations to develop as they like" – Churchill's own words – while in virtually the same breath he proposed, using matchsticks on the map, to set Poland's boundaries without consulting the Poles! Stalin could be forgiven for thinking that he was dealing with a cynic and a casuist as agile as himself.

Churchill's proposal for Poland would have meant either killing or deporting three million Germans from within what was still Germany proper. This mattered nothing to Churchill. The more bad blood there could be between postwar Poland and postwar Germany the better for Britain. It might also leave several million Poles under Stalin's control, although his proposal delicately provided for 'an interchange of population' from ethnically mixed areas of eastern Poland – a euphemism for that other euphemism of today, 'ethnic cleansing'.

Demythologising Churchillian rhetoric on World War II should not, of course, lead to new mythologies. That is the main problem with ideologically driven revisionism everywhere. It is by no means an exclusively Hibernian propensity. That Poland suffered savagely during the war is indisputable. The three million Polish Jews bore the full brunt of Hitler's genocidal policy. It was no accident that so many of the most infamous placenames in history were located in Poland – not only Auschwitz-Birkenau, but Belzec, Chelmno, Sobibor and Treblinka. But had not a single Jew been murdered, the combined death toll of the wanton slaughter by Hitler and Stalin of non-Jewish Poles would still have left Poland with the highest number of civilian casualties inflicted by the conqueror. The ratio of civilian war victims in Yugoslavia may have been as high as among non-Jewish Poles. But most of these were killed by other 'Yugoslavs' in a civil war, or rather in a series of civil wars.

That is not to say that Poland did not contain bitter internal conflicts of her own. She did. Poland was no democracy before the war. She had an authoritarian rightwing regime. There was widespread popular anti-semitism. Eastern Poland, in particular, was riven by ethnic tensions. Substantial numbers of Ukrainians and White Russians had found themelves corralled in Poland after 1920. Poland had eagerly seized the Czech part of Teschen as part of the booty in the destruction of Czechoslovakia after Munich, in what Churchill described as a "hyena-like annexation". But what term should then apply to his own proposal to lop off nearly half of Poland for the Soviet Union, compared with which Teschen was tiny? The Polish pre-war regime, for all its own crudities, couldn't hold a candle to Churchill's proposal of uprooting millions of people, and consigning millions of others to Stalin's tender mercies. Whether the relative legitimacy of the claims of the various ethnic groups involved, Churchill was not proposing to consult any of them. They were to be carted around the map like cattle. His proposals had little to do with right or wrong. They had to do with power relations.

Churchill was genuinely upset by Stalin's behaviour during the Warsaw uprising of August-September 1944. When the Poles of Warsaw rose, with Soviet encouragement, once Soviet troops reached the outskirts of Warsaw, Stalin halted his troops while the Germans, the SS at their head, pulverised the rebels, often in hand-to-hand sewer fighting. Stalin even rejected demands to allow Allied planes wanting to drop supplies to the rebels to land on Russian-held territory until he was certain it was too late to help the Poles. Stalin was happy to see the Germans and non-Communist Poles kill each other. It must rank among the most supremely cynical acts of even the supreme cynic of the century. Over 200,000 insurgents and civilians are estimated to have been killed.

There is no reason to doubt Churchill's dismay. But he soon shrugged it off, going in October to frolic in Moscow with Stalin "with whom, in spite of the Warsaw tragedy, I felt new links."

If Ireland was, in Woodrow Wilson's words, the great metaphysical tragedy of World War I, exposing the double standards of victors purporting to fight to make the world safe for democracy, Poland was the great metaphysical, as well as physical, tragedy of World War II. Here, more than anywhere else, was glaringly illustrated the opportunism of those now purporting to be fighting yet again to make the world safe for democracy, when democracy was simply the rhetorical facade behind which the national interest of the stronger states could be most fashionably served.

Chapter 22

Resistance *versus* collaboration

The size of the Resistance has swelled as spectacularly as the numbers in the GPO in 1916

I T IS natural enough to think of World War II mainly in terms of the clash of Titans, of the Panzers punching through the Ardennes, of Spitfires and Messerschmitts over the Home Counties, of the heroics and horrors of Stalingrad, of the clash of Tigers and T34s at Kursk, of the 1st US Infantry wading ashore at Omaha Beach, of the blanket bombing, culminating in Hiroshima and Nagasaki – and of Auschwitz.

But the vast majority of the peoples of western Europe, except for Jews, did not experience the war in that way. In eastern Europe, it was different, with so many civilians widely treated as sub-humans by both nazis and communists. But western Europe had a relatively short war as far as direct conflict was concerned. Norway and Denmark, Holland and Belgium were occupied in a matter of days, France in a month. It wouldn't be until 1944 or 1945 that they would experience ground warfare again. Italy did suffer war on the ground once British and American forces landed in Sicily in 1943, and the Germans moved in occupation forces when Mussolini was deposed. But for the vast bulk of western European civilians, the war was the choice between accommodation, collaboration and resistance. The responses tell us much about human nature, and are probably a good guide to how we ourselves might have behaved in similar circumstances.

For years after the war, the myth of the Resistance dominated public discourse. Except for a small number of repulsive collaborators, everybody had allegedly been in the Resistance, or had at least striven to help the Resistance. The size of the Resistance swelled retrospectively as spectacularly as the numbers in the GPO during Easter Week. The reality was different. It varied from country to country.

The most intriguing case of all was France. Indeed the very terms 'collaboration' and 'resistance' have a particularly French connotation.

'Collaboration' first gained semantic currency when Marshal Pétain, who presided over the Vichy regime, announced on French radio on 30 October 1940, following a meeting with Hitler, that he "accepted... in principle," the idea of "collaboration... between our two countries". But what did collaboration mean? Collaboration was, after all, a perfectly respectable term until it became tainted by the particular association with Nazi occupation, just as appeasement was a perfectly respectable term until it became associated with Neville Chamberlain and Munich. Pétain tried to persuade himself that it meant co-operation between equals.

When it patently did not, he tried to persuade himself that, as he put it at his trial after the war, "every day, with a knife at my throat, I struggled against the enemy demands." Reasonable men – and there are always reasonable men – urged that resistance was hopeless, that the only sensible course was to recognise reality. Was Germany not clearly going to win the war? Why alienate the inevitable victors? Why not adapt to their demands? They would be reasonable, after all, if one responded reasonably. Why provoke them unnecessarily? For that matter France, like much of western Europe, was doing quite well out of the war, thank you, until the tide turned in 1942-43. The extension of a war economy to depressed countries actually led to increased economic activity initially. Resistance could only jeopardise better employment and profit prospects. Would it not be madness to spurn all this in a hopeless defiance of an all-powerful conqueror on the basis of some absurd devotion to "a certain idea of France," as de Gaulle would phrase it in the first sentence of his memoirs. Why not cling to Pétain's much safer alternative?

There was, then, no lack of arguments for the realists of their day to advocate collaboration. And collaboration there was, in plenty. But it is probably true to say that the majority of the French people accommodated, rather than collaborated. One could not answer the realists of 1940 in realistic terms. One could only answer them in moral terms. And even though French public opinion assumed Britain would be beaten, and thought de Gaulle must be mad, nevertheless without Churchill's refusal to parley, collaboration would almost certainly have become much more widespread.

To gauge the full potential for collaboration not only in France, but throughout western Europe, we would have to know what the situation would have been like had Britain fallen. How would occupied peoples – including ourselves, for German occupation of Ireland would have followed immediately on the occupation of Britain – have behaved if there seemed to be no further hope? There had of course always been a handful to support the hopeless cause of Irish independence under British occupation, but one might choose to amuse oneself with listing the spiritual descendants of 'Castle Catholics' who would have sought to slither their way up the greasy pole of preferment.

Argument rages as to how far the British themselves would have accommodated, collaborated, or resisted occupation. Isaiah Berlin claimed that the game of asking who would have collaborated was the "most vicious an Englishman can play". But why? That tells us more about a man, or woman, than anything else in their lives. It is legitimate to speculate, if only because these are not latter-day musings, but were lively considerations at the time. Suppose the abdicated Duke of Windsor, an admirer of Hitler, were to have consented to become a collaborationist king. Would Lloyd George, another admirer of Hitler, have played the role of Pétain? Some believe that Britain would have replicated the compliance of the Channel Islands. Others indignantly retort that the analogy is false, if only because the Channel Islands were saturated with German soldiers. What we can say is that the British resistance would have had even less grounds for hope than the French resistance. For they could not have looked outwards to an unoccupied Britain that offered hope for the eventual defeat of Hitler. The United States could not come into a European war, even if she wanted to, without a large-scale European base. With that base gone, there was simply nowhere for her to go, even had Hitler still chosen to declare war on her.

Nor would the British Resistance have received a large influx of communists once Hitler invaded the Soviet Union in June 1941. Henceforth, communists would form a significant component in the French and Italian Resistance.

And the Resistance, very small initially, would receive another boost, from the demands of Fritz Sauckel, Hitler's labour supremo, that young men be delivered as forced labour to Germany from 1942-1943. Sauckel, both a thug and a thick, was the best recruiting sergeant for the Resistance throughout western Europe. If much of the history of the Resistance is a myth, the Resistance itself is not. And yet this too raises intriguing questions about the soft assumptions of western political thought.

The Resistance in countries with governments-in-exile in London could claim a degree of 'democratic' legitimacy. The French Resistance could not. It was a minority of a minority. De Gaulle, in London, to whom increasing numbers of the Resistance gave allegiance, had no democratic authority. On the contrary. He had been condemned to death, in absentia, by the legitimate French authorities. He had far less support in France than Pétain. It wasn't until October 1944 that America and Britain recognised his as the legitimate Provisional Government of France.

Democracy in France meant collaboration. One may say that the French people had no free choice, that they made their decisions under threat, to coin a phrase, "of immediate and terrible war". But that is no excuse, is it, according to fashionable current definitions of democracy? The Resistance had no democratic mandate. De Gaulle may have carried with him, as Churchill put it, "the honour of France." But where did he find this honour? He found it, to coin another phrase, by looking into his own heart. How inconvenient for what passes as Hibernian political thought! Collaboration was no small-scale activity.

The purge of collaborators in France notched up several thousand killed (executed? murdered?) by the Resistance before the judicial purge got under way. This in turn meted out some sentence in 124,613 of the 300,000 cases investigated. Nearly 50,000 were sentenced to jail, and 6,763 to death, of whom 767 were executed. Military tribunals executed about the same number. About 25,000 civil servants were purged – deemed to have been over-enthusiastic in the discharge of their responsibilities. Civil servants faced a peculiarly difficult choice in occupied countries. They were in the best position to assist the occupier. But they were also in the best position to frustrate him. Did they serve their country best by remaining at their post, or by abandoning it?

Nor were the French figures exceptional. In Belgium, 53,000 men and women were convicted of collaboration after the war. In Denmark 34,000 were arrested for collaboration.

Whatever the differences of definition, there is one test of collaboration under Nazi occupation that will resonate as long as a European conscience survives. That, of course, is the extent of collaboration in the Holocaust.

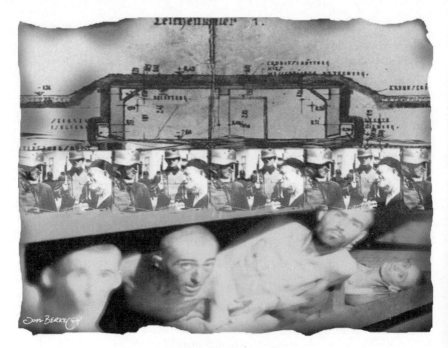

Chapter 23

Final solution that continues to haunt

The Holocaust is still one of the most debated episodes of history

MORE has probably been written on the Holocaust than on any other episode of the century. Research has been gathering increasing pace, with more written about it in each succeeding decade since, its power to transfix the imagination now ensured by memorials like the Holocaust Museum in Washington DC. Memory is further sustained by the claims for compensation against companies charged with using slave labour, and banks, especially Swiss ones, which are charged with the effective embezzlement of the wealth of the victims.

Whether we are much closer to understanding the Holocaust, however, may be debated, given for instance the violent controversy generated by the highly-publicised study Daniel Jonah Goldhagen's *Hitler's Willing Executioners*, a bestseller since its publication in 1996. Goldhagen claimed essentially that far from being ignorant of, or if they knew about it, opposed to, the Holocaust, "ordinary Germans" not only knew about and supported it, but that "millions" would have participated equally willingly, in the actual torture and murder, if only they had the good fortune to have had the chance.

This is an extremely comforting interpretation for the rest of us. It identifies the horror with one ethnic type, whose political culture can be made exclusively responsible for all that happened. It can even comfort the descendants of the willing executioners by insisting that political culture has changed fundamentally in Germany since 1945, and that therefore nothing similar could happen again. This gives a clean bill of moral health to present day Germans, while vigorously indicting an earlier generation.

Goldhagen's interpretation has been hotly challenged. The majority of authoritative historians of the Third Reich disagree far more than they agree with him. But he certainly raises issues that will not go away.

The Goldhagen debate follows hard on another debate that tore German historians apart a decade earlier, the so-called 'Historikerstreit', which revolved around not so much the motives of the killers, but the uniqueness of the Holocaust, and whether it should be singled out above all other mass slaughters, especially Stalin's, as incomparably evil. Even after the fallout from both debates, numerous questions continue to haunt posterity.

Why did it happen? Did it have to happen? Could the victims, or most of them, have been saved? How much did people really know about what was going on? Could the occupied countries have protected their own victims more effectively, or had they no choice? When did Churchill and Roosevelt know? Could they have bombed Auschwitz-Birkenau, the biggest single centre of mass murder? And even if they could, what difference would it have made?

Anti-semitic though Hitler was, the Nazis did not come to power on the basis of their anti-semitism in 1933. Widespread though anti-semitism was, in Germany it was probably less pervasive, and less vitriolic, difficult though it is to measure the intensity of public opinion on this type of topic, than over most of continental Europe north of the Pyrennees and the Alps. Incidentally, why Mediterranean Europe, no stranger to appalling blood-letting of its own, should have been relatively immune to anti-semitism, still remains worth pondering – even to the extent that the safest place in France for Jews until the Germans occupied it in 1943 was the area under Mussolini's control in the south east, or that the main escape route for such French Jews as managed to evade round-up for the death camps was through Franco's Spain, little compunction though Franco had about killing his Spanish enemies.

Several stages can be distinguished in the Nazi campaign against the Jews. The first included measures to deprive Jews of civic existence in general, all done in a manner reeking with the sadism of deliberate humiliation. More than half of the 500,000 German Jews, and of the 160,000 Austrian Jews trapped after the Anschluss in 1938, managed to emigrate before 1939. Many more found they could not, because other countries, including ourselves, would not take them in. There was no secret about what was happening. But at this stage, most of the rest of the world simply did not want to know, however much hand-wringing might go on.

Some of the reluctance derived from the continuing slump. But this argument could also disguise anti-semitic impulses. It is easy today to overlook the widespread persistence of anti-semitism in western society, often in the best social circles, no less. It is only since Hitler that anti-semitism has become unfashionable in the west, or rather only since Hitler began to threaten Britain and America.

It was the conquest of Poland that delivered into Nazi hands the biggest single haul of Jews they would ever make. One may speculate whether it would not have been better for not only Poland in general, but for Poland's Jews, if Britain and France had either not gone to war "for Poland" at all, or at least actually prosecuted it properly, instead of leaving the Poles bear the entire brunt of it until their own turn came. Initially all Poles, Jews and non-Jews, were at risk to almost casual murder. But by spring 1940, many of the 3,000,000 Polish Jews were being herded into the hideous ghettos, the two biggest in Warsaw and Lodz, where starvation rations soon led to famine conditions.

The conquest of France in June 1940 led to another proposed 'solution', the Madagascar Scheme. The idea was that all European Jews would be shipped to the French possession of Madagascar. Whether the scheme could ever have materialised is moot, but as it depended in any case on either the conquest of, or peace with, Britain, it remained academic.

Far from academic was what took its place following the invasion of the USSR. Himmler's SS killer squads, eagerly aided and abetted by many locals, set about mass murder of Jews, as well as of many others. However horrifically familiar the details by now, it still jolts one to read official reports of "seriously wounded people buried alive, who then worked their way out of their graves again". The second half of 1941 saw the eastern conquests turned into killing fields in an orgy of slaughter. Apart from the murders of civilians and Soviet prisoners of war, the best estimate seems to be that one million Jews were murdered in the wake of the German advance.

Even that pace of killing did not now satisfy the Nazi purists. It was now that the idea of the death camps began to be formulated under Adolf Eichmann's direction.

The first pure death camp, at Chelmno, began operations on 8 December 1941. Forty miles from Lodz, it would claim most of the unfortunates of the Lodz ghetto. It was in Treblinka, 45 miles from Warsaw, that the victims from the Warsaw ghetto would be murdered, while nearly a million more Jews from central Poland and Galicia were murdered in Sobibor and Belzec. So successful was the operation that some of the death camps could even be closed down by the end of 1943. There were no more Jews left to kill from their supply areas.

But of course all were not closed down. Above all Auschwitz, or rather Auschwitz-Birkenau, continued to suck in new waves of victims almost until the Soviet advance overran it in January 1945. But closure brought no relief for the inmates, who were forced into death marches in one of the most macabre of all features of the Holocaust, on which perhaps another 100,000 Jews died. By this stage one is so numb with numbers that the figures scarcely make an impact. And yet every one is a human tragedy, often involving entire families, in cultures where family feeling still provided the strongest of all human bonding.

In one way, it is curious that Auschwitz has come to stand for the entire genocide system. For the original Auschwitz was a concentration camp for Polish political prisoners in 1940. It was at the neighbouring camp of Birkenau, where gassing began in May 1942 for Jews alone, that the most horrific events took place. Birkenau was not technically a death camp in the full sense, for 'only' about half of each trainload was sent for immediate gassing. The other half were worked to death.

Birkenau was tragically the multi-cultural centre of Europe for two-and-a-half gruesome years. The cattle trucks rolled from every corner of continental Europe (British and Irish Jews would also have been dispatched if circumstances permitted), disgorging their freight from the trainloads from France and Slovakia, dutifully rounded up by French and Slovakian police, from Oslo to the ancient Jewish community of Salonika, from beyond Salonika again, from Crete and Rhodes, 400,000 in three months from Hungary after the German occupation in March 1944, from wherever the swastika flew and the jackboot strutted.

It would have been even worse but for resistance in the Netherlands, Denmark and Bulgaria. What more might have been done, and is Goldhagen right about the Germans?

1.) Banditen:					Jon Berkeley
a) festgestellte Tote nach Gefechten (x)					
August:	September:	Oktober:	Nov:		insgesamt:
227	381	427			1337
b) Gefangene sofort exekutiert					
125	282	87			737
c) Gefangene nach längerer eingehender exekutiert					
2100	1400	1595			
2.) Bandenhelfer und Bandenver...					
a) festgenommen					
1343	3076				16...
b) exekutiert					
1198	3020				142...
c) Juden exekutier					
31246	1652			8	363211
...läufer a.G.					
21				63	140

Chapter 24

The Holocaust and the nature of evil

It is not because the Holocaust was inhuman, but because it was so human, that it terrifies

PASSIONATE conflict still rages over the Holocaust. It is unlikely to abate if only because so many current interests are involved in stoking the flames. Even if they weren't, the common memory of mankind, to say nothing of specific Jewish memory, should surely sustain recollection of the most horrific single crime of this century, or of any century. The horror is not only because of the roughly six million Jews killed. On present estimates, Stalin murdered far more victims than Hitler. But his victims were not selected on racist grounds, though he could use anti-semitism for his purposes. He was simply the greatest all-purpose mass murderer in history. But never has a regime, not even Stalin's, set out so single-mindedly to kill every single person, from the youngest baby to the eldest living creature, of a particular fixed identity – Jews definitely, perhaps Gypsies, too – for the crime of simply being who they were, on purely biological grounds.

I mentioned in the last chapter Daniel Goldhagen's controversial work, *Hitler's Willing Executioners*. His material seems to me to make it very difficult to sustain the argument that the Holocaust was almost a bureaucratic accident, not fully intended by Hitler himself, but emerging as the preferred solution only in war circumstances, when all other options had been exhausted. Hitler envisaged extermination as the ideal solution from the outset. It was circumstances, not ideology, that changed.

Goldhagen is less convincing when he claims that 'ordinary Germans' actually knew about and supported the Holocaust, because they had been predisposed to this by centuries of genocidal anti-semitism, its flames fanned by the Christian churches, Catholic and Protestant alike, leaving the Holocaust the culmination of, rather than an aberration from, the main course of German history.

Anti-semitism does indeed seep like a foul stain through the history of Christianity. Vatican II repudiated all anti-semitic interpretations of Christian doctrine, but the struggle is still far from complete, despite the strenuous attempts of the present Pope to come to terms with the darker side of the Christian inheritance in that respect, not least through the work of the Commission for Religious Relations with Jews, and its most recent document, *We Remember: A Reflection on the Shoah*. This leaves more scope for debate, but at least it provides grounds for a genuine search for truth.

Even if Christian-Jewish reconciliation continues, this will not guarantee the end of anti-semitism. For the sources of much anti-semitism changed with the growth of racism in the 19th century, as indeed Goldhagen recognises. The springs of Nazi genocidal anti-semitism were more biological than theological, and therefore ultimately more potentially pervasive, for they transcend any particular religious belief.

Goldhagen's accusation that virtually all Germans were complicit in the

Holocaust remains not proven at this stage. So does his attempt to attribute unique genocidal lust to the Germans on the grounds of their centuries of alleged conditioning, if only because of his failure to engage in any systematic comparative study of anti-semitism or of the behaviour of the murderers of different nationalities. Many of the killers in the east weren't German at all, and many in occupied western Europe participated in the deportation of Jews.

What is unique about Germany is not popular anti-semitism, which could be found throughout much of Europe, often more virulently than in Germany, but a regime that adopted genocide as a policy.

Goldhagen makes much of the pleasure and pride some of the murderers took in their work. They even regaled girlfriends and wives with photographs of the killings, or invited them to come and celebrate the exploits. There is, sadly, nothing uniquely German about this propensity of killers to glorify their grisly triumphs in this manner. Their sheer pleasure in the suffering of others, and preserving mementoes of it, does not serve to distinguish the perpetrators of the Holocaust from, for instance, the Japanese engaged in the seven-week orgy of public torture of at least 260,000 victims in Nanking in 1937-1938, or the more individualised level of the lynchings of blacks in America, as a description of a lynching just 100 years ago, in 1899, reminds us:

"Sam Hose was lynched after church services in Palmetto, Georgia. Public interest was so aroused that special excursion trains were scheduled to carry curious spectators from Atlanta. Ladies clothed in their Sunday finery watched from carriages, gazing excitedly over the heads of men carrying small children on their shoulders as the ritual began. Hose was led to a stake placed in the middle of a dirt road. There he was bound with chains. Yelps and cheers rose from the throng of some two thousand people as Hose's ears were sliced off and thrown to anxious onlookers. As he writhed in agony, fingers and toes were amputated before the screaming man's tongue was removed with a pair of pliers. Only then was the coal oil poured over his prostrate body. There was a loud cheer as he was set aflame. When the flames receded, the charred corpse was eviscerated, an enterprising Georgian removing internal organs to sell as souvenirs. Bones went for a quarter; slices of his heart and liver were cheaper at ten cents each. And

141

there were buyers. All this was described in local newspapers. There were no arrests."

Whatever the differences between the state-driven murders of the Jews and this type of private enterprise lynching for an alleged specific crime, one of several thousand between the end of the American Civil War and the Second World War, sanctioned by local culture, there is no difference in the gloating of the perpetrators and spectators at human suffering.

What Goldhagen really does, in the course of trying to establish the unique evil of Germans, is remind us of the ability of humans of very different ethnic backgrounds to contribute to mass slaughter. It is not because the Holocaust is inhuman, but because it is so human, that it terrifies.

The comforting but groundless assumption that human beings are naturally good, that evil has to be explained as a deviation from 'normalcy', subverts serious understanding of the Holocaust as of all cruelty. Kindness requires as much explanation as cruelty.

If 'ordinary' Germans could not have ended the Holocaust in the circumstances, could Churchill and Roosevelt, who had far more copious information from their intelligence sources on the extermination of Jews than most ordinary Germans, have acted more effectively? Why did they not bomb Auschwitz, once that became technically feasible in 1944? There was of course always the argument that this could only kill the inmates and that it would divert resources from the most effective way of relieving the suffering, which was to win the war as quickly as possible.

Whatever about these arguments, the question is a false one. The war was not fought to save Jews. Jews would prove useful for propaganda purposes in presenting a war of national interests as a crusade for higher moral values. But the demand for 'unconditional surrender' which Roosevelt and Churchill proclaimed as their war aim at Casablanca in January 1943 removed whatever small chance there might have been of a non-genocidal alternative regime emerging in Germany. The prospects of that were very slim anyway. But the fate of the Jews, or any other victims, didn't count one way or the other.

The Jews featured at this stage no higher on their Richter scales of moral sensitivity than did the victims of Stalin's terror regime, or than had the horrors of Japanese atrocities in China. Nanking was no death camp concealed deep in Polish territory. It was front page news at the time. But nobody went to war against Japanese atrocities.

This was normal state behaviour, openly acknowledged as such at the time. The hypocrisy is not that of those, like Anthony Eden, who candidly avowed that the guiding principle in the conduct of foreign policy must be national interest, but that of those who wished to later pretend the war was fought to save the Jews.

The Jews themselves knew better. Jews were pawns in the game, insofar as they featured at all. That is why securing their own state was the only sure way of safeguarding their existence – where they too could have a national interest to defend. That did not happen without more injustice to many Palestinians. Nevertheless, the most striking institutional legacy of the Shoah is Israel itself, surely, all things considered, the most extraordinary state to be created in this, or any other, century.

Chapter 25

Britain's retreat from victory

The ultimate irony of World War II is that the apparent victor was one of the biggest losers

W E TRADITIONALLY assume that World War II began when Hitler invaded Poland in September 1939. It didn't. It began when Britain and France declared war on Germany in response to Hitler's invasion. The invasion would have remained merely a local conflict but for the British and French response – just as Stalin's invasion of Poland that same month remained a purely local conflict. Britain and France did not declare war on the USSR, because they didn't believe themselves directly threatened by Stalin. Their response to Hitler's invasion had nothing to do with Poland. Stalin could invade Poland, or wherever else he liked in Eastern Europe, and rule as brutally as he wished, without risking a world war, because he posed no perceived threat to the western allies.

Once France fell in 1940, Britain did, apart from her empire, stand alone.

She had good reason to take enormous pride in her resistance. Churchill might well echo Pitt's claim in the war against Revolutionary France, that she had saved herself by her exertions, and Europe by her example.

No one could grudge him the saying of it. Except that it would not be nearly as true as in Pitt's day. In Pitt's time, the USA didn't exist as a European power. But American entry was not only crucial for the defeat of Hitler. It also relegated Britain to secondary status among the Great Powers. The ultimate irony of World War II is that, in military power terms, the biggest loser, next to Germany and Japan, was the apparent victor, Britain.

Britain came out of the French Wars in 1815 as the greatest military power in the world. She came out of World War II playing a supporting role in a power play that had only two principals, the USA and the USSR.

This of course has been the essence of the charge against Churchill by critics who still contend that Chamberlain was more farsighted in striving to avoid conflict with Germany. Just a decade ago, Maurice Cowling, one of the most formidable English historians of the century, applied his ferocious historical intelligence to arguing "Why we should not have gone to war".

By sacrificing British interests to American ones, going to war allegedly hastened the decline of the British Empire. "He had not," said Churchill, in a celebrated dictum, become the King's First Minister "to preside over the liquidation of the British Empire". In the eyes of his critics, however, this was precisely what he did, however incongruous the image of a romantic imperialist waving his sword on the bridge as he steered the imperial vessel on to the rocks. According to this scenario, Britain found herself so financially drained by the war that it was only a matter of time before she would be obliged to abandon outpost after imperial outpost.

All that can be disputed. The benign alternative scenario, that Hitler would have left Britain alone, or that internal changes would have occurred in the longer term in Nazi Germany, which would have redounded to Britain's advantage, remains highly hypothetical. What cannot be gainsaid, however, is that the illusion that 'We won the war' did long blind many British policymakers to postwar reality.

Connoisseurs of delusions of grandeur in international affairs need look no further than the triumph of myth over reality in much British policymaking after the war – or indeed in a great deal of British writing about the war.

Liddell Hart, the renowned military thinker, graphically reflects this distortion of reality in his massive *History of the Second World War*. He devotes 210 pages to land campaigns involving British troops compared with only 89 to the war on the Eastern Front, even though the Germans normally deployed at least 30 times as many troops against the Soviets as they did against the British. Given this perspective, it is no wonder that so many British continued to persuade themselves for so long that they won the war themselves.

More evidence of this mindset, poignant in its way, can be found in the obituaries, now sadly following fast on one another, in the *Daily Telegraph*, custodian of the heroic national imperialist interpretation of the war.

Time and again, it is as if virtually the entire lives of men dying in ripe old age were packed into the few short years of the war.

Colonel Bill de Courcy-Ireland ("Commando whose unit captured the German navy's records") could count himself relatively lucky to have one-fifth of his *Telegraph* obituary devoted to his 54 postwar years. Compare that with the obituary of Major John Miller ("Officer who took 18 POWs on his own") on 4 May 1999, whose 54 years of life after 1945 were deemed to merit two lines out of nearly 50, or with countless others who are deemed to have had virtually no life after 1945, unless it continued to be a military one.

Not everyone succumbed to these delusions. But enough did to lose Britain decades in adjusting to reality. And yet, have we any right to grudge them their illusions? Had they not been prone to illusion, they might never have fought in the first place, but yielded to reality by compromise or surrender. The obituaries are nothing if not reminiscent of those of old IRA men whose lives also seemed to be packed, in an even more uneven struggle against the odds, into a few short climactic years. British or Irish, they knew for ever more they had done a great deed. Why should they not bask in the memory? Still, it would have been better for the British had they managed to blend the memory with a more realistic appreciation of postwar change.

The extent of that change was partly disguised by the towering reputation of Churchill, prime minister again from 1951 to 1955, after six years of Attlee's government following Labour's stunning victory in the 1945 general election. It was partly disguised too by Britain becoming the third atomic power, for all the good it did her in real power terms. But it was brutally exposed in the farce of the Suez expedition in 1956, an expedition launched by Anthony Eden on the false analogy of Colonel Nasser being a new Hitler, and his nationalising of the Suez Canal allegedly the equivalent of Hitler's grab for the Sudetenland.

Even those, like Harold Macmillan, who realised power had irrevocably shifted from Britain to America, found it difficult at times to grasp the full implication. "We will be Greece to their Rome," Macmillan's fatuous historical analogy, sought to conceal the wound of declining physical power.

The implication that Britain should compensate a physical decline by bringing to bear her unrivalled diplomatic skills, honed over centuries of dealing with crafty continentals and lesser breeds, to hold the trembling hands of an America bulging with muscle but sadly lacking finesse, was impossible to reconcile with the ineptitude of British policy towards the emerging European Economic Community in the 1950s.

Whatever one's views of European integration, centuries of diplomatic experience proved a poor guide to the almost pathological British incapacity to respond maturely to evolving European circumstances. The manner in which Britain has managed consistently to punch below her weight in European affairs, right down to the present, provides one of the most extraordinary exhibitions of foreign policy incompetence in modern history. Britain's failure, thanks in large measure to the continuing delusions of imperial grandeur, to accept the leadership of western Europe at a time when it was hers for the taking in the 1950s, would be brought home to her with a vengeance in 1963 when President de Gaulle vetoed her application to enter the EEC.

This was even more the moment of reality for Britain than the Suez fiasco when she had been forced to retreat by the combined threats of the superpowers, the Soviet Union and America. Now she suddenly found herself playing second fiddle to a France equally humiliated at Suez, and moreover in the person of de Gaulle, whom she had rescued in 1940. This was worse than injury. It was insult. The explosion of British outrage reflected the psychological shock of having to finally face the unpalatable truth that she seemed to count for less in the counsels of western Europe than the disdained French.

It was only now that the realisation began to strike home that the French, so humiliated in 1940, had learned to overcome the psychology of defeat – even if that shift in psychology owed almost everything in the circumstances to the impact of one of the most extraordinary personalities to play on the world political stage in the entire century, Charles de Gaulle.

In the image: ALGÉROISES, ALGÉROIS ! Le chef et quelques-uns de ses barbouzes L' OAS frappe où elle veut, quand elle veut, comme elle veut

Chapter 26

Charles de Gaulle's second coming

His 1958 constitution has helped bring 40 years of stability to France after endless turmoil since 1870

A CCUSTOMED to thinking of herself as Queen of the Continent for two centuries or more, France suffered a devastating blow to her *amour propre* from the crushing Prussian victory of 1870 which, at a stroke, shifted the centre of continental political power from Paris to Berlin. True, France would exact revenge in World War I. But it was a victory so dearly bought – the French suffered more than double the British death rate – that it soon came to loom more like a defeat in the

French psyche. In 1940, only a handful of French would rally to the call of the unknown General de Gaulle, who had fled to London to continue a hopeless struggle.

Four years later, of course, all was changed, as de Gaulle returned as the symbol of French resistance. But when he sought to establish a strong presidency above the parties, whose feuding he blamed for the pre-war failures, he found himself reduced to a type of internal political exile until fate summoned him – or more precisely, he summoned himself – to resolve the crisis of 1958, when civil war loomed as the French generals in Algeria threatened a coup against the despised parliamentarians in Paris whom they accused of failing to fully back them in the suppression of the Algerian revolt.

Despite a striking degree of economic success, the Fourth Republic had been racked by political instability, with governments falling every six months on average. Many French, like many British, still imagined themselves a great imperial power, despite the debacle of Dien Bien Phu in 1954, when General Giap flung them out of 'French' Indo-China, and the farce of Suez in 1956. Now nearly half a million men were engaged in a war of the utmost savagery in seeking to sustain the supremacy of the settlers in Algeria.

The threat from the generals, determined to expunge the memory of Dien Bien Phu in the killing fields of Algeria, forced the parties to turn to their most contemptuous critic, de Gaulle himself, to protect them from military dictatorship. The generals, for their part, accepted him with alacrity, convinced that he was one of their own. And why shouldn't they? Had he not sought the restoration of the French Empire after 1945, and was not his disdain for party politics legendary?

That was true. But the Second Coming of de Gaulle turned out differently from what anyone imagined. At the age of 68, having pondered the lessons of his political failure in 1945-46, he had drawn certain lessons with the remorseless logic, often disguised by the passion of his public performance, that had long characterised his thinking. De Gaulle was, first and foremost, an intellectual. Rarer still, he was an independent thinker.

A devout Catholic, he embraced the spirit of the Republic before 1914. His first book came to the conclusion, sacrilege for a soldier, that Germany had lost World War I because her soldiers had too much influence. He counted in the inter-war years among the small minority of military thinkers who sensed the potential of the tank for transforming static front-lines.

And of course he took the mutinous decision to head across the Channel in June 1940 to broadcast the defiance of the few in the face of crushing defeat. It would take him longer to abandon his imperialist assumptions. But he gradually, if privately, came to the conclusion that the empire might prove potentially more of a burden than an asset, jettisoning much of his imperialist baggage by 1958. This was not because he was reconciled to the idea of a modest international role for France. Quite the contrary, as the most celebrated phrase of his memoirs – "France cannot be France without greatness" – revealed.

The expression would be so reviled by his English critics, especially in their frothing fury at his imperious veto in 1963 of the British application to join the EEC, that they would regularly quote it as evidence of his megalomania. In fact, the sentiment, as so often with de Gaulle's most flowery phrases, served a highly functional purpose. It was rooted in the belief that the French were so prone to factionalism that they could be united only in pursuit of a great goal that transcended their inherent fractiousness. Hence his disdain for the political parties, who represented in his view the destructive factional impulses of a highly individualistic people. Hence too his insistence on the dominant role of a president who should personify the bonding influence of the pursuit of "greatness".

Whatever may be thought of de Gaulle's reasoning, his 'presidential' constitution of 1958 has been instrumental in bringing 40 years of remarkable stability to a France that had endured endless instability since 1870.

De Gaulle steered his own course – however reluctantly, for he would have preferred to keep it – towards eventual acceptance of Algerian independence in 1962, surviving at least three assassination attempts, facing down dissident generals and infuriated settlers, summoning all his own prestige as the de Gaulle of 1940 to rally the country, and the army, to him.

The loss of Algeria was objectively a crushing defeat for France. De Gaulle's political genius consisted in turning objective defeat into subjective victory. The ultimate irony was that the British, who apart from the experience of Suez, which the French fully shared, had suffered no Dien Bien Phu, no Algeria, no generals' revolts, no assassination attempts, nevertheless failed to psychologically disengage, as Dean Acheson, former US Secretary of State astutely recognised when observing that Britain had lost an empire and not yet found a role, whereas the French, humiliated time and again, managed to overcome the psychology of defeat in the enveloping embrace of Gaullist 'greatness'. An astonishing performance in terms of national psychology, it is doubtful if anyone but de Gaulle could have achieved it, by providing alternative images of 'greatness', thanks to his policies on nuclear weapons, anti-Americanism, and the leadership of 'Europe'.

He invested the French nuclear force with a symbolic significance, out of all proportion to its real military value, but indispensable in salvaging the self-respect of a military elite badly bruised by a succession of defeats, and exploited it psychologically far more effectively than did the British their bigger nuclear force. He also milked anti-Americanism for all it was worth. However much this infuriated Washington, it allowed the French, in reality making a potentially painful adaptation to the retreat from empire, to think of themselves as measuring up to the superpower.

Far from being incorrigibly anti-American, however astutely he played the tactical card, de Gaulle gave the Americans one of the best bits of advice they ever received, warning them at an early stage to get out of Vietnam before they became bogged down like the French had. Prisoners of their overweening self-confidence, the Americans dismissed the advice as the sour grapes of a poor loser who couldn't bear to see them succeed where the French themselves had failed. In fact, de Gaulle's belief that the Vietnam struggle was essentially a national rather than a communist one would prove the more percipient.

De Gaulle's handling of the EEC reflected the same willingness to adapt to changing circumstances that made this apparent icon of ideological rigidity so formidable a practitioner of realpolitik. Initially distrustful of the Common Market as a threat both to French sovereignty and the French economy, a vehicle by which West Germany would come to dominate Western Europe, he quickly came to realise how it could be turned to French advantage. Hence his veto on British entry, followed within days by the Treaty of Friendship with West Germany. It was as if the alliance situation of 1940 was utterly reversed, his changed attitude to Germany compared with his destructive impulse of 1945 again reflecting his willingness to adapt to changing circumstances.

There can be different views about the rights and wrongs of specific Gaullist policies, although they all served to keep France at the centre of western affairs and to burnish French self-esteem. If Britain punched far below her weight in the 1960s, France punched far above hers, thanks largely to the differences in their quality of leadership. Not that his virtuoso performance justified his attitude towards individuals, for he could discard even his disciples as coldly as his policies, as shown not least by his heartless treatment of Georges Pompidou, who held the fort for him when his own touch momentarily faltered during the student and worker unrest of 1968.

But at least he had the wit to draw the lesson that, at the age of 78, his powers were faltering, and to engineer a low-key exit from the revered presidency halfway through his term. De Gaulle's ingratitude paradoxically permitted Pompidou, as his successor, to lift the veto on British entry to the European Economic Community when he became president himself in 1969. With de Gaulle gone, France now needed a counterweight to the growing assertiveness of Germany. For Germany's phoenix-like recovery from the flames of 1945 was just as significant, psychologically as well as physically, as the French resurgence, a recovery that would also be personified by another remarkable individual, Konrad Adenauer.

Chapter 27

From catastrophe to miracle

And it depended heavily on Konrad Adenauer, who gave Germany back its self-respect and prosperity

N O COUNTRY had suffered so devastating a defeat as Germany in May 1945. She had lost 15 times as many men in action as Britain, and about 30 times as many civilians. Divided into four zones, the three western ones – American, British and French – had to endure a massive influx of refugees fleeing before the Soviets, whether from Eastern Europe, or from the Soviet zone itself. The 10,000,000 refugees constituted about 20% of the population in the three zones that would amalgamate to form West Germany.

So complete was the apparent destruction that the year 1945 was christened 'year zero', as if German life had been so obliterated that it had to begin from scratch again. But it was a false concept. For the survivors did not start from zero. They brought with them qualities that had long moulded German attitudes: commitment to hard work, determination, resilience, and organisational efficiency, only temporarily obscured by the racist inanity of Nazi ideology. Once the inane were crushed, these qualities could be harnessed for constructive purposes, if given the right leadership.

But that was a huge if. Where could constructive leadership come from? The inheritance did not seem promising. Democracy had been discredited before the rise of Hitler by the combination of political instability and economic hardship associated with the highly democratic Weimar Republic. Could a regime emerge to convince Germans that democracy was not synonymous with political and economic crisis? Nobody knew. How relations between the occupying western powers and the Germans would have developed had not the Cold War intervened, with the rapid worsening of Soviet-Western relations in the course of 1946-1948, culminating in Stalin's blockade of West Berlin in 1948-1949, must now remain hypothetical. It is highly unlikely, however, that West Germany would have emerged from the occupation zones nearly as quickly but for the perceived threat from Stalin. This threat forced the western allies, hard driven by the Americans, to treat the Germans generously, to ensure popular support against any Communist threat.

Even then, it is doubtful if the rapprochement with the west, or the recovery of German self-respect, could have proceeded nearly as smoothly but for the improbable emergence of Konrad Adenauer as the virtual personification of the new Germany. 'Improbable', not so much because the British Brigadier John Barraclough squeezed his way into the history books by dismissing Adenauer from his post in the re-established administration of Cologne for alleged incompetence – one of the less inspired personnel judgements in history – but because when Adenauer became Chancellor in 1949 he was already 73, and it was only natural that few expected him to prove more than a short-term, virtually caretaker, Chancellor until a more durable personality with better long-term prospects emerged. But *Der Alte*, the Old Man, as he came increasingly to be known, initially with some derision, increasingly with respect, and finally with reverence, would see off most of his younger detractors, remaining Chancellor for an unbroken 14 years, until his reluctant retirement in 1963, at the age of 87, when in his own mind he was only getting his second wind. More than anyone thought possible in 1949, he transformed the international image of Germany, as well as laying the basis for her re-emergence as the dominant influence on western European politics during the later Chancellorships of Willy Brandt, Helmut Schmidt, and Helmut Kohl, all of whom built on his legacy. Even Brandt's *Ost Politik*, ostensibly a reversal of Adenauer's hardline towards the East, would have been inconceivable but for the position of strength bequeathed by Adenauer. That legacy derived from his shrewd exploitation of the opportunity offered by international circumstances, together with the German sense of grievance at partition, a genuine sense of contrition for the horrors of Nazism, especially given that his own hands were clean, tactical skill in drawing the teeth of refugee revanchism, and exceptional party political skills in establishing his CDU as the dominant political force in Germany.

In retrospect, all this may seem natural, even close to inevitable. At the time, it was no such thing. It wasn't simply that Adenauer, reasonably enough, wasn't expected to last. It was also that there was far more initial continuity in German political behaviour after 1945 with the party anarchy of Weimar than we now like to remember.

Adenauer would, of course, duly prove himself the greatest electoral performer in German history. No other party leader would win more than 50% of the vote as he did in 1957, at the age of 81. But that vote did not descend from heaven. Eight years before, Adenauer and the CDU-CSU had won barely 30% of the vote, and Adenauer himself had been elected Chancellor by a majority of one. Ten parties, in best Weimar fashion, were represented in the 1949 parliament. Had Adenauer not succeeded in hoovering up the vote of the smaller parties, there could have been no guarantee that Bonn stability would succeed Weimar instability. None of that happened by itself. It helped, of course, that the German economy gradually recovered, after two dreadful post-war years. But it didn't recover automatically. It is true that West Germany did well out of Marshall Aid. But she did not receive any disproportionate amount. If she did better than Britain, for instance, it was because she chose, despite continuing consumer hardship, to use her aid more productively than Britain which chose to invest relatively far more in the immediate satisfaction of consumer goods or in reducing her national debt. She was lucky, too, in that the outbreak of the Korean War in 1950 created a market for the products of her traditionally superior engineering sector, powerfully reinforced by a strategically undervalued currency.

Although economic growth, fostered under the aegis of the corpulent Ludwig Erhard, was an important solvent of inherited suspicion of the efficiency of parliamentary democracy, it alone could not deliver political stability – witness the political shambles of the Fourth Republic in France despite an unprecedented rate of economic growth between 1946 and 1958. The real German miracle was more political than economic. Crucial changes occurred in the area of party politics and the constitution. The two great destabilising parties of Weimar, Nazis and Communists, now found little support, under whatever name. The blighting hand of the Soviet regime in East Germany sounded the death knell of communism in West Germany. The German Communist Party, the most vigorous in western Europe before Hitler's coming to power, was now among the weakest. More positively, the Catholic and Protestant parties, whose antagonism went back at least to Bismarck's assault on the Catholic Church in the 1870s, now buried the hatchet, with Adenauer's new CDU seeking to present a broadly united Christian political front.

The great institutional change was the Basic Law, in effect the new constitution, promulgated in 1949. Again in contrast to the French Fourth Republic, the Germans learned the lesson of earlier failure. The Weimar constitution had been too mechanically democratic, allowing representation in virtually perfect ratio to the number of votes cast, and thus in practice allowing quite disproportionate influence to small parties whose votes were necessary for coalition building, a democratic means leading to a profoundly undemocratic end.

Relatively harmless in a political culture of consensus, this could be lethal in a political culture of conflict. Adenauer himself had twice rejected invitations to become Chancellor in the 1920s, claiming that he enjoyed more real power as mayor of Cologne, where he was master in his own house, than he would as a Chancellor at the mercy of smaller parties snapping at his heels. The Basic Law drew the lesson of Weimar by so strengthening the position of the Chancellor that the Bonn regime came to be called the Chancellor Democracy. Reinforced by other provisions, especially the 'threshold' criterion, which required smaller parties to win a minimum proportion of the vote to secure representation in parliament at all, it has contributed to the remarkable stability of the Federal Republic, which has had effectively only seven governments in 50 years, compared with 14 in 11 years in Weimar.

But Adenauer did not succumb to the illusion that institutions on their own, or even the constitution, could resist new descents into horror if circumstances were to once again enhance the appeal of a demagogue in mass society. Hence his commitment to a European Union in which potential German revanchism should be submerged and suffocated. When the short cut of union through defence was torpedoed when the French National Assembly vetoed the idea of a European Army in 1954, still unable, perfectly understandably, to stomach the sight of Germans in uniform, even a European uniform, once more, he pursued the idea of European unity through economics in the Treaty of Rome in 1957.

By that stage there were already German soldiers in uniform again – and in German uniforms at that, once the Americans made it clear who called the tune by insisting in 1955 that, given the perceived continuing threat from the USSR, whatever the French might think, if the Europeans didn't want a European Army, then they would get a German army, and could lump it or like it. If Adenauer showed surpassing political skill in turning the post-war course of events to German advantage, that course of events was itself largely determined by Stalin's post-war policy and the American responses to it.

Chapter 28

The inevitability of Stalinism

In 1945 Stalin had a choice: his decision had nothing to do with ideology and all to do with his personality

THE FUTURE of the post-war world in 1945 depended on Stalin more than on anyone else. His decision on what policy to pursue after the war had an exceptional influence on the course of postwar history, in some respects right down to the present. The war left Stalin in a unique position. Not only did he command far and away the biggest and most triumphant army on earth, which had borne the brunt of the war against Hitler and had played the crucial role in his defeat. Now it controlled much of eastern Europe, with far more firepower than the western allies.

True, America had the atomic bomb from July 1945. But Stalin was not particularly bothered about this. He knew, from a spy network that had penetrated virtually all the innermost recesses of the atomic programme, that America had very few bombs, and lacked the ability to destroy more than a handful of Russian cities.

Nuclear destruction on the scale then feasible paled into insignificance compared with the destruction the USSR had already suffered from Hitler during the war, and indeed from Stalin himself since 1929.

Moreover, Stalin had achieved a certain rapprochement with the majority of his subjects during the war, even with those who had suffered hideously from his campaign against "the enemies of the people".

The wanton savagery of German behaviour had succeeded in forging an unprecedented degree of popular support for Stalin himself. He had the wit to relax the reins to some extent, and to conscript the traditional heroes of Russia into the pantheon of Soviet resistance.

He even suspended his anti-religious campaign. The 'Great Patriotic War' sought to mobilise all elements in Russian society, binding up the wounds of the virtual civil war that Stalin had waged with collectivisation and the purges.

He therefore enjoyed at home a degree of respect, even of reverence, as the supreme victor in the greatest war of all time which, added to his virtually total control over the political system, gave him greater scope for individual initiative than any other of the victors.

Even had Roosevelt lived, even had Churchill won the election of 1945, even had de Gaulle got his way about a new French constitution, even had Chiang Kai-shek measured up to the challenge of waking the sleeping giant that was China, they could have exercised nothing like the virtually untrammelled authority that Stalin enjoyed.

Stalin found himself in a position to make, indeed of having to make, a historic choice. Would he try to build on the wartime spirit of solidarity, or would he revert to the essentially Mafia-type rule, as the biggest godfather of them all, ruling through the terror of the secret police?

No longer desperately fighting for his own survival, no longer threatened objectively by external or internal enemies, he was free at last to reveal his true colours. Would he rule through fear of the Gulag, or would he seek to build, for the first time in the history of Russia, a truly civic society? This was the historic choice now confronting Stalin.

Historians have speculated endlessly about whether alleged western intransigence drove Stalin back into his pre-war mood of hostility and suspicion. Were not his conciliatory gestures on Greece and Czechoslovakia evidence that he sought co-operation rather than confrontation with the West?

The problem with positing that conclusion is that Stalin expected the Americans to withdraw completely from Europe, as they had after World War I, an expectation apparently borne out with spectacular speed, leaving only a handful behind by 1947, so eager were the boys to get home, and so impossible would any American politician find it to keep them in uniform. It was very much in Stalin's longer term interest to behave reasonably in the short term.

Even then, it quickly emerged that Stalin had no intention of continuing wartime relaxation within the USSR. He would indeed show his true colours. They were the old familiar ones. A terror dictatorship was reimposed, and Stalinism turned inwards to live ever more in the paranoid dementia of its creator.

This is not to say that Stalin posed a military threat to any adequately armed adversary. He didn't. There are many similarities between Hitler and Stalin. But there is a striking difference in their attitude to risk in international affairs. Where Hitler was reckless, Stalin was cautious. Wedded to no ideology except his own supremacy, he would cling to all the power he had, but he wouldn't risk it by seeking confrontation with any enemy who might successfully defy him. Nevertheless, it was understandable enough that to many western Europeans, left virtually defenceless after American demobilisation, Stalin appeared a looming threat, particularly following the communist coup in Prague in March 1948.

Given the rhetoric of world revolution routinely deployed by communist ideologues, given the strong communist votes in France and Italy, it is understandable how the Americans themselves were increasingly gripped by fear concerning the potential threat from Stalin, provoking a reversal of their disengagement from Europe during 1947, and leading to the rearmament of the West through the founding of Nato. But Nato wasn't established until 1949, four years after the end of the war in Europe, and nearly a year after Stalin began his blockade of West Berlin in June 1948.

For all their fear of Stalin, many western Europeans were still as suspicious of a revitalised Germany as they were of a perceived Soviet threat. There was much truth in the caustic aphorism that they envisaged Nato as a mechanism for "keeping the Americans in, the Russians out, and the Germans down".

But as Adenauer's Germany groped its way to respectability, the Soviet threat loomed ever larger in western minds, further stoked by Stalin's presumed support for Mao's conquest of China in 1949, and the North Korean invasion of South Korea in 1950 in what was seen as a strategy of sustained communist expansionism in pursuit of global conquest. Western observers could be forgiven for assuming the worst.

After all, Soviet propaganda proclaimed incessantly the inevitable triumph of communism over capitalism. What the observers failed to understand, not unreasonably, was that Stalin was no communist, or at least no Marxist. The issue was Stalin's character, not his ideology.

Stalin had a crystal clear view of the meaning of politics, in international as in domestic affairs. Politics was all about power, above all holding it once one had it. There were incidental ideological implications. But ideology followed power, rather than vice versa. "This war is not as in the past," he observed during the manoeuvring over the postwar territorial settlement. "Whoever occupies a territory also imposes on it his own social system. Everyone imposes his own system as far as his army can reach. It cannot be otherwise."

With this lapidary formulation, Stalin stood Marx on his head. For classical Marxism, political power followed from victory in the class struggle, which was itself based ineluctably on economic factors. Economics determined politics and society. For Stalin, the reverse was the case. Armed force determined the nature of the social system. This, at a stroke, subordinated communist ideology to Russian national interest.

The Soviet army would determine social reality. Stalin, if anything, was even more suspicious of independent communists – of communists whom he could not control – than he was of capitalists. Hence his failure to support the communists in the Greek civil war in 1947, and above all his break with Tito of Yugoslavia, once he realised he could not control him, in 1948. Hence too his terrorist purges and show trials of independent communists in occupied eastern Europe. The irony, and the tragedy, was that the supreme ruler of the Soviet Union in 1945 might just possibly have turned Russia into a genuine long term superpower if only he had pursued a different policy and did not equate power essentially with military power.

Though modified to some extent by Stalin's successors, this was a lesson the suppressed peoples of Eastern Europe would have to learn again and again, from East Berlin in 1953 to Budapest in 1956 and Prague in 1968. The regime rapidly crushed the East Berlin workers' rebellion shortly after Stalin's death. Who did these workers think they were? The proletariat?

It was precisely because Stalin disposed of so much power, and precisely because he had a good deal of choice as to the use of that power within the Soviet Union, that his decision to opt for more of the same, to continue making the secret police the cornerstone of Soviet society, marks one of those fateful turning points in history when history failed to turn.

Chapter 29

The birth of the American century

It was only after WWII, and the Truman and Marshall Plans, that the US became a permanent world player

IF Stalin had more options open to him than any other national leader in 1945, it was the United States that emerged as the single most powerful state at global level. If the US president had less room for manoeuvre in the use of that power, given the constraints imposed by a democratic system compared with the decision-making atmosphere in which Stalin operated, nevertheless he had more power potentially at his disposal if he could find the means of mobilising it. That was much easier said than done. For if Henry Luce had already

164

proclaimed in *Time* magazine in 1941 the arrival of the 'American Century', that was still by no means certain in 1945, despite the prodigious powers of military and economic mobilisation shown by the United States during the war. And even if Americans could be persuaded to embrace the idea of the American Century, what type of American Century would it be?

So habituated are we now to America's world role that it is difficult to grasp that the first thing on the minds of most Americans in 1945 was to bring the boys back home. In contrast to Europeans, Americans weren't accustomed to their boys, to say nothing of some of their girls, being in uniform. As late as 1940, the United States had fewer men under arms than the Netherlands.

No American president, and certainly none catapulted from obscurity into the White House like Harry Truman, vice-president for only 83 days when Roosevelt died, could ignore the passionate desire to bring the boys back home, as Roosevelt himself recognised when bringing a gleam to Stalin's eye at Yalta in February 1945 by announcing his ambition to withdraw all US troops from Europe within two years. Within these two years, the 8,500,000 military of 1945 had shrunk to virtual vanishing point. Of course, America still had a monopoly of the atomic bomb. But her diplomacy was not atomic based. None of the dozen A-bombs in her stockpile in 1947 was immediately operational, and it would not be until Stalin blockaded West Berlin in June 1948 that the United States set out to accumulate a massive nuclear arsenal.

It was in Europe that the United States had to first come to terms with the changed power realities following the war. At first sight, she was ill-equipped to do so. Not only was Truman himself so inexperienced in foreign affairs that he had to rely heavily on his advisers, these advisers themselves were also highly inexperienced. Nevertheless, their inexperience did not in general weaken American diplomacy. Blunders can certainly be cited, like the brusque termination of Lend-Lease to Britain. But it is one of the amiable fallacies of the European self-image that long experience of international relations necessarily breeds superior diplomatic skills. The ineptitude of the French and British performances between the wars, to say nothing of their frequent ineptitude after the war, scarcely sustains that assumption.

In the event, American policymaking on Europe would prove outstanding for several years. In responding in 1947, firstly through the Truman Plan to support Greece and Turkey against presumed Soviet subversion, and then the Marshall Plan, American policymakers displayed a striking creativity in the face of unprecedented circumstances. When carried through the Berlin Airlift in 1948-1949, and the formation of Nato in 1949, European policy provided the Truman presidency with a series of notable achievements that have led to the gradual growth of Truman's own retrospective reputation until today he comes very close to featuring in the front rank of American presidents.

Dean Acheson, at the centre of policymaking throughout the period, may have sounded vainglorious in calling his memoirs *Present at the Creation*, but one can see why the American decisionmakers of the time felt themselves to be at the centre of the creation of the American Century, one destined moreover to survive into an indefinite future.

Of all the initiatives of these years, what has become known as the Marshall Plan has strong claims to be considered the most imaginative and creative. The most important fact about the proposal in June 1947 was that it was Marshall who made it. For Marshall was the most respected American public servant of his generation. He had served as Chief of Staff during the war, the single most important person, apart from Roosevelt himself – indeed often including Roosevelt himself – in determining American war policy. Once Marshall gave his imprimatur to an idea, it tended to become policy.

"The most unsordid act in history", Winston Churchill called the Marshall Plan. Churchill's criterion, at least if confined to behaviour in international relations, was not in truth very demanding. Few states act out of sheer altruism in the conduct of their foreign policy, and those who do are not likely to flourish for very long. The American policymakers were, ironically enough, less impressed by their own virtue. Will Clayton, the official most directly involved, put it brusquely: "Let us admit right off that our objective has as its background the needs and interests of the people of the United States. We need markets – big markets – in which to buy and sell."

That was certainly part of American thinking. Expectations of impending slump, similar to the slump after World War I, were still widespread in early 1947. A poverty-stricken western Europe, desperately short of dollars, found it virtually impossible to buy from a United States that, in turn, needed 'big markets'. The $12.5 billion pumped in between 1948 and 1951 certainly lubricated the wheels of US-European trade.

But Clayton was actually too caustic about the totality of his own country's motivation. Self-interest there undoubtedly was, but it was enlightened and imaginative self-interest. Marshall's address was entitled 'Against hunger, poverty, desperation and chaos'. And the Marshall Plan was against all of those – even if the motivation was partly fear of communist exploitation of economic hardship.

The plan was full of paradoxes. Here were the Americans, reputedly the high priests of the free market, to whom planning was allegedly anathema, insisting that only European states that submitted 'plans' would be eligible for assistance. While some Americans denounced the Monnet Plan in France as too dirigiste, Marshall himself thought it might actually serve as a model for his own plan! Marshall, like many other military men, had no doctrinal distaste for planning. In fact, military men were often among the most enthusiastic advocates of planning, having found themselves obliged to plan big during the war. They were far more interested in getting the job done than in worrying about the doctrinal purity of the means by which they did it.

However rudimentary many of the 16 country 'plans' submitted – several were simply shopping lists – the Marshall Plan, allied to the gradual infiltration of Keynesian thinking about the ability of governments to engineer full employment, fostered the creation of a new mindset among European policymakers concerning the role of the state in economic growth. The direct economic impact of the Marshall Plan was originally exaggerated – all plans tend to be hyped up – for the western European economies had begun to recover anyway, even before the impact of the plan, but this doesn't mean the $12.5 billion pumped in didn't significantly affect the pace and direction of growth.

It does warn, however, that calls for new 'Marshall Plans', to help revive the Russian economy, for instance, or indeed Balkan economies, are largely misplaced. The already highly developed state of western European economies and societies, including relatively well educated labour forces, familiarity with the rules of the market, even if often breached, and considerable entrepreneurial potential, left western Europe already primed to take advantage of the American impact. Similar preconditions do not exist to anything like the same extent in many of today's ravaged economies, which need much longer-term programmes with much more focus on human capital.

The final paradox of the Marshall Plan was that it encouraged Europeans, and especially French and Germans, to work together for the first time. Americans, used to thinking big, found difficulty in grasping how so many Europeans could think so small. As western Europeans gained experience of working together, and observed American attitudes at first hand, they felt impelled all the more to think in terms of the idea of an ever closer union to which the six founding members of the European Economic Community committed themselves in the Treaty of Rome in 1957.

Indeed, the preamble of the American European Recovery Act of 1948 had urged a United States of Europe! It is ironic that one of the first fruits of the American Century was to provide momentum for European integration.

Chapter 30

How Europe had history happen to it

For the first time in centuries Europe was having history happen to her as much as she was making it herself

IT IS tempting to become Eurocentric in discussing World War II and its consequences, and this despite the fact that the war was the first truly global war. World War I is something of a misnomer for the war of 1914-18. Although it involved some fighting in Africa, the Pacific, and the Middle East, this fighting was ultimately Eurocentric, in that it involved conflict over German colonies in these far-flung places, or with Turkey, still a quasi-European power, in the Middle East.

Apart from the fact that the scale was incomparably smaller than that of the Pacific conflict in World War II, the big difference was that it was now an Asian country, Japan, that was the driving force in the Pacific and East Asian conflicts this time around.

Japan had, it is true, fired a warning shot across European ambitions by her defeat of Russia in 1905, and she had duly established herself as the leading regional power with her invasion of Manchuria in 1931, and of China in 1937. But these did not fully impinge on western European consciousness, given the deeply ingrained assumption of the British and French of their essential superiority over the lesser breeds.

Japan's bid for Pacific hegemony with her attack on Pearl Harbour in December 1941 would fail disastrously in the face of the American response. Although America was ultimately likely to succeed, given the discrepancy in resources between the two countries, the timing of her success nevertheless owed much, in the way it actually occurred, to some brilliant military leadership, identified in the impressionable public mind with the bravura persona of Douglas MacArthur, but most effectively by Admiral Chester Nimitz.

Nimitz was arguably the most impressive American military commander of the century, as he showed above all at Midway in 1942, where despite having an inferior force he made early effective use of Ultra intelligence to pull off an extraordinary victory over the formidable Admiral Yamamoto.

It was Europe, however, rather than America, that suffered the main consequences of the Japanese bid for imperial hegemony in the East. America could look after herself. But for the French in Indo-China, the Dutch in Indonesia, the British in Burma, Malaya, and most spectacularly, Singapore, where the surrender of General Percival in 1942 symbolised, for European supremacists, the world turned upside down. The native image of European invincibility was shattered.

The European imperialist mind failed, for the most part, to recognise the winds of change in Asia, despite the fact that the signs were already apparent before the war in the brightest imperial jewel of all, India.

The Dutch, the French, and to some extent the British, all sought to roll back the tide of history, Canute-like, for a decade or more after the war, even if the British had the wit to salvage what credit they could – and for some Indians it was a great deal – by withdrawing from the sub-continent with some speed in 1947.

In the longer span of history, the escape of the Asian states from the military control of the European empires, as well as the assertion of Chinese independence by Mao Zedong after 1949, are likely to loom as the most significant shifts in political power of the century – indeed of several centuries – whatever impact cultural and economic trends towards globalisation/Americanisation may have on their lifestyles.

In the shorter term, however, the postwar struggle between the USA and the USSR kept Western Europe at the centre of global politics, even if now, for the first time in centuries, she was having history happen to her at least as much as she was making it herself. This would probably have been the case in Europe even had the USSR not preached a globalist ideology. Once the Atlantic had become a bridge rather than a barrier, the United States could no more tolerate the dominance of the European continent by a single power than had Britain historically, even if that power were to have ostensibly no immediate aggressive intentions towards the USA.

East Asia was different. It wouldn't have mattered tuppence to the USA whether Korea was unified under a North Korean dictator in 1950, any more than it would have mattered if Vietnam were united under a North Vietnamese dictator, but for these being communist dictatorships, and thus seen as merely stepping-stones to an ideologically driven communist bid for global hegemony.

It was this ideological threat that induced a subtle but profound change in American mentalities. Traditionally an anti-colonial power in principle, deeply suspicious of British imperialism even during World War II, she gradually became a defender of the status quo as she slipped into the mindset of 'containment'.

Even when the rhetoric of 'rollback', potentially revolutionary in its own way, became fashionable in the Washington of John Foster Dulles, Eisenhower's belligerent Secretary of State, the reality remained very different.

The decisive moment was President Truman's sacking of General MacArthur when the veteran war hero proposed atom-bombing China as

American troops were driven back from the Yalu River by the Chinese.

It was a logical conclusion of this thought process for Eisenhower to accept a return to the status quo ante in the 1953 settlement in Korea. For the first time in their history, the Americans had fought a war not for victory, but simply for a draw.

Anyone still beguiled by the rhetoric of rollback had their eyes opened by the American failure to support the Hungarian rebels in 1956, deluded by Dulles-type rhetoric, and duly crushed by Soviet tanks.

Even while simultaneous American displeasure at the gunboat Anglo-French adventure in Suez reminded the western European powers that their imperialist pretensions were now doomed, American motivation was now based less on revulsion at Western European imperialism than on the calculation that native nationalism offered a better bulwark against communism than imperialist occupation.

If America had become a largely conservative power by this stage, there was no chance whatever of her becoming more reckless once the Soviets sent Sputnik into space in 1957. Sputnik was a chilling moment for America. Despite the Soviet acquisition of both atom and hydrogen bombs, Americans could still feel themselves secure in Fortress America because the Soviets lacked the delivery capacity to actually destroy American cities.

What changed the assumption, at a stroke, was not Sputnik itself but the revelation that the USSR possessed the rocket power to put Sputnik into space. If she could do that, she could certainly hit America.

It was no coincidence that Khrushchev, by now secure as Stalin's successor, should initiate a Berlin crisis within a year of Sputnik. He was confident that in the new age of perceived Soviet rocket superiority, the USA would not dare risk destruction over Berlin. Why risk Washington and New York going up in flames simply to save a couple of million people in the middle of Europe?

Of course Khrushchev himself didn't want nuclear war, being quite sane behind the public displays of braggadocio. But with the new, young, untried President Kennedy in 1961, he sensed an opportunity for a diplomatic kill that would enhance his power at home.

Up to a point, he judged his man correctly. Kennedy was terrified of the threat of nuclear war, as indeed any rational leader had to be, and Kennedy was the epitome of rationality. The militant rhetoric of his inaugural address, calling Americans to "bear any burden, pay any price" in defence of freedom was a facade behind which he mounted a frantic search for compromise on Berlin.

But the Berlin crisis remained a rhetorical one, for all the nervousness in Washington, and even more in London, where Harold Macmillan was ready for virtually any compromise. Kennedy's nerve held sufficiently for Khrushchev to effectively concede defeat by building the Wall to keep East Germans under control.

Even at the height of Soviet nuclear prestige, and of the apparent credibility of Khrushchev's claims that "We will bury you", the Berlin Wall was a confession of the ideological and practical bankruptcy of communism. It exposed the hollowness of the rhetoric of burial.

But the next, and climactic, confrontation was not merely rhetorical. However much mythology has encrusted the Cuban crisis, it remains the moment, at nearly 40 years distance, when mankind has come closest to nuclear conflict.

Who knows what the consequences for the entire human race might have been? Kennedy's handling of the Cuban crisis was arguably not only the defining moment of his presidency, but of the Cold War itself.

Chapter 31

A safer world after the Cuban crisis

*The way Khrushchev and Kennedy handled the
missile crisis led to greater trust between the powers*

THE Cuban Missile Crisis broke in public on 22 October 1962 when President Kennedy went on television to announce that Soviet missiles capable of striking most of the USA had been discovered in Cuba, that he was insisting on their removal, and that he had imposed a quarantine around Cuba to prevent the arrival of any further Soviet material.

For six days the world lived through the most dangerous crisis – simply because the price of getting it wrong was so high – it had ever confronted. Then, on 28 October, the crisis ended as abruptly as it began when Khrushchev agreed to dismantle the missiles and return them to the USSR. The crisis transformed the standing of Kennedy in Moscow's eyes. At a stroke, the impression that Khrushchev had formed of Kennedy as weak when he did not respond in kind to Khrushchev's blustering style at their Vienna summit the previous year, and which was a factor in Khrushchev deciding to see how far he could push him, had rebounded with a vengeance.

In fact, contrary to their rhetoric, both leaders knew full well for at least a year that the Americans held the advantage in intercontinental missiles, and it was partly in an effort to compensate at a stroke for this American superiority that Khrushchev sought to put medium range missiles, in which the USSR was relatively strong, in Cuba.

Kennedy was infuriated when he heard on 16 October that aerial photography had identified the missiles, and reached the immediate determination that they must be removed. But how? It was in his handling of this issue, in identifying the right balance to strike between firmness and restraint, that Kennedy revealed qualities of leadership that many had hitherto doubted. For the manner in which the issue was handled was itself central to the outcome.

A way had to be found of enabling Khrushchev to withdraw with some semblance of his dignity preserved, allowing him to claim a major gain from his initiative, while at the same time ensuring that he did withdraw, and leave him with no illusions that any further nuclear adventurism could gain him any possible advantage. For the appalling vista that opened up in front of Kennedy when he heard the news was not only what those rockets might do to the USA, but what Khrushchev might be tempted to try next if he got his way on Cuba. Kennedy was clear from the outset on his objective, but not on how to achieve it. The shrewdest immediate decision he made was not to go public with his information until he had decided what he was going to do.

It was due to this that the first news the American public got of the missiles was coupled with a declared plan of presidential action as to how he proposed to deal with it. Had he gone public, or had news leaked out, before he had determined on his response, not only would Khrushchev have been given more time to respond, but policy would have had to be devised in a goldfish bowl with all the extra pressures from a raucous and hysterical public, particularly as the mid-term electoral campaign was in full swing.

Indeed, during the six days in which the president and his advisers wrestled with alternative responses, he fulfilled most of his own election-eering engagements in order to preclude the media pack from instantly raising questions about his change of plan. But it was a close run thing. Both *The New York Times* and *The Washington Post* had got a sniff by 22 October. It was only Kennedy's personal influence with their proprietors and reporters that prevented a leak. For the six days from 16 to 22 October, therefore, Kennedy had to wage a two-front battle, the first to prevent Khrushchev knowing that he knew about the missiles, so that he would retain the initiative when he went public by dictating the desired outcome, the other against an American media already habituated to assume that a scoop was a scoop was a scoop, irrespective of the consequences.

Kennedy was as prudent in public affairs as he was often reckless in pri-vate ones. He usually sought the middle ground between the recommenda-tions of his advisers. It was therefore crucial to the quality of his decision-making that he had sufficient self-confidence to surround himself with advisers of varied opinions, and ones moreover with sufficient independ-ence of mind to be willing to express their own viewpoints fairly forcefully. This was one of the main differences between Kennedy and his successor Lyndon Johnson. Whatever accounts for it, Kennedy had such a remark-able sense of self-confidence and security that he not only tolerated, but encouraged, the widest possible range of viewpoints among his advisers, whereas Johnson, a remarkable personality in his own way, was racked by an extraordinary sense of insecurity, and consequently chose advisers whom he felt would see things his way, thereby reducing the options pre-sented to him.

This has tempted some historians to speculate whether, for instance, Kennedy would have pursued any different policy to Johnson on Vietnam had he not been assassinated. But this is an invalid procedure. Historians can, indeed must, speculate about alternative courses that might have been chosen by decision makers who actually contemplated alternative possibilities and opted for one rather than another, perhaps by the closest of margins. Historians must encompass the alternative possibilities confronted by live decision makers to understand how their minds worked. But they cannot ponder, except as the purest speculation, what dead men might have done had they lived. That is not reconstructing a real historical situation. That would cross the divide between legitimate speculation on real alternatives, and fantasy history, perhaps a fit subject for the novelist, but not for the historian.

We don't know what Kennedy might have done, or not done, on Vietnam, had he lived. We do know what alternatives he confronted on Cuba. Advice ranged from the Joint Chiefs of Staff, on the one hand, who wanted to 'take out' the missiles by bombing, and not only the missiles, but the Castro regime itself, to some diplomats who wondered if Kennedy shouldn't approach Khrushchev directly before going public with a view to trying to avoid any public confrontation. Kennedy rejected both extreme courses. His room for concession was limited in terms of domestic politics in any case, not so much because it would be gleefully seized on by his Republican opponents in the mid-term elections, but because he was bound by massive congressional votes the previous month declaring any attempt to place missiles in Cuba unacceptable.

The only public concession he was prepared to make was to guarantee that the USA would not invade Cuba, which allowed Khrushchev to trumpet this as a major victory for Soviet policy. Privately, Kennedy went a shade further, accepting a Russian demand that America withdraw Jupiter rockets from Turkey. As these were already obsolescent, their withdrawal made no difference in the power balance between the two giants. But it would give Khrushchev some more ammunition against internal critics of the failure of his gamble by pointing to this 'concession'.

Put like this, the crisis appears almost an academic exercise. But it was, of course, nothing of the sort. Kennedy did not know how far Khrushchev would, or could, go. Would Khrushchev march into West Berlin, and turn the Cuba crisis into a Cuba-Berlin crisis? After Kennedy's broadcast on 22 October the British Foreign Office, that repository of centuries of experience, "expected to a man that the Russians would be in West Berlin the following day". How could Kennedy know that Khrushchev would revise in a single week the image of Kennedy he had built up over two years. The price of a Kennedy miscalculation could have been catastrophic.

What strikes one most in working on Kennedy's Papers is his luminous intelligence. Analytical intelligence alone does not by any means guarantee political intelligence. It was the combination of the two that marked Kennedy's handling of the Cuban crisis. His masterly broadcast conveyed that sense to the wider public, however little they could be aware of the detail of the decision-making, just as his general handling of the crisis helped explain his rapturous reception in Europe the following summer and also the sense of loss caused by his death.

The consequences of the crisis would survive the assassin's bullet in Dallas right down to the present day. For it was the realisation by two essentially prudent leaders, Kennedy and Khrushchev – despite Khrushchev's intimidatory style – of how easy it would have been to have gone over the brink through miscalculation, that led to the dramatic improvement in speed of communication between Moscow and Washington – delays in translating Khrushchev's responses in the American Embassy had threatened to escalate the crisis.

Ironically, Kennedy's outrage at the fact that Khrushchev had blatantly lied to him about putting missiles into Cuba in the first place, and Khrushchev's realisation that Kennedy not only exercised restraint in his response, but also in sharing public credit with himself for the resolution of the crisis, instead of gloating, as a lesser president might have done, led to a growth in trust between the two men.

The fostering of the mindset in both the Kremlin and the White House that this type of confrontation must never be allowed develop again contributed significantly to making the world a safer place despite all the crises that would blow up during the rest of the Cold War, even if none of us can predict what the future may bring – because the nuclear age has not gone away.

Chapter 32

Prague candles still shine brightly

Human nature can never live up to ideals. But it does matter what ideals it fails to live up to

THE Cuban Missile Crisis did not cause the immediate overthrow of Khrushchev, despite the damage to his prestige. He clung on for two more years, and might have survived longer but for the harvest crisis of 1964, which was seized on by his critics as the occasion to dismiss him. Yet Khrushchev's fate itself reflected the distance traversed in the 11 years since the death of Stalin.

Whereas Stalin presided to the end over a gang headquarters, in an atmosphere dominated by fear, conspiracy and ingratiation, which carried over into the decision of the survivors to kill the murderous secret police chief, Beria, in 1953, the atmosphere in Khrushchev's Kremlin was much more relaxed, and he himself was allowed to live in comfortable retirement after his deposition.

That was only fair, in that he had not climbed to power over the corpses of his main rivals, Malenkov and Molotov, but had instead pensioned them off. His deStalinisation campaign after 1956 made it difficult for anyone to revert to full-blooded Stalinism, however callous the treatment of millions of prisoners in the Gulag continued to be.

Nevertheless, the Brezhnev regime that succeeded him, if it did not revert to total terror, certainly halted the thrust of Khrushchevisation. For the basis of Brezhnev's power was a deal with the military, who now came to enjoy unprecedented influence in Soviet affairs.

Deeply disturbed at Khrushchev's desire to restrict military spending in favour of investment in consumer goods and especially in agriculture, they threw their support to Brezhnev on the understanding that he would respond sympathetically to their demands for an intensified armaments drive. The deal was essentially that the military would get their money, and that consumer goods would have to come second. But this in turn meant taking no chances with public expectations, and a consequent slowing down of the move, however modest, towards civil rights under Khrushchev. It was no accident that show trials of writers and intellectuals resumed in the mid-1960s.

This was why the timing of the Prague Spring in 1968 challenged the Brezhnev leadership to define the essential meaning of Soviet communism for their generation, and as it so happened, possibly forever. The obvious precedent was Khrushchev's crushing of the Hungarian Revolt in 1956.

But there were basic differences between Budapest and Prague that raised more fundamental challenges to the nature of Soviet communism. For the Hungarian rebels were posing more of a challenge to the USSR than to communist doctrine. Their rising was largely fuelled by hostility to their ancestral enemy, Russia.

The types of reforms they were proposing were not much different from Khrushchev's own deStalinisation programme. The revolt was as much a national as a social one, and it was their proposal to leave the Warsaw Pact that stung Khrushchev into action.

The Czechs and Slovaks, on the other hand, were the most genuinely ardent admirers of Russia in Eastern Europe. Where Russia was Hungary's hereditary enemy, she was the hereditary friend of Czechs and Slovaks. There were no Soviet troops in Czechoslovakia, so confident were the Soviets of Prague's loyalty.

True, the Czech communists had come to power through a coup in 1948, and had never inflicted the burden of democratic choice on their people. But there was much greater popular support, nevertheless, for the Soviet Union there than anywhere else in the Soviet empire. Prague was the last place Moscow expected trouble.

The Prague Spring began as a reaction to a repressive turn in internal policy by the Communist boss, Antonin Novotny, in power since 1953. Novotny was merely sniffing the Moscow winds, but he met more resistance than did Brezhnev in the Kremlin.

In the resultant conflict in the Czech party, Alexander Dubcek, the Slovak party boss, emerged as a compromise candidate in January 1968, apparently a safe choice who would steer a cautious course and rock no boats.

The irony was that this virtually unknown Slovak became in a few months the idol of the Prague populace, as much to his own astonishment as everyone else's, the symbol of socialism with a human face. His instincts were genuinely decent, and as his decency came through almost despite his lack of artifice in public, the Czechs warmed to him as they had to no politician since the death of Thomas Masaryk in 1937.

Dubcek became something of a living folk hero in a matter of months, among a people starved of any living idol except athlete Emil Zatopek. A cult of personality developed around Dubcek – but it was a spontaneous cult from the ground up, not one cultivated from the top down, through layers of oleaginous lackeys.

The other fleetingly familiar faces of the Prague Spring, like Josef Smrkovsky and Ota Cernik, radiating hope for not only a new Czechoslovakia, but a new Europe, added to the aura of expectation.

It is impossible to recapture today the sense of excitement, even exhilaration, generated among many socialists, and even among liberals, in Western Europe no less than in Eastern, at the promise of the Prague Spring.

But of course it all went horribly wrong. Dubcek suffered two disadvantages.

First, he so genuinely admired Russia that he could not bring himself to believe that Moscow could regard him as a threat. He either failed to take sufficiently seriously himself, or to persuade his colleagues to take sufficiently seriously, the repeated warnings from Moscow of the dangerous route Prague was taking.

Second, he failed, or refused, to recognise that Moscow could not tolerate free speech in its version of socialism for the very good reason that it feared the whole edifice would come tumbling down.

The collapse of censorship in Czechoslovakia therefore sent the alarm bells clanging in Moscow. True, the reformers reiterated their loyalty to the Warsaw Pact, in contrast to the Hungarians in 1956. But free speech alarmed neighbouring collaborationist regimes, especially that of Walter Ulbricht in East Germany, as well as the Soviets themselves. Needlessly provocative phraseology, like that in the party's April Programme, that "the party's aim is not to become the universal administrator of society, to bind and shackle the whole organisation of society by its directives...", was a red rag to both the Russian and East German bulls.

Calling elections for an Extraordinary Congress to be held on 9 September raised for Moscow the appalling vista of an overwhelming popular vote for the Prague route. It could not be allowed meet. Brezhnev would take no further chances, having from his perspective behaved with considerable restraint.

Militarily the USSR recorded a walkover. There was no military resistance. Despite surmises that the Soviets would not risk an invasion if they had feared resistance, this seems unlikely. After all, they sent in over half a million of their own troops, with about 200,000 more from East Germany, Poland, Bulgaria and Hungary – more than Eisenhower assembled for D-Day.

But politically it turned into a fiasco. For the challenge posed by the Prague Spring was not a territorial one. It cut right to the aortic core of the

Soviet meaning of communism. If Moscow could not abide communists who were fundamentally loyal to itself – Dubcek was naïve enough to find it almost impossible to doubt Moscow's goodwill – then whom could it abide?

The members elected to the September Congress immediately met in secret and completely gave the lie to the standard specious Soviet claim that they had come in response to an invitation from the Czech people.

By rejecting collaboration, they forced Moscow into revealing its true colours through the enunciation of the Brezhnev Doctrine, proclaiming the Soviet right – "sacred duty" no less – to intervene militarily in any socialist country which failed to follow correct socialist doctrine – in other words, the Moscow line – not only in foreign policy, but in domestic affairs.

Prague had forced Moscow to drop the mask completely. There could be no more eloquent commentary on the bankruptcy of the Soviet version of communism, the 'inevitable' victory of socialism according to infallible Marxist laws now reduced to dependence on Soviet bayonets. It would take 21 years for the Soviet Union to repudiate the Brezhnev Doctrine, with the statement that "the entry of the armies of the five socialist countries into Czechoslovakia in 1968 was unjustified".

No doubt the Prague Spring would have failed to achieve many of its objectives. "Bliss was it in that dawn to be alive" would have been followed by the harsher light of common day, as indeed the Velvet Revolution of 1989 has been. Human nature can never live up to its ideals. But it does matter what ideals it fails to live up to, and how it fails to live up to them. The route of the Prague Spring offered hope of an alternative to the route of the Brezhnev bayonet.

The candles lit in the Prague Spring were to be soon snuffed out. But when the history of 20th century Europe can come to be seen in proper perspective, and when a full reckoning can be made of how the human spirit can preserve a vestige of decency under the heels of totalitarian thuggery, they will shine among the brightest lights of all.

Chapter 33

Reversal of fortunes

In 1968 it was the USSR, not the US, which was calling the shots. How times have changed

WHEN Alexander Dubcek was criticised for refusing to resist the Warsaw Pact invasion of Czechoslovakia in August 1968, he replied that resistance would have been absolutely useless because no one would have come to his country's aid, and that while hundreds of thousands of lives were blighted by the subsequent crackdown by the Soviets and the collaborationist regime of Gustav Husak, this was still better than hundreds of thousands of corpses on the streets. The West was lavish, of course, as was its wont, with sympathy. But there was no question of its putting its gun where its mouth was.

For one thing, the United States, whose response was naturally crucial given the utter ineffectuality of the western Europeans, for all their Eurorhetoric, was virtually prostrate. The Vietnam war was ripping the country apart. Lyndon Johnson had become a lame-duck president once he announced his intention in March of not running again. There was a combination of genuine humanitarian revulsion at the horrors of the war with an intellectual rejection of the arguments advanced by the Johnson administration that appeasement of Ho Chi Minh would be tantamount to a second Munich; it is startling how often this false analogy was invoked by intelligent people, unfortunately unable to think historically. These arguments provided cover for millions of potential draftees of the first 'me generation' anxious to avoid dying for their country.

The change in the mood of America in the 15 years between the end of the Korean War and 1968 was unprecedented. The case for fighting in Vietnam was at least as strong as the case in Korea, perhaps stronger. The suffering of the civilian population in Korea, as well as of American troops there, was at least as great. The difference was a combination of the role of the media in general, and of television in particular, in exposing the horrors of Vietnam, and the greater receptivity of the first post-war generation to the argument for self-interest rather than national interest, at least as defined by the political establishment. They were not disposed to weigh lightly what they gave, now that the good life beckoned as never before.

When that was the case in an area the administration deemed, rightly or wrongly, crucial to American interest, there wasn't the slightest chance of mobilising American public opinion for an attempt to support any putative Czech resistance behind the Iron Curtain, even had Washington wanted to, which it didn't. It was stretched enough in Vietnam as it was.

Dubcek was absolutely right about the utter political indifference, in the real world, to the fate of Czechoslovakia. Nevertheless, the Soviets took no chances. They were shrewd enough to know that they, and their collaborationist regimes in eastern Europe, ruled by force, and that if anything did go wrong, and resistance started, one could never know where it might end, either in Czechoslovakia or in other satellite states. More troops flooded into Czechoslovakia in a week than the Americans ever had in Vietnam. Indeed, if the Americans had shown the commitment in Vietnam that the Soviets did in Czechoslovakia, the outcome would have been very different.

But the next 20 years would record an extraordinary reversal of fortunes. Sceptics might select August 1968 as a case study in the hazards of prediction. Who would then have surmised that by 1989 it would be the USSR, apparently so overwhelmingly dominant in its sphere, so internally solid, that would collapse? And that the United States, so riven by internal dissension, with Robert Kennedy and Martin Luther King falling to assassins' bullets in that *annus horribilis* of 1968, with the Democratic convention in Chicago virtually a battleground for demonstrators and police, would emerge as the victor in the Cold War?

Nor could the prophet of 1968 be blamed for myopia. For that remained the consensus view long after 1968, indeed to the virtual moment of Soviet and satellite collapse, which few anticipated even a year, much less 20 years, beforehand. One of the liveliest debates in the USA of the late 1980s revolved around the thesis of Paul Kennedy's celebrated 1987 book, *The Rise and Fall of the Great Powers*, with its ominous analogy between contemporary America and the vanished claims to hegemony of Spain, France, Britain and Germany. Could the USA avoid its fate?

The foreign policy of Richard Nixon, the victorious candidate in 1968, and his chief strategist, Henry Kissinger, was based on the premise of parity between the two superpowers. Indeed, so pessimistic was the prognosis for the preservation of parity, much less the securing of supremacy, seen to be, that Nixon was prepared to jettison the cherished truths of 20 years, and play the Chinese card, when he made his dramatic visit to Beijing in 1972. Ironically enough, it was in this respect that the Soviet invasion of Czechoslovakia, and the subsequent formulation of the Brezhnev Doctrine, in effect giving Moscow *carte blanche* to invade any socialist country whenever it wanted, rebounded to American advantage. Beijing had no intention of becoming a second Prague, and its opening to Washington was partly a rational response to what it saw as potential Soviet aggression.

Kissinger, brooding on the lessons of history – he had written brilliantly incisive studies of Metternich and Bismarck, statesmen devoted to preserving the status quo, even if in Bismarck's case it was his very own new status quo, built on the ruins of the one he himself had earlier demolished – had come to the conclusion that parity of military power was in the best interests of both the United States and the entire world.

In Kissinger's concept of international relations, reinforced all the more by his reflections on the implications of nuclear weapons, stability through co-operation between the superpowers was the only safe way of managing a nuclear world. This meant that neither should feel threatened by the other – which meant that even seeking superiority was essentially destablilising, and therefore dangerous. In this model, in a nuclear world, at least once mutually assured destruction had been achieved, parity was safer than superiority. The ideal was a sort of joint global condominium, where the superpowers co-operated in managing a nuclear world, rather than striving to constantly upstage the other.

But Kissinger also believed that a willingness to compromise at global level could only have credibility if sustained by a clear willingness to defend the territorial status quo at local level. He may well have been right, for there were surely elements within the Soviet Union who saw no reason why they, the rising military power, should stop once they had achieved parity unless convinced of the determination of their rival/partner to defend their interests. Willingness to compromise can, after all, be only too easily interpreted as weakness.

Nuclear parity should not, therefore, be seen as a cloak behind which manoeuvres continued to weaken the other side, even though one might take advantage of local circumstances to try to ensure stability at local as well as global level, as with Kissinger's handling of the 1973 Israeli-Egyptian conflict to lure President Sadat away from exclusive reliance on the USSR.

This emphasis on the status quo at almost any price led the Nixon regime into a series of measures of dubious legality, perhaps sometimes counterproductively in the longer term. It required, for instance, a dual approach to Vietnam. Nixon and Kissinger were anxious to extricate the USA from the Vietnam imbroglio. But how could one do that without sending all the wrong signals? After all, the USA became involved in the first instance precisely in defence of the status quo there. It was, therefore, essential to show that Vietnam was a once-off, not a case study in American retreat. There could be no domino effects from American withdrawal. Otherwise the flight from Saigon would simply prove the prelude to costly conflicts elsewhere. This led to all the harsher exhibitions of power, directly or indirectly, in Cambodia, Laos and, probably not least, East Timor, in response to any perceived threat to stability.

Though Kissinger himself was a European, a refugee from Germany, Europe engaged him to a lesser extent than almost anywhere else. True, he proclaimed 1973 the Year of Europe, whatever that was supposed to mean. But the fact was that the status quo was least under threat in Europe, which therefore attracted his attention least. It also impinged on him that, in foreign policy terms, there was no Europe. The answer to the question, 'Who speaks for Europe?' was a cacophony of discordant voices, which meant no voice at all. He could hardly be blamed for failing to find Europe when the Europeans themselves didn't know what it was.

In the event, 1973 became not the 'Year of Europe', but the Year of the Oil Crisis, which turned out to have unanticipated consequences not only for the Arab world, but the European worlds also, east and west, and for their societies and politics no less than for their economies.

Chapter 34

Slippery slope of the 1973 oil crisis

Coinciding with the economic slowdown of the 1970s, the crisis played a part in a drift to the right

THE 1973 oil crisis was no ordinary economic crisis. It heralded seismic shifts in the functioning of the world economy and, through unforeseen repercussions, in the functioning of world politics. It all seems such a long time ago now, but much of our world view today remains coloured by the consequences of this event. It would be too much to ascribe everything that has happened since then to the oil crisis, but it seems certain that the world today would be a very different place but for its occurrence.

The crisis was itself the unanticipated consequence of the Israeli-Egyptian war of 1973. The oil producers managed to co-operate sufficiently to rapidly raise the price of oil by 70% after the war. It would rise three-fold within a decade, accelerated by a second oil crisis in 1979. Crisis is, of course, a highly ethnocentric way of looking at it. The oil producers might claim, and with some reason, if so many had not been so corrupt, that they were simply righting an historic wrong, having been ripped off for so long themselves.

Whatever about that, the crisis could not have come at a worse time for the industrial world. Both the US and Western Europe had been living high on the hog for several years. The great post-war boom was already running out of steam by the late 1960s. The Vietnam War had driven up American government spending, weakening the once almighty dollar to such an extent that dollar surplus had superseded dollar shortage as a major headache. A generation reared on ever rising expectations had come to take the good times for granted, with rising income demands adding to the spiral of inflationary public expenditure in several countries.

The 1970s were going to be in for a bumpy ride in any case. Already in 1972, Britain had seen her highest number of days lost through strikes since the general strike of 1926, as the government of Edward Heath engaged in what then proved to be futile conflict with the miners' union, a conflict instrumental in losing the election he called in 1974, an election that would prove so fateful for Northern Ireland in the immediate aftermath of the Sunningdale Agreement.

It would take a tougher operator than Heath, and a shift in public opinion, as the shambles continued through the farce of the three-day week and the headless chicken imitation of the Labour governments of Wilson and Callaghan, for the power of the most conservative trade union movement in the world, still intent on fighting the battles not of yesterday, but of the day before yesterday, to be broken. It was a case of cometh the hour, cometh the woman. Margaret Thatcher of course demonised the trade unions to sway public opinion in her favour. But they had given her the rope to hang them.

Even then, the hour would hardly have come but for the oil crisis. It was this that finally impressed on public decision makers, and on a growing number of the public, that the Keynesian recipe for recovery no longer worked – or one should rather say, the bastard Keynesianism that had now superseded the real thing. John Maynard Keynes, one of the truly luminous intellects of the century, will continue to be read, whatever the vagaries of fashion, long after most of his detractors have been forgotten. Keynes had shown in 1936, in contrast to the then conventional wisdom, that in certain circumstances governments could solve slumps by spending more instead of less. But it all depended on circumstances, and on the nature of the unemployment.

Politicians, as is their wont, had increasingly chosen to ignore the qualifications, and had got it into their heads that the solution to any recession/depression was to fling money at it. When they tried this in response to the oil crisis, they found to their consternation that it didn't work. In fact, it seemed to make things worse. The classic slump brought unemployment and deflation. The slump of the 1970s, or at least the spending response to it, brought unemployment and inflation. It was the worst of both worlds, as the new Mitterrand government in France would discover to its cost in 1981, forcing it to make a U-turn and jettison cherished truisms of socialism within a year of taking office.

Yet while there was failure, both intellectual and political, to cope with the worst crisis since the 1930s, what didn't happen is also instructive. Contrary to widespread foreboding, a social crisis of the 1930s vintage did not erupt. There was no rush to a right wing dictatorship. In fact, it was right wing dictatorships which proved particularly vulnerable in the 1970s – although not all as the direct consequence of the crisis – in Portugal, in Spain, and in Greece.

What didn't happen is therefore as striking as what did. But if right wing dictatorships failed to flourish, there was a drift to the right politically, especially in Britain, America, and Scandinavia, and economically virtually everywhere. The failure of the pseudo-Keynesian response allowed the social Darwinian fundamentalists among economists to resurrect long dormant theories of monetarism, and to apparently reduce economic policy to a formula, if only governments would generally keep out. Right wing politicians on the prowl for a usable alternative to the patently failed formulae, like Thatcher and to some extent Ronald Reagan in the US, sensed the electoral potential of this for an appeal to the self-interest of the better off sectors of society, whose natural response to the depression was to protect themselves by demanding reduced taxes, reduced welfare expenditure – except on those measures perceived to be of direct benefit to themselves – and the general 'rolling back' of the state. While much of this remained rhetorical, there is no doubt that a shift in public attitudes, most laconically summarised as 'privatisation', did occur.

When its appeal to the comfortable classes could be combined with the powerful suppurating nationalism, or rather jingoism, of a section of the English working class, incarnated in the tabloid headline 'Gotcha' during the Anglo-Argentinian war, it made for a lethal electoral cocktail.

Reagan would likewise prove a past master of playing on the resentments of an American middle class that had seen an actual decline in living standards under the Carter administration, combined with a feeling that it was time for America to stop being pushed around, a sentiment crystallised by the humiliating spectacle of the American hostages in Tehran following the sensational collapse of the American supported Shah regime and the descent from on high, as it were, of Ayatollah Khomeini. Carter paid the price for the frustrations engendered by the sense of economic and psychological battering among the American electorate that resulted in Reagan's landslide victory in 1980.

Thatcher clung closely to Reagan in foreign policy. She didn't have much choice, because she needed him. But it is a profound mistake to view Thatcher as a conservative. She was a radical, not a conservative, far more hostile towards existing institutional privilege than the Labour Party, particularly under that epitome of romantic conservatism, Michael Foot. And for all her bullying instincts, for all her crudity and callousness – exposed yet again in her recent championing of Pinochet – Thatcher was the first British prime minister since Churchill, or perhaps even before, who did not believe in the inevitable decline of Britain, whose mission was not to manage decline, but to reverse it. However hamfisted her handling of Europe, which would eventually be the issue used to bring her down, there was something magnificent about her determination to defy the drift to mediocrity of a once great state.

Ironically, her greatest legacy at home may well be Tony Blair's Labour.

The idea of the Labour of Michael Foot ruling Britain in the 1980s makes the mind boggle. It would take a succession of pulverising defeats for Labour to grasp the nettle to turn itself into a potentially radical force again. And while change was inevitable for Labour, it is quite possible that little would have happened in the way that it did, but for the general sense of disillusionment with Labour fostered by the impact of the oil crisis.

It is natural enough for us to be fascinated by Thatcher. But for all her valiant efforts to restore Britain's role as a dominant player, she remained marginal to the events that are likely to loom largest in historical reconstruction of the 1980s, a decade in which global affairs seemed to recover a sense of direction following the floundering of the 1970s. This was partly because of the emergence of two strong leaders simultaneously in the US and the USSR, Reagan and Gorbachev. It was also due to the gradual re-emergence of Deng Xiaoping as *de facto* ruler of China following the deaths of both Mao and Zhou Enlai in 1976, and the arrest of the 'Gang of Four', including Mao's widow, on the date of their own planned coup. China had been wracked by not only Mao's 'cultural revolution' but by bitter infighting among Mao's aspiring heirs.

Given China's potential weight in global affairs, anything that happens there is potentially of world-historical importance, particularly as so much depends on the fortunes of so relatively small a number of protagonists. And potentially as important as any of them in longer historical perspective would prove to be the election of an obscure Polish cardinal as Pope in 1978, who would be known to history as John Paul II. Stalin had once sardonically inquired, revealing once again his sensitive reading of Marxist texts, "how many divisions has the Pope?" The 1980s would provide a surprising answer.

Chapter 35

Reagan: America's representative man

He was a celebrity, blessed with luck, who believed in survival of the fittest. In short, the perfect president

THE ELECTION of Ronald Reagan as President of the USA in 1980 turned out to be one of the turning points in the history of the 20th century. Or did it? The question resurfaced in 1999 with the publication of the highly controversial authorised biography, *Dutch: A Memoir of Ronald Reagan* by Edmund Morris. The 'liberal' media, and 'leftist' intellectuals, real or self-imagined, regularly, indeed ritualistically, ridiculed Reagan, the B-movie actor, as a caveman running wild in civilised society. And there was much to ridicule. Or at least there would have been, if one were to judge politicians by cultural criteria. But we don't.

If culture were the criterion, in the sense of a value system based on a profound knowledge of the history of civilisation, of communing with the seminal minds of the ages, how many American presidents in this century would one bother crossing the street to meet? Only Woodrow Wilson would have recognised the range of intellectual reference, only Kennedy and Clinton had the intellectual calibre or curiosity to even care. Nor is this the product of some peculiarly American crassness. How many British prime ministers would qualify by this criterion? How many political leaders anywhere? But one does not judge political leaders in this way. Politics is about power, not culture. Deriding political performance by cultural criteria is usually an acknowledgement that one's own side has been worsted at the political game. By that criterion, Ronald Reagan left a trail of not just defeated, but devastated, enemies behind him.

Nor was the fact that Reagan was a B-movie actor any argument against him becoming president in American political culture, towards which we are all likely to be headed. He could have been a Z-movie actor for all the difference it would have made. It is not acting that is the name of the game, though there is of course a high element of acting in all politics, which has, and has to have, an element of show business about it anyway. It is celebrity that is important, and Hollywood is the quickest route to celebrity in a film and television age.

Culture is in no condition to denounce this. For culture too has in large measure caved in to celebrity. Where the market rules, celebrity sells, in culture just as much as in politics. Name recognition, face recognition, voice recognition, count for far more than profundity of thought. Far from lacking the qualities prized by American culture, much less politics, Reagan incarnated them.

For that matter, and for what it mattered, Reagan did not come straight from Hollywood to the White House. He put in time as governor of California, a state with a bigger population than most countries, including the likes of Canada and Australia. He was at least as qualified as most presidents to conduct whatever passed as domestic policy. True, from his essentially social Darwinist perspective, the weak might go to the wall, but that didn't bother the majority any more than it bothered himself. It is one of the founding principles, one might say founding myths, of America, that opportunity is boundless in the land of opportunity, and that those who don't make it are responsible for their own failure.

The myth allows a wonderfully convenient evasion of collective responsibility with an absolutely clear conscience. What is more, there is a good deal of truth in the myth. But it is not the whole truth. The dogs in the street know that as so much American poverty is clustered among blacks, life chances are not equal.

How can babies born to single black mothers – a frightening number themselves illiterate, thanks to the historical legacy of slavery and the denial of civil rights until a generation ago – growing up in wretched circumstances, 'educated' in rotten schools, often flung onto the street illiterate in turn, be expected to compete with babies of identical innate ability born in far more salubrious circumstances? Reagan, and his type, didn't care. The result was that the United States was one of the worst countries in the western world in which to be poor during the Reagan years. But politically it didn't matter. The victims were not his constituency.

Debate continues among the cognoscenti as to whether Reaganomics was soundly based or not. Invoking the rhetoric of fiscal responsibility, but grounded in the reality of tax cuts and deficit spending, and the ethos of enrichessez vous, it did the trick electorally. Reagan was re-elected with a massive majority in 1984, and his legacy allowed George Bush romp in after him.

In any case, it is not on his economic policy, insofar as he had any idea what it really was, that history will judge him. It is above all on his foreign policy, the area in which he had no experience before becoming president. Was he the man 'who won the Cold War', as his followers, many of whom verge on idolatry, claim? Or did he just happen to be around when deeper forces, tides in the affairs of men, tectonic shifts, happened to break through to the surface, and he had the good fortune to coincide with them, however uncomprehendingly, his role being simply to smile at the camera?

Rarely has the contrast between the Great Man model of history, and the Inevitability model, been so sharply profiled. Those who dismiss Reagan's role argue that the Soviet Union was doomed due to its own internal weakness, and that Reagan's campaign against 'the evil empire' had little to do with it. Before we can evaluate that argument in detail, it is necessary to sketch in the background from which Reagan launched his assault on the USSR, breaking with the dominant conventional wisdom that victory in the Cold War was impossible, or at least lay far in the future.

He was in many respects lucky in the timing of his election. Jimmy Carter might well have won re-election but for the change in the mood of the country in 1979-80 due to two factors. The first was the second oil crisis, driving up petrol prices. Petrol, or gas, is so central to the American way of life, in a country of vast distances and little public transport, that it is only modestly stretching the analogy to say that it approximates to the role of bread in the French Revolution. Petrol prices are probably the single best guide to the mood of America. The image of the Clinton impeachment farce that most lingers in my mind is the response of the garage customer to the TV interviewer shoving a microphone into his face, demanding his views on whether the president should be impeached over the Monica Lewinsky affair. "With gas at 99 cents a gallon? Are you crazy?" Never has the political philosophy of the Founding Fathers in drawing up the constitution been so pithily summarised!

To add collective insult to individual injury, the kidnapping of American diplomats in Tehran, and their parading on television, compounded by the spectacularly failed rescue attempt that left American helicopters grounded in the desert in April 1980, doomed Carter's chances of re-election. The simultaneous blows to pocket and psyche created a mood receptive to Reagan's campaign rhetoric that America should no longer allow herself be pushed around. He could, in addition, point to the Soviet invasion of Afghanistan in 1979 as support for his accusations about Soviet expansionism. He was lucky too in that the swing in the public mood not only sufficed to sweep him into the White House but allowed the Republicans recapture the Senate, greatly simplifying his relations with Congress.

All this good fortune was consolidated right at the outset of his presidency. Iran released the hostages on the day of his inauguration. The decision had already been taken, but so determined was the Ayatollah to deny Carter any credit that the actual event was delayed until the moment he departed from office. This allowed Reagan bask in the glow of popular approval. It also saved him from the immediate decision of what to do about the hostages if the Iranians held on to them. Would he have put his gun where his mouth was? Could he have afforded to be seen to back down after all his rhetoric? Almost certainly he would have had to do something, or be instantly dismissed as another paper tiger. And almost equally certainly, the 'something' would have been in danger of escalating, because 'something' thinking is always in danger of being swept along by factors beyond one's control.

Reagan would ride his luck. Strictly speaking, it wasn't in Reagan's presidency that the Berlin Wall came down, or that the Soviets withdrew from eastern Europe, or that the Soviet Union disintegrated. All these happened during the Bush presidency from 1989 to 1993. And yet, in popular perception Bush remains a footnote to Reagan in Cold War history, so completely did Reagan stamp his personality on western policy during his tenure of office. Love him or loathe him, it is the B-movie actor whose shadow looms over the most momentous episode in world history since the Cuban crisis of 1962.

Chapter 36

Right man, right place, right time

By happy coincidence, Ronald Reagan turned out to be just the right US president in the 1980s

IT SEEMS absurd to those who think of Ronald Reagan as a goofy nonentity who ought never to have been President of the United States, that his presidency could be deemed epoch-making. It somehow offends the sense of propriety of those reared on the image of presidents as sentient beings to think of him as president at all, much less as a highly successful one. Is nothing sacred any more? If a B-movie actor can swan through the presidency so successfully, couldn't any clown do it?

The short answer is probably, well actually, yes, with two provisos. The first is that the clown has to be a consummate media performer. Reagan's sobriquet, the 'great communicator', virtually said it all. Communication was the name of the game. But it was emphatically not the case that the medium was the message. For Reagan had a very definite message. He was the first president actually to believe that the Cold War could be won.

No American president could publicly proclaim that the Cold War could not be won, or declare that the USA was only playing for a draw, that stalemate represented the best option available. But that was the reality of day-to-day American policy since World War II. The balance of terror was a doctrine of stalemate.

A more optimistic gloss could be put on this by citing the doctrine of containment. The argument was that if the USSR could be 'contained' long enough, it would become more internationally amenable, through the inevitable emergence of a civil society. On this projection, the USSR was bound to evolve from a dictatorship into a democracy, once a civil society emerged.

A civil society was one in which a sufficient number of people were sufficiently educated to demand a voice in decisions affecting their fate, which was bound to occur as the USSR developed the cadres necessary to turn it into a fully industrialised country. It was only a matter of time until these educated people would insist on some form of representative government. Until then, she had to be contained.

Containment, in short, turned Marxist doctrine on its head by contending that history was on the side of what communists disdainfully dismissed as bourgeois democracy. No more than Marx, however, could it predict when this triumph would occur, when history would remember whose side she was on, or how exactly it would occur. The containment model appeared to envisage a gradual shift, though without specifying the modalities of political change involved. And it was as curiously impersonal as that of Marx himself.

The Soviet Union was, in practice, a caricature of Marxism. It turned out to be Marx's great misfortune – for many of his insights into the human condition remain valid – that it was in Russia his ideology was taken up, and that the liberating potential of Marxism was crushed beneath the claws of the Russian bear. Ronald Reagan was blissfully oblivious to all this. His mindset derived far more from the film world, and often from his own roles.

He justified his Star Wars initiative in 1983, so derided by his critics, when he proposed to build an invulnerable defensive shield over America, by citing the quintessential movie analogy that the USA and the USSR were like two gunfighters facing each other "across a table, each with a cocked gun, and no one knowing whether someone might tighten their finger on the trigger". Here was a highly personalised process of right and wrong, with ideally the good guy thumping the bad guy, of good triumphing over evil. His description of the USSR as the "Evil Empire" was classic film script.

The indignant reaction of many socialists and even liberals in the West to Reagan's description casts a baleful light on the willingness of people who are not themselves evil to accommodate to injustice as long as their own comfort is not disturbed. What else was the Soviet empire but evil? It denied freedom not only to the peoples of the satellite states, but to its own citizens. It was still essentially a system that, in the last resort, depended on the secret police.

Brezhnev's immediate successor, from 1982 to 1984, was Yuri Andropov, the first secret police chief to rise to the very top in the USSR. True, Andropov was not Beria, and the USSR was no longer Stalinist. But that is not exactly a testing criterion of civility. It still had political prisoners, Andrei Sakharov, one of the truly great Russian spirits of the century, the most prominent. What sort of human beings made, for the most part, their careers in these regimes?

Much of the Soviet population may have been reasonably satisfied with their lot. Their only criterion, after all, was what they had come through, and how their present compared with their past. There is a comforting illusion in the West that the end of communism was due somehow to greater exposure to the western way of life through the invincible power of information technology which could penetrate all Soviet barriers. And it is the case that a small number of Soviet thinkers, who would surface after Gorbachev assumed power in 1985, would be greatly influenced by their knowledge of the West. But it all depended on politics, and the mass of Soviet citizens was far removed from philosophic, or any other, contemplation, of the good life.

Not only that. Many in the West were indifferent, or downright hostile, to attempts to give the peoples of the Soviet empire the type of political choices they themselves enjoyed. The massive campaigns against the deployment of cruise missiles in the early 1980s were only partly inspired by Soviet agents, much though we are now learning about the activities of the KGB. They were also driven by not only genuine fear of nuclear conflict, even if far fewer cruise were deployed than SS-20s, but by either indifference to the idea of freedom, or actual sympathy with the Soviet system.

Remember how many West Germans, including virtually all the SPD intelligentsia, had comfortably adapted by the mid-1980s to the idea of not only the partition of Germany, but to the principle of a one-party state in East Germany, preferably of course with a little bit of loosening of restrictions on human contact across the frontier. Needless to say, revisionist historians were in the forefront of finding justification for the existing power realities.

Contemplation of the 1980s, so near chronologically, so distant psychologically, is a purgative experience. Far from there being a surge of western pressure towards freedom of choice in Eastern Europe, predominant opinion in the West was against rocking the boat. That was why Reagan was initially an isolated voice among the policy elite in raising the possibility, or even the desirability, of shifting the status quo. Fat cats were not risk-takers for freedom or anything else, except more fat.

His critics could naturally, and rightly, point to Reagan's support, in Central America in particular, for equally evil regimes or movements. But there was a vast difference in scale, and in their systemic nature, between the two situations.

The second proviso for success for an intellectually challenged president is that he find himself in situations requiring qualities of character rather than intelligence. The situation he inherited was tailor-made for Reagan. It was to be the misfortune of the Soviet leadership cadre at the end of the Brezhnev era, that they now met, for the first time, an enemy not only as resolute, but as primitive as themselves, whose perceived qualities of toughness, combativeness and resoluteness were certainly influential in leading to the shifts in Soviet perceptions of the way forward under Gorbachev after 1985.

But remember that the Soviet leadership was not exactly lining up to jump into Gorbachev's arms in the early 1980s. After all, when Andropov died in 1984, it was not to Gorbachev, but to the decrepit Chernenko, so goofy that he made Reagan appear an intellectual, that the Politburo turned.

It was a situation ideally adapted to Reagan's skills as not only the great communicator, but as a great simplifier. Most of the time his simplifications would have been a recipe for conflict and chaos in international affairs. By the happiest, or at least most extraordinary, of coincidences, it turned out to be just right, or as right as anything can be in an imperfect world, for the 1980s.

Where Reagan was instinctively and indubitably right was in realising that image and expectations count for so much in power. Their image of Reagan was crucial to Soviet calculations. And it wasn't Reagan's Hollywood past that determined their perception. The collection of thugs and thicks that constituted the bulk of the Soviet leadership at the end of the Brezhnev era in 1982 would not themselves, after all, feature too prominently in the ranks of the intelligentsia, for whom they had even greater contempt than had Reagan himself, if that were possible.

What they understood was power. And in Reagan they confronted the most single-minded of all power players among American presidents, his nose for the jugular as unburdened by intellectual baggage as their own. At last they faced someone as primitive as themselves, with both the determination and resources to have the bigger gun. That they could understand. But did it require a Reagan to bring forth a Gorbachev, or would the processes of 'civil society' have thrown up a reformist leader at this stage anyway?

Was Gorbachev the justification of 'containment' doctrine, or of Reaganism?

Chapter 37

Soviet openness spelt closure

In 1982, when Leonid Brezhnev died, there was little sense of the impending decline of the USSR

THE prospects of the USSR at the time of Brezhnev's death on 10 November 1982 did not appear remotely as gloomy as the wisdom of hindsight decrees must have been the case. The obituaries convey little of that sense of impending doom that so many commentators would later claim to have detected. The occasional hints at a loss of energy in Brezhnev's later years, and a certain sense of likely change under his successor Yuri Andropov, were no more than might have been expected after the death of anyone holding office for 18 years. Brezhnev had, after all, seen four American presidents through his hands before Reagan, having begun as long ago as Lyndon Johnson.

Far from anticipating decline, the obituaries generally describe Brezhnev as a strong leader, who had created an apparently invulnerable internal stability and raised the USSR to at least military parity with the USA, its navy now for the first time carrying the hammer and sickle to all the oceans of the world, reminding the USA of the Soviet presence not only on land and in the air, but at sea as well.

There was, it is true, some comment on the economic stagnation of the final Brezhnev years. But the West itself had had a bumpy '70s, and wasn't exactly booming in the early '80s. There were, too, unruly elements in Poland, where a trade union – God help us, what was communism coming to? – called Solidarity, personified by an obscure welder – an actual working man, no less, called Lech Walesa, had had the infernal cheek to demand workers' rights, a logical contradiction, surely, in what was already a proletarian state, the spirit of popular resistance fired by a visit in 1979 from a Polish pope, of all things. But General Jaruszelski had declared martial law, and if that failed there was always the Brezhnev Doctrine, formulated in the wake of the invasion of Czechoslovakia in 1968, under whose banner of doctrinal purity the Soviet army could crush any threat to socialism – and which Jaruzelski himself implied had been the alternative to his own crackdown on Solidarity.

Poland was, nevertheless, a nuisance because there was always the danger that 'terrorists' among the Poles, a notoriously combative and impulsive people, would resist, and while they would stand no chance against superior Soviet power, the publicity would be bad for the USSR. But in the end, what did Moscow have to care? The Soviet invasion of Afghanistan in 1979 was intended, apart from sorting out an unruly neighbour, to warn the West of the continuing determination of the USSR to brook no nonsense. The West would no doubt register its usual quota of self-righteous shock/horror, if the Polish situation had to be regularised, before resuming business as usual, however many Poles were killed.

Surely the Soviet military build-up under Brezhnev ensured even more total military control of its own satellites? It did indeed. The Soviet empire in eastern Europe could never be brought down by revolt. It could only be destroyed by change at the centre, in Moscow itself.

There was precious little sign of that in 1982. The USSR incarnated stability and durability. And yet it would all have vanished within a decade. Never in history has so militarily superior an empire retreated so rapidly from its conquests – and then imploded itself. How did the inconceivable happen?

It is conventional wisdom to claim that the pressure piled on by Ronald Reagan, in the form of another round of weapons competition, made it clear to Gorbachev, when he succeeded Chernenko in 1985, that the Soviet economy, with its hugely inferior level of productivity, simply could not sustain the competition without devoting so high a percentage of total resources to military expenditure that civil unrest was likely to follow. Therefore, goes this reasoning, Gorbachev's gamble on Perestroika, economic restructuring, from which everything else followed, was really the result of Reagan's determination not to settle for a draw, contrary to the consensus view among previous American administrations, in the Cold War. Hence Reagan's deification, in this account, as the man who won the Cold War.

Up to a point, this is quite valid. The prospect of a massive further military drain on the stagnating Soviet economy not only concentrated Gorbachev's mind, but doubtless allowed him concentrate the minds of reluctant colleagues, on the need for rapid change. And even though he had no real idea on the best way to achieve change – but then nobody had – he realised that the only way to overcome the opposition from the bureaucrats, managers and *apparatchiks* comfortable with the old system, was to launch *Glasnost*, openness, in effect a form of political restructuring, although in contrast to *Perestroika*, where the results were very mixed, this developed such a breakneck speed of its own that it would restructure Gorbachev himself out of a job.

But this does not answer the question of why or how it happened that particular way. The most urgent need for the USSR, in the face of the Reagan build-up, was to achieve arms control. Here Gorbachev's willingness to compromise through accepting verification procedures that permitted closer scrutiny of Soviet weapons than ever before, helped overcome the fear, and the risks, associated with the balance of terror. But this did not require the collapse of the Soviet empire, much less of the Soviet Union itself.

Empires have, of course, frequently collapsed. Even apparently strong states have sometimes cut and run, like Britain out of much of its empire, without actual, or even prospective, experience of military defeat. But never in history has an empire enjoying such unquestioned military superiority withdrawn so fast as the USSR from eastern Europe, something that did not even come onto the agenda until well into the Gorbachev period, and essentially after the threat of a renewed arms race had been blunted. That the USSR could not embark on a new arms race did not oblige it to abandon its eastern European empire.

Glasnost, it is true, required greater openness of debate in the USSR itself, and might seem incompatible with the idea of empire. But democracies have never had any problem justifying, or at least rationalising, their own imperialism. *Glasnost* did not require withdrawal, much less the collapse of the USSR itself, which Gorbachev opposed to the end. It must be doubtful if Britain or France would ever have withdrawn from anywhere if they had such overwhelming military superiority at their disposal as the USSR had in eastern Europe.

One can point to some pragmatic reasons for withdrawal. Eastern Europe had become an economic drain, with subsidies now flowing out from the USSR. Long gone were the days when Stalin could suck the empire dry. But this was still a relatively minor factor, and perhaps only a temporary one.

It was only Gorbachev's insistence on non-interventionism after 1988, reversing the Brezhnev Doctrine, that gave most eastern European peoples the courage to actually drive out their local communist regimes.

Permitting the communist regime of East Germany to fall was the most extraordinary bouleversement of all. Permitting is even too weak a term. Gorbachev could be regarded as the gravedigger of the East German regime, given his patent disdain for Erich Honecker, the hard-line East German leader. Nothing signalled more the dramatic shift in foreign policy than the Soviet acceptance of the unification of Germany, for so long demonised as the ultimate enemy.

These were the consequences of individual decisions, taken by a relatively small number of people, ultimately by Gorbachev himself, over a very short period. There is a natural reluctance among social scientists to accept that, in this modern world, a small number of individuals, perhaps even one, can make such a difference. But it is personalities, and their understanding, right or wrong, of the direction of history, much more than processes, that determined the extraordinary events of the three years from 1988 to 1991.

The argument that a seismic shift in the nature of the Soviet regime was inevitable, thanks to the rise of an educated civic society demanding greater political participation, has its attractions. The USSR was indeed highly educated in the sense of having produced a massive cadre of technically trained graduates. But these remained politically illiterate for the most part, poorly prepared to engage in sophisticated debate on the nature of political systems.

Politics, contrary to a widespread technocratic illusion, is the most demanding of all activities. It is the truly 'hard' science, again contrary to popular assumptions. It is much easier to develop, or import, technology than to develop, or import, genuine democracy. Even the rise of civil society by no means necessarily brings with it the political culture necessary for the combination of freedom with progress and stability. The 1990s have hardly provided decisive evidence of the success of civil society in most of the post-Soviet states.

Of course, purely short-term power players may argue that an internationally despised Russia suits the West far better than an internationally respected one, that a fractured, almost paralysed political system, poses far less external threat than one with a sense of direction under vigorous leadership. In the short term that may be true. Preferring a weak but potentially unstable Russia to a stronger but more stable one is playing high-risk politics, however. It is far too early to pronounce confidently on the longterm consequences of the collapse of the Soviet Union.

Chapter 38

European integration, but only in the west

The Wall is down 10 years but many central and eastern states have still not been allowed join 'Europe'

BLISS was it in that dawn to be alive, etc. Such was the initial euphoria over the fall of the Wall, the most evocative symbol of oppression in the world since 1961, when Khruschev and Walter Ulbricht, the East German boss, could think of no other way to keep East Germans inside East Germany, as they voted massively with their feet to get out. Khruschev probably underestimated the emotional and symbolical impact of the Wall. After all, citizens of the Soviet Union had no right to emigrate en masse. Indeed, they had no right to unrestricted travel inside the USSR.

The high profile incidents at the Wall over the following years, with border guards routinely murdering East Germans desperate or foolhardy enough to try to escape, served regularly to rake the wounds. One could hardly think of a way of ensuring more frequent own goals than the Wall. But why should Ulbricht or his successors care?

Across the border, many in West Germany became reconciled to the idea of two states on German soil, learning to bring verbal democracy to a refined pitch of perfection in deploring the dictatorial regime while co-existing comfortably with it. The collaborationist mentality can spread across borders as well as behind them.

Many more in western Europe shared this complacency... western leaders had so regularly gone through the ritual of deploring German partition as long as they were certain it was here to stay, that when the scenario changed at bewildering speed, with all the familiar, and by now comfortable, landmarks, of the Yalta settlement suddenly submerged beneath the tumultuous waves of change surging from Moscow, they were left floundering when the hollowness of their rhetoric was abruptly exposed.

Hence the squawking when the unthinkable happened, and Gorbachev withdrew the Soviet veto on German reunification, shocking Thatcher and Mitterrand, who otherwise had so little in common, into a futile effort to stave off the unthinkable. Was nothing sacred any more? The irony is that, had it depended on the West, Germany would probably still be divided, with a communist dictatorship still in power in East Berlin, while Bonn's western allies continued to go through the hand-wringing exercises about how wonderful democracy is and wasn't it terrible to have that odious regime still in power in East Germany?

The denouement was even more embarrassing for Mitterrand than for Thatcher. A cultured man, widely read, even if permanently scarred by what he had seen of human nature in Vichy during World War II, Mitterrand had long sailed under the European flag with Helmut Kohl. Thatcher carried no such baggage. A magnificent savage, she had never made any pretence of her disdain for either Europe or culture, British, or rather English, power being the only value she cherished.

The American administration of George Bush, although equally bewildered by the pace of change, did not share European fears about a resurgent Germany. The USA had not suffered directly from German attack during the war, nor did it view a reunited Germany as likely to relegate itself to a lower rung on the international ladder. It was prepared to sail in Bonn's slipstream, although it would be taken aback by the navigational agility displayed by Helmut Kohl as the helmsman steering so nimbly through the currents to guide the boat safely ashore as Germany achieved unification by October 1990.

So inevitable do we make it all seem in retrospect, it is difficult to remember now that, even as the Wall came down in November 1989, just how slow Washington, Paris, London, even Bonn itself, were to anticipate the speed of likely change.

As with the collapse of the USSR, it is far too early to pronounce definitively on the historic significance of German reunification. The apocalyptic fears expressed by alarmists at the time have patently not been realised, though pessimists might respond that it is indeed early days yet. Of course, East Germany is still proving more a drag on, than a stimulus to, the German economy, and there is still plenty of eastern grumbling about western arrogance, some of it quite justified. But this too will pass.

What will be slower to pass, in central and eastern Europe in general, perhaps in former East Germany in particular, is the culture of suspicion, not only of the state, but of human nature. The saddest revelation of the Stasi files is of how the secret police corrupted an entire society by getting neighbour to inform on neighbour, spouse on spouse, children on parents. Nothing serves better to remind us of the fragility of the human spirit under pressure, of the impulse to collaboration with power in the human breast, than this type of revelation.

The real wonder is not that collaboration occurs, but that any fraction of any occupied people preserve sufficient self-respect, and sense of dignity, to resist the threats and blandishments of power. Lord Acton's dictum that all power corrupts, and absolute power corrupts absolutely, is normally taken to refer to the impact on the wielders of power. But it applies with almost equal force to the victims of power. It is no wonder that the psychological consequences of the powerlessness induced by occupation or dictatorship can survive so much longer than the physical consequences.

The German question virtually vanished from public concern during the 1990s. This is partly because Germany itself has been wrestling with economic difficulties, partly because of the gingerly manner in which it has adopted a more active military role, partly because the continued presence of American forces in Europe, have assuaged fears.

It is curious in a way that the newly liberated central and eastern European peoples have shown less trepidation about German intentions than some western European commentators, given how much more they suffered from Nazi racism than the west. Slavs, after all, ranked only slightly above Jews in the Nazi biological order. Poles and Ukrainians, in particular, suffered savagely at Nazi hands. But then they suffered savagely at Soviet hands as well, however much western allies of Stalin sought to gloss over that. Circumstances have compelled central and eastern Europeans to adapt a more balanced view than western Europeans of the human capacity for barbarism.

The timely German renunciation of territorial claims on both Poland and the Czech Republic, as well as lingering fear of possible Russian expansionism, and the importance of German investment for their attempts to build their economies following the ravages of communism, all enabled central and eastern Europeans to take a benign view of Germany as more a potential support than a threat.

The central and eastern European states have queued up to try to get into the European Union. Brussels has responded with an arrogance of style that reminds one of the imperialist lineage of many Europeans. There have been few more demeaning spectacles for any genuine European in the past decade than the scene where the applicant – or should one say supplicant – states were ranked in terms of their fitness to join 'Europe' on the basis of how far they satisfied the superior western standards, in terms of 'democracy plus the market'.

It wasn't quite the last judgement. The rejects were not condemned to eternal perdition, but merely to a spell in purgatory where they could cleanse themselves further to raise themselves to the level of political and economic purity that would make them worthy to join 'Europe'. Nevertheless, it conveyed in chilling cameo the mindset of at least some of the new mandarins of Europe.

Map 7   Germany's shifting frontiers 1914 - 1990

The great irony of all this is that immediately after liberation, many central and eastern Europeans, or at least their intellectuals, were probably far more genuine 'Europeans', than the more cynical westerners. Of course their Europe, like that of many an Irish intellectual, real or *soi-disant*, throughout the 20th century, was largely myth, not reality. It was an idealised alternative to their own real world. Like Seán Ó Faoláin at home, they imagined their ideal world, and called it Europe. But it was not entirely myth. There might be no common European home, of the type Gorbachev liked unavailingly to invoke, but there was, after all, a common European culture, however thin the crust.

This was the idea of Europe that Václav Havel sought to summon, a Europe drawing on history, on the diversity of cultures and languages, to distil the richest possible brew from all the ingredients, Europe as an orchestra in constantly creative harmony. His audience at his Trinity College Dublin discourse in June 1996 may recall his analogy between Europe and a Gothic cathedral. "It is as if the builders of a Gothic cathedral had forgotten they were building a cathedral and had begun to think of it as no more than a high and solid building with space for many people. With such a state of mind, their creation would inevitably cease to be a cathedral and would gradually turn – as in a fairy tale – into a mere mass of stone."

Havel's call for the injection of some transcendental idea into the meaning of European integration evoked no response in Brussels. Instead, there came Agenda 2000, the bureaucratic image of "a stronger and wider union", a body without a soul.

Chapter 39

Union, beyond the millennium?

Europe may be a big player now, but with a declining population and creativity in ideas, this could all change

W HATEVER the ultimate fate of European Monetary Union, the drive to achieve it between the Treaty of Maastricht in 1991 and the introduction of the Euro on 1 January 1999 dominated the policy thrust of the Union itself and of the member states throughout the 1990s, as they strove, with varying degrees of ingenuity and success, to present figures that appeared to satisfy the Maastricht criteria. The next treaty after Maastricht, that of Amsterdam, was largely a holding operation while preparations for the EMU went ahead, as an Irish official deeply involved in the negotiations, Bobby MacDonagh, vividly illustrated in his judiciously sardonic survey of the modalities of the decision-making of deferral.

The longer the Euro stays in place the more it will come to be taken for granted and become an essential building block of the 'ever closer union' towards which the various EU treaties ritualistically aspire. Indeed, several of the EMU's champions see the currency union as the engine that will pull the political union in its train. There is no necessary reason why EMU should lead to a political union. Currency union did not suffice to keep Ireland clinging to membership of the United Kingdom.

Indeed, we have become even more derivative in relation to English thinking in some ways since we broke with sterling in 1979. Nor has currency union sufficed to undermine the Scottish demands for devolution, or even independence, nor to endear Flemings and Walloons to one another in Belgium. Currency union is no substitute for political will. On the other hand, it can help foster the preconditions for closer political union if the opinion makers succeed in guiding public opinion in this direction on other grounds.

What sort of Europe will emerge from the currency union therefore remains uncertain. The European Union, for all its manifold incongruities, is a truly astounding achievement. How many predicted 50 years ago the degree of integration today? But how the Union will affect Europe's place in the world, only time will tell. Although it has certainly helped bring a resurgence of European self-confidence following the disastrous wars, the direction of history, insofar as history has a direction, may not seem to be in favour of an enhanced global role for the European Union. It is not only that the individual empires through which European states dominated the world a century ago have floundered. It is also that the population of Europe has shrunk as a proportion of global population. The European Union today accounts for no more than about 6% of world population. And as the populations of the individual member states have been virtually stagnant for 30 years, while that of the rest of the world has grown sharply, its demographic weight is likely to continue declining, even when it admits its present applicants.

Of course population does not translate directly into power. But it may be that in the 21st century it will come closer to doing so than ever before. If economic globalisation continues, it seems plausible to assume a growing convergence between living standards worldwide. Much will naturally depend on what happens in China. Even if the European Union expands, it will come nowhere near matching China's population. If China achieves its economic potential it will gradually come to dwarf the Union, virtually irrespective of what the Union does.

The relationship between China and western Europe has already changed dramatically in the course of this century. Although China remained nominally independent a century ago, the manner in which the European powers strutted their stuff in suppressing the Boxer Rebellion left little doubt who the real masters were. That has all changed out of recognition. The lowering of the Union Jack on the Governor's Residence in Hong Kong on 1 July 1997 symbolised the definitive end of an era.

It seems likely that when the 20th century can come to be seen in proper historical perspective Chinese names will loom much more prominently than they do now. Japan has, of course, been a major economic player for a generation. But Japan, although a population of 130,000,000 is hardly tiny, simply isn't big enough to remain a dominant player, even in east Asia, if China learns to achieve its potential.

India remains an unpredictable quantity. It passed the one billion population mark in 1999. It has some remarkable political achievements to its credit, but its economic potential remains significantly under-realised. Who knows whether it will come close to punching its potential economic weight in the next half century?

There isn't, in one sense, much that the European Union can do about these matters. It can mobilise its own economic potential as far as possible. But once its citizens have chosen to opt for a more or less stable population, in contrast to the rapidly increasing ones of China and India, as well as the rest of south-east Asia, they set a limit to their total economic power. Presumably the growth rates in India will level out, as they already have to an extent in China – but they will reach a plateau at a far higher level than in Europe. In short, the more global economic convergence occurs, the smaller Europe's weighting at global level.

Europe still exerts disproportionate influence in the world of ideas, which are not nearly as potentially dependent as economics on mere numbers. But this is the dimension of European activity which is at present least encouraged by a European Union which, if Agenda 2000 is to be taken as a guide, thinks in predominantly material terms, and whose idea of intellectual 'relevance' is confined to the factors influencing short term economic growth. This is understandable. It is also myopic.

Of course the United States has an even smaller population than the European Union. But there are big differences between the power position of the USA and that of the Union. The rise of the USA has been the most striking single shift in power relations in the 20th century. The biggest single question for the next century is whether American hegemony can continue to the same degree. It is truly astounding that a country with 5% of the world's population should exert such dominance in so many areas of global affairs. It is precisely the fact that in every major realm of power – military, political, economic, financial, scientific, technological, intellectual, cultural – the USA is the world leader, that makes it so remarkable.

It must also make one wary of prediction simply because it is unique, and we don't have even one plausible comparison against which to test our assumptions. We know that every great power, and every empire, has declined. But then there has never been a great power like the USA. It may be observed, however, that although the populations of the European Union and of the USA are broadly similar, comparison ends there. In striking contrast to Europe, American population continues to grow at a rapid clip, renewed directly and indirectly through immigration. Some of this occurs in the traditional manner of coming in at the bottom of the ladder. But it is striking how many immigrants, particularly Asians, are now graduates.

Europe has nothing to rival this magnetic attraction for international talent. Indeed, England in particular has devised means to drive many of its best university minds to America through low pay and the declining status of knowledge workers, the very people crucial to the knowledge industries that now drive the American economy, as Peter Drucker stresses again in a recent *Atlantic Monthly*. Prognosticating on the European Union's prospects in the new century depends at least as much on what others do as on what Europe does. In the end, if the Union loses relative status in the economic and political power pecking order it is likely to be largely because there simply won't be enough Europeans around, unless it expands beyond any present expectations. But if it loses out in the world of ideas, if it finds history happening to it rather than it making its own history, it will have nobody to blame but itself – at least partly as a result of the obsession of its practical men with the purely practical.

Chapter 40

1989 and all that

The tenth anniversary of the fall of the Berlin Wall has prompted some poor historical analysis

IT WAS intriguing to read the reflections on the 10th anniversary of the fall of the Berlin Wall. They may not tell us a great deal about the deeper meaning of the events of 1989, but they do reveal a certain amount about the events themselves, and even more about who we are now. Anniversaries are wonderful for the way in which they induce us to flights of careless exposure even while we delude ourselves that it is on the past rather than the present we are throwing fresh light.

Many of the assessments were what one might expect as the conventional wisdom. The delirium of delight that accompanied those first few heady days after the fall of the Wall has now well and truly vanished into the disillusion of East Germans trapped in an 18% unemployment level, deprived of the cradle-to-grave security the communist regime provided, cheated of the instant riches portrayed on West German television as the essence of West German capitalism, with many of the best jobs in the East now taken by Westerners, who in turn look down on the backwardness of their sometime sundered brethren, whom they treat as virtually an internal colony. *'Tarcuisne'* is even harder to bear than *'bochtaineas'*, as Eoin Rua Ó Súilleabháin once said, if in somewhat different circumstances. It has gone so far that it has now become fashionable to refer to 'the wall in people's minds'.

These verdicts are all based on assumptions about what should have happened if only things had been handled better – if only Helmut Kohl hadn't rushed unification, if only there had been a step-by-step integration of the two German economies, etc. The London *Times* unhesitatingly proclaimed that "the 'cost of Kohl' to Europe had been exorbitant". It knows, you see, what would have happened for the past ten years, if only Kohl had followed a different path. It is truly wonderful how commentators who could not predict a week, or even a day, in advance what was going to happen in 1989 itself, are now able to predict what would have happened over ten whole years in retrospect if only their recipes had been applied!

But all these verdicts are based on assumptions about alternatives that we have no way of testing. Readers of this book and my *Sunday Tribune* column will be aware of the fact that all historical judgements are based on the idea of might-have-beens. It is therefore important these be specified systematically instead of arbitrarily. The might-have-beens have to be credible. They cannot be simply a wish list of what should have happened. The trouble with the criticisms of Kohl's approach is that they try to freeze politics in the East, as if everything else would have stood still in the following years. These are invalid types of 'virtual history'.

For that matter, expecting some uniform type of response in East Germany is in itself unhistorical. For the East is not a monolith. There are quite sharp differences in both living standards and mentalities between the old industrialised Saxony in the south, and the more traditionally agrarian north east. Differences within the former East Germany are quite likely going to become more prominent in this coming decade.

What emerges clearly from the reconstructions of the fall of the Wall is how contingent, almost accidental, everything was. The long recent interview on German television with Lieut Col Harold Jaeger, the commander on the Wall, was particularly revealing. He now lives as a newspaper and magazine vendor in Berlin. He has the mind of one of nature's junior clerks. How insignificant these one time lords of creation look when they can no longer strut in their uniforms and clasp their guns! He is proud of his service with the elite border guard. He had no compunction about killing – provided he got his orders.

As the crowds built up, he scratched around desperately for someone to give him orders. He didn't mind what the orders were, as long as he could have the psychological security of orders. But no orders came on 9 November 1989. He had to actually think. In those circumstances, the line of least resistance recommends itself to essentially dependent minds. In the end, the system, devised to destroy the independence of mind of all its subjects, destroyed the capacity for independent action of its own defenders. Hannah Arendt's celebrated phrase about the banality of evil takes on a new meaning in these circumstances.

But Jaeger merely reflected the entire East German system. If they had minds of their own, they would probably have used force. And nobody in the West would have lifted a finger to deter them. It is sometimes said that the revolutions of 1989 were characterised by no new idea. It has been retorted that their novelty lay in the idea of non-violent revolution, that ends and means were so intimately intertwined, that they could not be separated, or as Adam Michnik, the leading Polish dissident intellectual, put it, those who begin by storming bastilles will end up building new ones. One might retort in turn that those who cannot storm bastilles are stuck with the old ones. The sad fact remains that what allowed successful revolutions in 1989 was not *their* emphasis on non-violence. It was Gorbachev's insistence on non-violence. The East German leadership was paralysed because Gorbachev had effectively forbidden the use of force at his Moscow meeting with Egon Krenz, the new East German leader, on 31 October. Nor is there any reason why the Soviet empire had to implode in an orgy of non-violence. Whatever its economic circumstances, it still disposed of the military power to crush all challenges. This makes Gorbachev's role all the more crucial. After all, the students in Tiananmen Square, slaughtered on 4 June, the day of the historic Polish elections, were not exactly revolting. Much good it did them. The difference in Berlin was that the guards did not open fire.

But it is not only the Colonel Jaegers who expose themselves in retrospectives. Commentators, who after all are actually paid to think, can be equally careless. Mark Steel in the *Independent* couldn't see what the fuss about the Wall was all about. After all, wasn't Reagan as big a tyrant as Stalin, so what was the point of exchanging one tyranny for another? The communist and post-communist systems in eastern Europe are, apparently, 'fundamentally... the same system'. With such searing insights, political philosophy is in safe hands! And yet Steel's approach, for all his blithe disregard for the scale of Stalinism, marks at least a flicker of intellectual independence, compared with the unctuous self-righteousness of most western commentaries, whose only concept of 'progress' in central and eastern Europe is how like 'us' the backward creatures have become, and how far more they have to go before they reach our standards of civilisation.

Michael Gove in the London *Times* cast his net more widely, seizing the opportunity to protest at the unfair treatment of poor General Pinochet compared with Nelson Mandela. After all, Pinochet had prevented a communist coup in Chile by Allende, and while his regime may have been 'brutal' that was an understandable price to pay for his services to humanity. Mandela, on the other hand, had been a communist, who had engaged in guerrilla activity – actual violence – unlike Pinochet's regime, for torture is not of course violence – and South Africa today has "the highest incidence of rape in the world". Ulster Unionists, whose cause Gove so passionately champions, may be moved to wish for a more circumspect exhibition of values in their delicate circumstances.

Arguments from history often take a battering on occasions like this. Even John Simpson, writing earlier in the *Daily Telegraph*, managed to insert into an otherwise sensitive account of the fall of the Wall, the observation that "in unifying his country after the Wall came down, Helmut Kohl wrecked the balance of Europe as much as Bismarck did in 1870". This is apparently because when Germany will have 90 million people, France, Britain and Italy will have only 60 million each. But this, frankly, is an absurd analogy. Germany's power after 1870 was based on her military superiority. Her relations with other states were very different indeed from today. False analogies by the ignoranti are bad enough, but at least understandable. It is when those who ought to know better indulge them that one despairs of the possibility of ever learning anything from history.

It was a bad week for historical analogy all round. Michael Gove apparently considers Allende the Chilean Hitler, a strikingly ambitious analogy indeed. Still, he isn't safe for the prize of the analogy of that week. For in a letter to *The Times*, Lord Hooson, QC, took analogy to unplumbed depths by detecting a "strange parallel" between "the wave of Euroscepticism which has characterised the last quarter century of the second millennium" and "the wave of angloscepticism which seems to have charactersised the end of the first millennium in England", when "those within Wessex, Northumbria, Mercia, Kent and so on were much concerned to maintain their equivalent of sovereignty...".

Ardent an advocate though an historian must be of efforts to learn from history, one is tempted to wonder, in the face of such examples, if one cannot overdo appeals to history.

Maybe, after all, commentaries on the fall of the Wall were wise to mostly confine themselves to the events of the century rather than the millennium.

Chapter 41

The coming decline of the US?

The biggest question for the new century is: will China rise and the USA fall? And how far and how fast?

A S WE draw towards the close of a book that has sought to provide glimpses into crucial episodes in this century, one becomes more conscious of just how little control the human race exerts over its collective fate, and this despite the fact that never has so much scientific or material progress occurred so quickly. The collapse of the Soviet Union impressed the fragility of even the most apparently permanent of political systems on our consciousness. And yet here we are, only a decade later, indulging in an orgy of predictions about what lies beyond the millennium. Indeed, within a year of the implosion of the USSR, Francis Fukuyama was positing western, liberal capitalism as the eternal victor, its blend of 'democracy' and 'the market' destined to survive in a form of materialistic hubris, however boring, until the end of time. Four years later, in 1996, Samuel Huntington was in turn repudiating the Fukuyama vision, equally confident that what was in store was a conflict of civilisations, with the USA as the standard bearer of western civilisation – Western Europe in this scenario, incidentally, featuring as little more than a spear-carrying appendage to the USA.

Who knows which, if either, of these scenarios will eventuate? Huntington can interpret events in the Balkans, Chechnya and Kashmir, as support for his model. The Fukuyama model appeals more to proponents of globalisation theory, convinced of the inevitable triumph of the American version of capitalist democracy as the type to which all mankind is destined to belong forever and ever, Amen.

But models tend to be abstractions. What most of us want to know is how will whatever changes that may occur affect the balance of power between states? Who wins and who loses? Will, in the most widely speculated scenario, the USA decline and China rise, and if so, how far and how fast in both cases? That remains, in purely state power terms, the biggest single question for the next century. Will the chronicler of 2099, assuming the world has survived until then, begin by describing the decline of the USA in much the same terms as we now describe the decline of the British Empire, which a century ago covered a quarter of the globe and today is reduced to a few specks on the map? Or will observers still call the American president a century hence, as some Greeks called President Clinton, *planitarchis*, the ruler of the planet?

The contrasts with 1900 are actually more striking than the similarities. In 1900 there were five major powers, and the USA patently had the potential to be one. Today, there is only one superpower. The putative rise of China, therefore, poses a direct challenge to the solitary superpower. It does not simply involve a realignment within an existing system. But the nature of power has itself changed. The USA covers a much smaller land area than the British Empire, and controls a far lower percentage of world population than did Britain. Yet its relative power on the world stage is vastly greater than was Britain's at its height.

That is because global power no longer depends so heavily on military power. It is indeed crucial. But it is more a prerequisite for world power, than world power in itself, unless its possessor is willing to embark on high risk wars of conquest. Global power and influence depend partly on economic power – if only because military power is unlikely to survive long without economic power. But cultural and intellectual power become relatively more important in a globe where war between major powers has become increasingly risky.

Globalisation implies that not only are we becoming more homogeneous, but that we are doing so along a single predictable path, ineluctably determined by the triumph of western lifestyles in general and American values in particular. That lifestyle, however, is not carried on the point of American bayonets, but through a combination of American cheque books, the influence of American mass visual media, and the spread of English as the global language.

But how does that translate into the political power of states? Take China. It has nearly one-quarter of the world's population. If it got its act together, it could become much the biggest market in the world in the next generation. American companies are already salivating at the prospect of China entering the World Trade Organisation. But would a China achieving its economic potential be a more or less serious threat to American hegemony, or to western lifestyles? Would a prosperous China copperfasten the triumphant march of westernisation through globalisation, with its own replication of American lifestyles as the pinnacle of civilisation, or would it find a Chinese way to emulate western material standards without wholly embracing American media values?

Can China effect the shift from her inherited security culture to a market economy culture without experiencing political upheaval? China has had, after all, far more instability than stability in this century. It is only 30 years since the chaos of Mao's Cultural Revolution. Has she any chance of combining a shift to market with a shift to democracy, or does the shift to market require political dirigisme to keep the losers in their servile places? Would China be as big a mess today as Russia if the Tiananmen Square students had not been suppressed in 1989? Is Chinese dictatorship more in the interests of western capitalism, or even of the USA as a state, than democracy? Or would the first ever democracy in China release, or inspire, unprecedented energies that would translate into a Chinese power position more rapidly, but also more unpredictably, than China under dictatorship?

Nobody knows. This is because China is striving to change its entire social system while simultaneously striving toward superpower status. The challenge is unprecedented. Soviet Russia, and Japan, tried something similar at different times. But they did not face the challenge of doing so in the white hot glare of the Internet.

The outcome will depend not only on political skill and economic performance. It will also depend heavily on how effectively China can respond to the other sources of American dominance today – intellectual, cultural and social power. It is not American military power, or even economic power, that effectively means that globalisation means Americanisation. It is that the bulk of the western, and increasingly of the non-western, intelligentsia and media have accepted the dominant American concepts of the nature of the good society. A key determinant of how world society develops in the new century is likely to be the nature of social thought emanating from the Chinese intelligentsia. Will it be heavily derivative from American intellect, or will it achieve independent status?

It is easy enough to understand the obsession of the Chinese leadership under Deng Xiaoping with economic growth at all costs as a prerequisite for military power. But the epoch-making test for the quality of Chinese leadership will be how it translates economic performance into intellectual performance, and whether it will be a leader or a follower in terms of global lifestyles.

If China is to offer an alternative to US lifestyles and value systems, the struggle for global influence will be mainly a struggle for the hearts and pockets of Hindus and Muslims. For it is the populations of India, on the one hand, and of Pakistan and Bangladesh, as well as Iran, Nigeria, Indonesia and Egypt, that are projected to rise most spectacularly in the next half century. How many of us realise, given our Eurocentric focus, that by 2050 Pakistan is projected to have treble the population of Russia, and more even than the USA?

It may be that none of this will come to pass. Population growth, which today is bounding along fastest of all in the Muslim world, may slow down there. Population won't matter greatly anyway if the Muslim world remains mired in economic backwardness. But if Pakistan and Iran, for instance, succeed in achieving sustained economic growth, with its implications for military power, then the relative skill with which China and the West relate to them will make for interesting times.

India appears less a potential rival to western interests today than China. But the Indian population is growing faster, and may even overtake the Chinese in another generation. That won't matter, unless India achieves sustained economic growth. But if she does, she too will carry immense weight in determining the outcome of the globalisation stakes in the next half century. May it be that the Hindu and Muslim worlds will hew their own paths, equally independent of American and Chinese influence?

One of the ironies of globalisation is that the West is wagering on dominating world value systems at a time when its own population is projected to shrink rapidly in relative terms. The fascinating question that will still remain, if these countries do achieve growth, is what will they do with it? Is there a law of human nature which states that the only route to take is the western one? Are there any alternatives? These are huge questions in terms of the potential, for better or worse, of human nature. They are likely to come closer to being answered in the next half century than ever before.

Chapter 42

Searching for the person of the century

Mandela or Gandhi? De Valera or Smuts? Roosevelt or King? Lenin or Stalin? Or perhaps a medical pioneer?

ONE would think that selecting the person of the century should be a fairly straightforward task. In my innocence, I tried it out on a friend. Who would our person of the century be, we asked ourselves. A lot of people would opt for Nelson Mandela, we thought. But then doubts set in. An extraordinary man, indeed. His ability to forgive, combined with his tactical and communication skills, was astonishing. But his actions, however remarkable, directly affected only a small

230

number of people. This instantly posed the problem of what criteria to apply. Should scale matter?

Nicholas Mansergh, probably the internationally best known Irish historian of the century, Foundation Professor of Smuts Chair Commonwealth History at Cambridge, author of the still standard history of the Commonwealth, met every Prime Minister of a Commonwealth, or sometime Commonwealth, country over a generation. His short list of the three outstanding personalities among them all was Jawaharlal Nehru of India, Jan Smuts of South Africa and Eamon de Valera of Ireland. But remarkable careers though they carved out – Nehru, the Harrow- and Cambridge-educated President of the Congress movement for Indian independence who would spend a total of nine years in jail before duly becoming first Prime Minister of India for 17 years; Smuts, the Cambridge graduate who would die as Chancellor of the university, having served as a Boer guerrilla commander against the British, Prime Minister of South Africa for 13 years, a member of the British Imperial War Cabinet in 1917-18, a drafter of the Charters of both the League of Nations and the United Nations; and De Valera, of the even more improbable life story, one of the, if not the, most extraordinary in the entire history of the public affairs of the century. But if our criteria must include the number of people affected, then only Nehru could conceivably remain on a final short list, simply because of scale, his actions affecting the lives of so many more than Smuts or De Valera.

By this criterion, a prominent personality in a big country will outrank one in a small country, even though the one in the smaller country may objectively be the more remarkable. For if it were remarkable personalities we were looking for, the criteria would be far different from influential ones. Many remarkable personalities may not be influential outside very small circles. How many mothers may be truly remarkable people, but only their families will ever know?

But then, how does one assess scale even on the public stage. Who knows whom Mandela might inspire beyond South Africa? Would one rank Nehru above his patron, Gandhi, even though Gandhi never held office, as the Indian of the century? Does the light from Gandhi's star not belong to the ages – however dimly it may shine among the yuppies of India today? But then Gandhi was not only a pacifist prophet: his career subverted British power in India.

The British retreat from southern Ireland in 1922 had been an extraordinary event by world historical standards, but it made little difference to the real bases of British power, whatever its impact on the psychic income of irreconcilable imperialists. But India was different. She had been the brightest jewel in the imperial diadem. More than any other individual, Gandhi effectively broke the back of the British Empire, a tectonic shift in world history. His influence doesn't simply depend on how long his teachings serve as inspiration in a materialist culture.

Likewise the career of Martin Luther King didn't simply serve to lift American blacks off their knees. It marked a fundamental change in the ethos of American society, however much racism remains widespread among individuals. It recalled the USA to its founding principles, however often breached in the observance. It is hard for us today to conceive the intensity of American racism, particularly in the South.

Southern whites had little to learn from South Africa about the tricks of the racist trade. The shift in perspective, however incomplete, is of historic significance, for it is a perspective that affects the attitude and behaviour of all other races in the USA towards blacks. It obliges them to accept a different world view. That will never be completely achieved, at least as long as human nature remains what it is, because there will always be those who so need to feel superior that they will embrace racism. Nor does it mean that blacks themselves, any more than people of any other colour, are not capable of racism. Nevertheless the historic inheritance of racism in the USA has been smashed, however many fragments remain. And because the USA exerts world historical influence, King's achievement has implications far beyond America's borders.

But size is actually the simple bit. What about time? Supposing a once glittering reputation fades quickly or suddenly? Would that not place the personalities earlier in the century at a possible disadvantage? Ten years ago, how many still worshipped at the shrine of Lenin, or even Stalin? Today, they seem to belong with Ozymandias in the garbage bin of history. But that does not lessen the influence they wielded on the lives of multitudes. Perhaps Lenin's star will rise again. Would that enhance his ratings – even though he be the same Lenin? Suppose the handiwork of Mandela crumbles in the next century. Should he then too recede in importance?

That will not be his fault. But will it affect the perception of his legacy? Should it?

If the person has to come from a big power, because it is some sort of measurable influence, and not 'greatness' by some abstract formula, we are assessing, one could say the main event of the century has been the rise of American power. Should it not, therefore, be the president who presided over the rise of that power, Franklin Roosevelt, who should top the list? None could deny the extraordinary personality of FDR. But should one not also ask, what difference did the person make? Might one not then say that the USA was bound to rise, and it was almost incidental who happened to be president when events pulled the US into world affairs, given that the decision to intervene in World War II was made for the USA by the Japanese at Pearl Harbour and by Hitler's declaration of war? No American president could have responded other than as Roosevelt did.

Should it be a public figure at all? Few can surely query the reduction in suffering due to medical advances this century. Should then the palm be awarded to the medical profession, on the grounds that it has done most tangible good? What about, as a symbolic nominee, Dr William Osler, the Canadian doctor who died in 1919, having done more than anyone, his admirers claim, to create "a united profession working in many lands, doing more for the race than has even been accomplished by any other body of men".

Advances in medicine are presumably among the least controversial – until one confronts the claim that by keeping so many more people alive, they are threatening the very survival of the species. There are ways of responding to this claim, but it helps remind us how uncertain almost any criterion can be.

The inventor of the contraceptive pill has probably done more to alter women's lives, and consequently not only sexual behaviour, but family structures and family relations, even if the longer term consequences are still unforeseeable, than all the legislation ever passed. But as with all discoveries, even those with the most far-reaching consequences, it is not the discovery itself, but the use made of it, that determines its historical significance. Who determines the value systems which decide how the human race will respond to the choices science and technology make available?

233

What will the new century make of the possibilities opened up in genetics by Crick and Watson's discovery of the structure of DNA? The impact on values is likely to be even more profound than the impact on genetics – but who will decide, and by what criteria?

To return to the public sphere, if by the person of the century we mean the individual who made the most difference, for better or for worse, we are instantly back into 'virtual history' because our criterion then has to be what would have happened if this person had not been there. Any judgement on the significance of any individual involves judgement of likely alternatives, a truly daunting challenge, to which we will try to respond in the next chapter.

Chapter 43

Hitler: person of the century

As frightening as it was, he did have the greatest impact on the lives of the largest number of people

PICKING the person of the century becomes indulgently subjective unless one can cling to tightly specified criteria, which may of course be eternally debated. My criteria are the difference the individual made, and their impact on the lives of the largest number of people within their own lifetime and for some sort of reasonable period of time thereafter. An element of fuzziness creeps in even here, for one may well ask, what is a reasonable period of time? The reason for including it is that the further one gets away from the person, the more are other things likely to happen that blur the picture.

This criterion inevitably favours the policy maker over the thinker. It may serve to make a communist dictator the person of the 20th century, but not Marx the person of the 19th, because his ideas, real or imagined, did not directly affect people's lives until implemented. It is in any case difficult to assess the influence of thinkers. Marx was claimed as an inspiration for many policies he may have repudiated, just like Adam Smith, whose *imprimatur* Thatcherites like to invoke. Burke, for instance, enjoys periodic resurrections among politicians. But does he come into fashion from time to time because they have come to broadly similar conclusions, and are scratching around for a good quote, rather than actually having been influenced by, or even read, the original, an even more pervasive occupational hazard for thinkers in these days of speechwriters excavating books of quotations to embellish the pronouncements of their political masters and mistresses with the veneer of philosophical profundity.

It is even more difficult to gauge spiritual impact. John Paul II is clearly one of the most extraordinary personalities to have appeared on the world stage during the century. He will always feature in studies of the fall of communism. How he will feature beyond that, however, depends partly on the fortunes of the Catholic church, and more broadly on the fate of the values he champions.

These criteria, it must be readily conceded, load the scales in favour of public figures in big countries, and sadly, of those who inflict suffering and death much more than those who do good. Death, after all, is the ultimate impact on the individual, and it is so much more specific than the more diffuse concept of good.

The choice has therefore nothing to do with the intrinsic ability or attraction of the individual. In public affairs, Charles de Gaulle had not only an extraordinary career, making and remaking himself not once, but twice, in 1940 and 1958, to incarnate France. He had, too, a much more original and better stocked mind than most leaders of greater powers. But that is the rub. France was no longer a great power in de Gaulle's day. His performance could astonish and dazzle. But it did not have enough specific wider impact to qualify him by our criteria.

One would have to consider Churchill for his epic defiance of Hitler in 1940. But apart from the fact that we do not know how the alternatives would have worked out – although I adhere to the view that Churchill was right to have rejected Hitler's peace proposals in 1940, given that he would have broken any agreement as soon as it suited him – as indeed would Churchill, but it would not have suited him as soon as Hitler – the fact remains that it was by the USSR and the USA the war was decided.

Should Roosevelt and Stalin therefore joust for the prize? It is difficult to dispute Roosevelt's primacy among American claimants, not for his wartime leadership alone, for that was mixed, but for his restoration of hope to a deeply demoralised and divided society on assuming office in 1933. Who knows how ugly an already ugly situation might have become had disillusion and despair persisted?

Even Roosevelt's claims must recede, however, before those of the five dictators of the century who made the most dramatic impact on most people's lives, Lenin, Stalin, Hitler, Mao and Gorbachev. But consider here how time changes perspectives. If the USSR were still in existence, Lenin's claims would rank very high indeed. His supporters could claim he virtually brought a new world into existence, and launched the political career of a doctrine which dominated the lives of one-third of the world's population, and influenced, if only in reaction, the lives of very many more.

Stalin's star too would shine brighter if the USSR had survived. In contrast to Lenin, Stalin did not create a new regime. He inherited a party in power, even if he had to claw his way to the top within it. Even without Stalin, dramatic change was likely to have occurred in the USSR of the time. Whether it would have left the USSR stronger or weaker must be a matter of surmise. Some might even wish to argue that when his legacy can be fully assessed, Stalin will be found to have lost Russia time both in terms of global power and of human development, and at a horrific human cost to boot.

Maybe the same will come to be said of Mao, although his claims will depend in large measure on what happens China in the new century. It remains unclear whether the dreadful price millions of Chinese have paid for his indifference to human life will yield many enduring benefits that could not have been achieved at a less savage cost. But the alternative was probably a bloody shambles and if China does turn into an economic and military superpower under Communist auspices his name may loom large, his millions of victims either forgotten, or deemed an acceptable price to pay.

Gorbachev's position is different. His crucial decision in principle was not to use force to sustain Soviet control of the satellites. That was an extraordinary decision by world historical standards. It certainly marked the end of an era, and carried within it the seeds of the destruction of the Soviet Union itself. Who knows what the ultimate consequences will be? All one can say is that it was a historic decision, which probably only a handful, if that, of people in the same position would have taken. It has already left its imprint on world history, and may affect the fate of millions unborn. But we cannot risk peering too far ahead.

That brings us, inescapably, to Hitler. The difference he made cannot be disputed. If anything can be safely surmised in history, it is that without Hitler, who was effectively, unlike Stalin, his own creator, nazism would not have triumphed in Germany. Had Hitler never gone to war, his regime would still have been remarkable. If we credit Roosevelt with restoring hope in the USA, we must credit Hitler with restoring hope in Germany, sharply reducing unemployment even before his rearmament drive. Who knows how international affairs would have developed but for him? Germany might well have embarked on an expansionist policy under alternative, presumably military, leadership. But it is difficult to believe it would have embarked on such high risk gambles as Hitler. Would Stalin in the 1940s, for instance, have felt confident enough to have launched strikes of his own, or would he have concentrated to the end on 'building socialism in one country'?

What we do know is that Hitler set the pace and determined the framework within which others would have to react, in a manner unmatched by any other political figure of the century. It was he who introduced genocide on biological grounds into European history – not that Europeans had not indulged genocidal impulses in the colonies, but without formulating the biological determinism of Hitler as a basis of policy. Even if the number of his victims was less than that of Stalin, the basis of their extermination was even more chilling. Communism too involved the principle of mass slaughter, but the definition of legitimate victim was a shade more flexible. If the price paid by Hitler's victims was frightening, what would his victory have meant?

Hitler's legacy determined the map of world power long after his death. It also happened to undermine the attraction of racism in western culture. It is unfashionable now to recall how racist much of western thought was before Hitler. References to caucasians and aryans litter the literature of empire. Think of the Reverend John Laputa in John Buchan's *Prester John*, or of Rider Haggard's *Queen Sheba's Ring*. The concept of negroid-Jew had become pervasive in European literature. The eugenics movement, with its obsession with 'improving' the race, its breeding programmes to produce better 'stock', breathed the same foetid air. Inferior types should be weeded out. Churchill himself often sniffed from the same pot, without fully inhaling, of course.

Hitler made all that line of thinking unfashionable for at least a generation. But it was touch and go whether it was racism or communism that would become public enemy number one in the West. Many would have preferred Hitler to have been on 'our' side against Stalin, not because Stalin's crimes were far more heinous before 1939, but because racism caused them far less concern than communism's perceived threat. It was only in retrospect, given the glorious propaganda opportunities provided by the pictures of the concentration camps, that the war became a war to end racism. It could hardly be claimed to be one to end communism, given the wartime alliance with Stalin. But once the war was proclaimed a crusade against racism, it became more awkward to sustain racist doctrine, including anti-semitism, at home. It is doubtful, for instance, if the move towards Civil Rights in the USA could have made as much progress but for the USA being hoist on the petard of its own anti-racist rhetoric.

Intense though the competition be, it is for these and similar reasons that it seems to me Hitler has the strongest claim, however frighteningly, to be considered the person of the 20th century – in so many ways the greatest, in so many the most terrible, of all centuries.

Chronology of the 20th Century

1900   Boxer Rebellion in China.

1901   Commonwealth of Australia established.
Boxer Rebellion crushed by consortium of western powers.

1902   Britain and Japan enter into Anglo-Japanese Alliance.
Treaty of Vereeniging brings Anglo-Boer war to an end.

1903   Assassination of King Alexander of Serbia, leading to expansionist Serb policy.

1904   Russo-Japanese war begins.
Entente Cordiale between Britain and France.

1905   Japan defeats Russia at Port Arthur. Revolution in Russia leading to
Tsarist acceptance of constitutional government in October Manifesto.
Sweden concedes independence peacefully to Norway.

1906   Election of first parliament *(Duma)* in Russia.
Labour Party formed in Britain
Muslim League formed in India.
Finland becomes first European country to introduce female suffrage.

1907   Anglo-Russian Convention regulating their respective spheres of
influence in Asia.

1908   Young Turk revolt.
Habsburgs annex Bosnia-Herzegovina.

1909   National Association for the Advancement of Colored People (NAACP)
established in USA.

1910   Union of South Africa established.
Japan annexes Korea.
Portuguese monarchy overthrown and Republic proclaimed.

1911   Agadir Crisis between France and Germany (Second Moroccan Crisis).
Chinese Revolution overthrows Manchu Dynasty.

1912   Sun Yat-Sen becomes provisional President of Chinese Republic, but superceded
by a warlord.
Alliance of Balkan states launches war against Ottoman Empire.
Woodrow Wilson elected President of the USA.
South African Native National Congress established (later African National
Congress, ANC).

1913   Balkan Wars drive Ottoman Empire out of most of Balkans, and lead to Serbian
expansion.

1914   First World War breaks out.
Battle of the Marne halts German advance on Paris. Battles of Tannenberg
and the Masurian Lakes halt Russian advance into Germany.

1915 Sinking of Lusitania by German submarine.

Secret Sykes-Picot Agreement on post-war carve-up of Middle East between Britain and France.

Italy enters war on Anglo-French side.

Turkish mass slaughter of Armenians.

1916 Battle of Verdun.

Easter Rebellion in Ireland crushed by British.

Battle of Jutland.

Sharif Hussein launches Arab revolt against Ottoman rule with British support in Arabia.

Battle of the Somme.

Germany becomes virtual military dictatorship under Ludendorff.

Home Rule Leagues established in India.

Woodrow Wilson re-elected President of USA.

1917 Germany launches unrestricted submarine warfare.

Russian Revolution breaks out.

Tsar Nicholas II abdicates.

USA enters war against Germany and Austria-Hungary.

Kerensky offensive collapses. Russian army begins to fade away.

Bolshevik Revolution under Lenin in Russia.

Balfour Declaration in favour of a Jewish homeland in Palestine.

Finland declares independence from Russia.

1918 President Woodrow Wilson proclaims his 14 points plan for peace and reconstruction.

Germany imposes punitive Treaty of Brest-Litovsk on Russia.

Russian civil war breaks out, lasting until end of 1920. Western aid for counter-revolutionary Whites proves futile.

Whites under General Mannerheim defeat Reds in Finnish Civil War.

Ludendorff's Spring offensive halted in France.

Western Allies counter-offensive begins.

Habsburg Empire disintegrates.

Turkey agrees to armistice.

German Revolution: Kaiser Wilhelm II abdicates.

Germany signs Armistice to end First World War. Germany becomes a republic.

Austria, Poland, Hungary, Czechoslovakia, Yugoslavia, Estonia, Latvia, Lithuania become independent states during next year.

Female suffrage for first time in a British General Election.

1919 Assassination of Zapata, Mexican peasant leader.

Amritsar massacre of 300 Indian demonstrators by British forces.

Whites unleash anti-Jewish pogroms in Kiev.

Treaty of Versailles.

War victors impose treaty of St Germain on Austria.

Female suffrage introduced in USA.

Trotsky counterattacks White Army at Petrograd.

Lenin establishes the Comintern to promote world communist revolution.

1920 League of Nations established.

Gandhi launches civil disobedience campaign in India.

Polish-Russian war begins.

War victors impose Treaty of Trianon on Hungary.

Pilsudski defeats Tukhachevsky at Warsaw.

War victors impose Treaty of Sèvres on Turkey. Mustafa Kemal I (later Atatürk) leads Turkish resistance.

Bolsheviks win Russian Civil War.

British Government of Ireland Act partitions Ireland.

1921 Kronstadt rebellion crushed by Bolsheviks in Russia.

Anglo-Irish Treaty.

1922 Lenin suffers serious stroke. Stalin becomes General Secretary of Communist Party.

Michael Collins killed in ambush in Irish Civil War.

Mustafa Kemal abolishes Ottoman Sultanate.

Expulsion of Greeks from Turkey.

Lloyd George deposed as British Prime Minister in favour of Andrew Bonar Law.

Mussolini appointed PM of Italy by King Victor Emmanuel.

1923 French occupy Ruhr.

Gustav Stresemann, German foreign minister 1923-9, pursues conciliatory policy towards western powers

Free State Government wins Irish Civil War

Turkey declared a Republic, with Kemal as first President

Treaty of Lausanne recognises Turkish Republic

'Exchange' of ethnic populations between Greece and Turkey

General Primo de Rivera establishes dictatorship in Spain.

Ramsay MacDonald becomes first British Labour Prime Minister.

Hitler launches failed coup in Munich

German inflation reaches its peak. Old currency abolished, and new currency accepted by public, ending inflation.

1924 Lenin dies. Succession struggle in USSR between Stalin and Trotsky.

Greek Republic proclaimed.

Murder of opposition deputy Giacomo Matteoti by Fascists in Italy.

1925 Stalin wins succession struggle.

Locarno Conference guarantees existing boundaries of France, Belgium and Germany.

1926 Reza Khan proclaims new Pahlavi dynasty in Iran.

Defeat of General Strike in Britain.

Pilsudski becomes dictator of Poland.

Chiang Kai-shek leads campaigns to rescue China from rule by warlords.

1927 Trotsky expelled from Soviet Communist Party.

1928 Stalin launches first Five Year Plan in USSR.

Chiang Kai-shek becomes President of China.

Muslim Brotherhood established.

1929 Lateran Treaties recognise Vatican as a state.

Arab-Jewish conflict in Jerusalem.

Revolutionary National Party established in Mexico, holds power for rest of century.

Gandhi begins Salt March, campaign of civil disobedience in India.

Stalin launches forced collectivisation of farms in Soviet Union.

1930 Parliamentary Democracy collapses in Weimar Germany. Heinrich Bruening becomes Chancellor, ruling by emergency decree.

General Primo de Rivera resigns in Spain.

1931 Japan invades Manchuria.

King Alfonso XIII abdicates in Spain. Second Spanish Republic declared.

Britain abandons Gold Standard. National Government under Ramsay Macdonald comes into office.

Statute of Westminster recognises Dominions right to self-government within British Empire.

British imprison Gandhi.

1932 De Valera elected President of the Executive Council of Irish Free State.

Franklin D Roosevelt elected President of USA.

1933 Adolf Hitler appointed Chancellor of Germany.

Enabling Law invests Hitler with dictatorial powers.

Roosevelt launches 'New Deal'.

Germany formally becomes one party state.

1934 Night of Long Knives in Germany.

Hitler proclaims Third Reich, with himself as Fuehrer.

Chinese Communist Long March begins.

Assassination of Kirov. Stalin launches mass purges.

1935 German troops reoccupy Rhineland.

Hitler introduces conscription in Germany.

Pilsudski dies. Succeeded by a Colonels regime in Poland.

Nuremberg Laws against Jews introduced.

1936 Popular Front government in France under Leon Blum.

Italy annexes Abyssinia.

Generals rebel against Republic, beginning Spanish Civil War.

Stalin begins show trials in Moscow.

Germany and Japan sign anti-Comintern Pact.

1937 German bombing of Guernica.

Italy joins anti-Comintern Pact.

Japan invades China.

'Rape of Nanking'.

1938 Hitler annexes Austria *(Anschluss)*.

Munich Agreement conceding Sudetenland to Germany.

Atatürk dies.

Kristallnacht.

1939 Germany annexes Czechoslovakia.

Franco captures Madrid. End of Spanish Civil War.

Anglo-French guarantee to Poland.

Nazi-Soviet Pact to partition Poland.

Germany invades Poland.

Britain and France declare war on Germany.

USSR invades Poland.

USSR occupies Estonia, Latvia, Lithuania.

USSR attacks Finland.

1940 Finnish-Russian Peace Treaty.

Germany invades Denmark and Norway.

Winston Churchill succeeds Neville Chamberlain as British Prime Minister.

Hitler attacks Netherlands, Belgium and France.

Dunkirk.

Italy declares war on Britain and France.

De Gaulle flies to London.

Armistice between France and Germany.

Battle of Britain.

German bombing of London begins the 'Blitz'.

1941 US Congress authorises Lend-Lease programme of aid to Britain.

Germany invades Yugoslavia and Greece.

Germany invades USSR.

Roosevelt and Churchill issue Atlantic Charter, listing post-war aims.

Japan attacks USA.at Pearl Harbour.

USA declares war on Japan.

Germany declares war of USA.

1942 Wannsee conference to plan genocide of European Jews.

British surrender to Japanese at Singapore.

USA interns Japanese Americans.

Admiral Nimitz defeats Admiral Yamomoto at Midway.

Montgomery defeats Rommel at el Alamein.

1943 Roosevelt and Churchill announce unconditional surrender policy at Casablanca Conference.

Field Marshall Paulus surrenders at Stalingrad.

Bombing of Hamburg.

USSR defeats Germans at Kursk in biggest tank battle in history.

US and Britain invade Italy. Fall of Mussolini. Germans occupy Italy.

Bengal Famine in India – last major Famine in British controlled territory.

Tehran conference. Churchill proposes Stalin annex Polish territory post war, and Poland annex German territory.

1944   Siege of Leningrad ends after more than two years and one million dead.

Rome captured by western allies.

D-Day. Western Allied forces under General Eisenhower invade France.

Assassination attempt on Hitler fails.

Warsaw Rising.

De Gaulle establishes Provisional French Government.

1945   Yalta Conference.

Bombing of Dresden.

Bombing of Tokyo.

Death of Roosevelt. Succeeded by Harry Truman.

Mussolini executed by Italian partisans.

Hitler commits suicide.

Official German surrender.

United Nations Charter signed at San Francisco.

Labour defeat Conservatives in British General Election, with Clement
Attlee succeeding Churchill as Prime Minister.

Potsdam Conference.

Atom bombs dropped on Hiroshima and Nagasaki.

Japan declares intention to surrender.

President Truman ends Lend-Lease to Britain.

Formal Japanese surrender.

Coalition government under Christian Democrat Alcide de Gasperi comes to
power in Italy.

Nuremberg War Crimes Trial begins.

Tito declares Republic of Yugoslavia.

1946   De Gaulle resigns as Head of French Government.

Tokyo War Crimes Trial begins.

Chinese Civil War between Mao Zedong's Communists and Chiang Kai-shek's
Nationalists breaks out.

Juan Peron elected President of Argentina.

Italy abolishes monarchy in plebiscite, becoming Republic.

Ho Chi Minh launches revolt in 'French Indochina' against French occupation.

1947   George Marshall's Harvard Speech announcing idea of Marshall Plan.

India under Nehru and Pakistan under Jinnah established, as British withdraw
from India.

Mass slaughter in Kashmir.

Greek Civil War between communists and royalists leads to Truman Doctrine.

1948   Gandhi assassinated by Hindu fanatic.

Tito breaks with Stalin.

Czechoslovakian Communist coup.

State of Israel proclaimed.

Stalin imposes Berlin blockade. Truman responds with Berlin Airlift.

Afrikaner National Party wins election in South Africa and institutionalises apartheid.

Malayan communist revolt begins.

1949 USSR becomes atomic power.

Ireland becomes Republic and leaves British Commonwealth.

India become Republic but remains in British Commonwealth.

NATO established.

Stalin lifts Berlin blockade.

Federal German Republic (West Germany) established. Konrad Adenauer elected Chancellor.

German Democratic Republic (East Germany) established.

Mao proclaims Peoples' Republic of China as Chiang Kai-shek driven to Taiwan.

Hungary taken over by Communists.

Indonesia wins independence from Holland after post-war conflict.

1950 Robert Schuman, French Foreign Minister, proposes 'Schuman Plan', devised by Jean Monnet, for pooling of French and West German resources to form European Coal and Steel Community.

China occupies Tibet.

North Korea invades South Korea. USA leads response.

1951 Mohammed Mossadeq becomes Prime Minister of Iran, and nationalises oil.

Truman dismisses General MacArthur for advocating use of atomic weapons against China.

Conservatives win British General election, with Churchill succeeding Attlee.

1952 Egyptian Revolution overthrows King Farouk after British troops kill police.

Mau Mau rebellion breaks out in Kenya.

Britain becomes atomic power.

USA tests hydrogen bomb.

Dwight D Eisenhower elected President of USA.

1953 Stalin dies from stroke. Malenkov succeeds.

Mossadeq overthrown in British and American organised coup. Shah resumes control in Iran.

Korean War ends.

USSR tests hydrogen bomb.

Malenkov and Khruschev, General Secretary of Communist Party of USSR, have Beria, secret police chief, shot.

1954 French surrender to General Giap at Dien Bien Phu. Vietnam partitioned into North and South.

Col Gamal Abdel Nasser supplants figurehead Gen Neguib as Egyptian President.

US Supreme Court declares segregation in public schools unconstitutional.

Algerian insurrection begins.

French Assembly rejects European Defence Community.

1955 EOKA insurrection begins in Cyprus against British rule, seeking union with Greece.

Four Power Occupation of Austria ends. Austrian neutrality declared.

West Germany joins NATO.

Warsaw Pact established.

Military coup ousts President Peron in Argentina.

Churchill resigns as British Prime Minister, succeeded by Anthony Eden.

Boycott of buses by blacks in Montgomery, Alabama, after Rosa
Parks refuses to surrender her seat to a white man.

1956 Sudan declares independence.

Khruschev denounces Stalin in 'Secret Speech' at Party Congress.

Morocco becomes independent from France.

British deport Archbishop Makarios, Cypriot Greek leader, to Seychelles.

Gomulka comes to power in Poland.

Hungarian Revolt. Crushed by Soviet forces.

Attack on Egypt by British, French and Israeli forces following nationalisation of
Suez Canal by President Nasser. Invasion crumbles under US pressure.

Eisenhower re-elected President of USA.

1957 Harold Macmillan succeeds Anthony Eden as British PM following Suez fiasco.

Treaty of Rome establishes European Economic Community.

Gold Coast becomes independent as Ghana under Kwame Nkrumah.

Federal troops compel desegregation of public schools in Little Rock.

USSR launches intercontinental ballistic missile, and puts Sputnik into orbit.

1958 European Economic Community comes into existence.

General Charles de Gaulle becomes Prime Minister of France. Fourth Republic
succeeded by Fifth Republic with new 'Presidential' Constitution, with de Gaulle
elected first President.

Eamon de Valera resigns as Taoiseach of Irish Republic. Succeeded by Lemass.

Monarchy overthrown in Iraq.

Khruschev provokes Second Berlin Crisis, demanding withdrawal of all western
forces from Berlin.

Mao's Great Leap Forward.

Death of Pope Pius XII, succeeded by Cardinal Roncalli as Pope John XXIII.

1959 Fidel Castro enters Havana in triumph as Batista dictatorship ousted – and
establishes his own, but at least initially more popular, dictatorship.

Chinese crush Tibetan Revolt. Sino-Indian border war. Dalai Lama flees to India.

Cyprus become republic under presidency of Archbishop Makarios.

1960 Congo Crisis.

Harold Macmillan's 'wind of change' speech in South Africa.

France's first atomic test.

Sharpeville Massacre of at least 60 peaceful demonstrators by police
in South Africa.

Nigeria becomes independent.

John F Kennedy elected President of USA.

Chaos of Mao's Great Leap Forward causes massive famine in parts of China.

1961 USA severs diplomatic relations with Cuba.

Sino-Soviet public split.
Britain applies for entry to EEC.
Bay of Pigs invasion of Cuba.
East Germany builds Berlin Wall.

1962 Algeria becomes independent.

Second Vatican Council begins.
Cuban Missile Crisis.
Yuri Gagarin becomes first man in space.

1963 President de Gaulle vetoes British application for entry to EEC.

Franco-German Friendship Treaty.
Death of Pope John XXIII. Succeeded by Cardinal Montini as Pope Paul VI.
Adenauer resigns as German Chancellor, succeeded by Ludwig Erhard.
US President Kennedy assassinated. Lyndon Johnson succeeds .

1964 Palestine Liberation Organisation (PLO) established.

Civil Rights Act in USA.
Labour defeat Conservatives in British General election for first time since 1951,
with Harold Wilson becoming Prime Minister.
Khruschev deposed in USSR. Leonid Brezhnev succeeds.
Lyndon Johnson elected President of USA.

1965 Indo-Pakistani war over Kashmir.

Army under General Suharto assumes de facto power in crushing attempted
communist/junior officer coup in Indonesia.

1966 Mao launches Great Cultural Revolution, which paralyses China for several
years.
'Great Coalition' in West Germany under Kiesinger allows Social Democrat
participation in government for first time since 1930, with Willy Brandt as
Foreign Minister.

1967 Nigerian Civil War begins.

Military coup in Greece inaugurates brutal dictatorship.
Israel defeats Arabs in Six Day War.
Harold Wilson announces withdrawal of Britain from 'east of Suez', except for
Hong Kong.

1968 Alexander Dubcek appointed First Secretary of the Czechoslovak Communist
party. 'Prague Spring' follows.
Martin Luther King assassinated.
Student and worker demonstrations in Paris.
Robert F Kennedy assassinated.
Richard Nixon elected President of USA.

1969 Nixon appoints Henry Kissinger his chief foreign policy strategist.

Soviet-Chinese border conflicts.
President de Gaulle resigns. Georges Pompidou later elected as successor.
Yasser Arafat becomes leader of PLO.
Neil Armstrong first human to set foot on moon.

First deaths in latest Northern Ireland Troubles.

Muammar al-Qaddafi comes to power through coup in Libya.

Strategic Arms Limitation Talks between USA and USSR begin.

Social Democrats become main party in government in Germany for first time since 1930, in coalition with Free Democrats, with Willy Brandt as Chancellor.

1970 Nigerian Civil War ends with defeat of Ibo breakaway state of Biafra.

US invasion of Cambodia.

Salvador Allende elected President of Chile.

President Nasser of Egypt dies suddenly. Succeeded by Anwar Sadat.

Edward Heath becomes Prime Minister of Britain as Conservatives win Election.

Willy Brandt pursues a conciliatory *Ostpolitik* towards eastern european states, including East Germany, and recognises Oder-Neisse frontier with Poland.

1971 Civil War in Pakistan, with East Pakistan becoming independent as Bangladesh.

Kissinger's secret visit to Beijing to arrange Nixon's visit.

1972 'Bloody Sunday' in Derry. British paratroopers kill 14 demonstrators. Britain subsequently suspends Stormont parliament and assumes direct responsibility for Northern Irish affairs.

President Nixon visits China.

Nixon and Brezhnev sign Strategic Arms Limitation Treaty (SALT).

1973 Britain, Ireland and Denmark join EEC.

US agrees to Paris Accords, providing for withdrawal from Vietnam.

Coup led by Gen Pinochet overthrows and kills President Allende in Chile. Torture regime begins.

Willy Brandt resigns as German Chancellor following spy scandal, succeeded by Helmut Schmidt.

Valery Giscard d'Estaing elected President of France in succession to Georges Pompidou who died in office.

Israel defeats Egypt and Syria in Yom Kippur War. Arab oil producers organise oil embargo of west in retaliation for American support for Israel. 'Oil crisis' follows.

1974 Richard Nixon resigns as President of USA under threat of impeachment over Watergate affair. Gerald Ford succeeds as President.

Military dictatorship in Greece collapses following abortive coup in Cyprus. Constantine Karamanlis returns from exile to be elected PM, 1974-80.

India becomes nuclear power.

Alexander Solzhenitsyn driven into exile from USSR for publishing *The Gulag Archipelago*.

1975 North Vietnam captures Saigon and unites all Vietnam under Hanoi regime.

Communist Khmer Rouge conquer Cambodia, initiating mass state terror, murdering possibly up to two million victims.

Indonesia occupies East Timor.

General Franco dies. Parliamentary democracy established in Spain with monarchy restored under King Juan Carlos, with Adolfo Suarez as Prime

Minister (1976-81).

1976 Col Ramalho Eanes becomes Portugal's first democratically elected President since Antonio Salazar assumed power in 1933. Mario Soares becomes Socialist Prime Minister.

Mao Zedong dies.

Military regime in Argentina tortures and murders thousands in 'dirty war'.

Jimmy Carter elected President of the USA.

1977 Charter 77 Declaration in Czechoslovakia, challenging government of Gustav Husak to honour human rights accords.

1978 Aldo Moro, Christian Democrat PM of Italy, kidnapped by Red Brigades and later murdered.

Deng Xiaoping wins power struggle in China to succeed Mao.

President Sadat of Egypt and Prime Minister Begin of Israel sign Camp David Accords.

Cardinal Karol Wojtyla of Krakow becomes first non-Italian Pope since 1522 as John Paul II following deaths during year of Popes Paul VI and John Paul I.

1979 Vietnamese invasion overthrows Khmer Rouge regime in Cambodia.

China and USA establish diplomatic relations.

Ayatollah Khomeini returns to Iran, Shah overthrown by popular revolt.

Margaret Thatcher becomes British Prime Minister.

1980 Iraq under Saddam Hussein invades Iran. Murderous war lasts eight years.

Solidarity Labour movement emerges under Lech Walesa in Poland.

Rhodesia becomes independent as Zimbabwe under Robert Mugabe.

Quebec votes to remain part of Canada.

Death of Marshall Tito.

Ronald Reagan elected President of USA.

1981 Greek Socialist Party, PASOK, comes to power under Andreas Papandreou.

Greece enters EEC.

IRA hunger strikes in Northern Ireland.

Francois Mitterrand elected President of France.

Indonesian suppression of East Timor rebels.

President Sadat of Egypt assassinated by Muslim fundamentalist.

General Jaruszelski declares Martial Law in Poland.

1982 Britain defeats Argentina in Falklands War. Military Junta in Argentina discredited.

Helmut Kohl displaces Helmut Schmidt as Chancellor of Federal Republic of Germany.

First Socialist government, with Felipe Gonzales as PM, elected in Spain since Civil War.

Brezhnev dies. Succeeded by Yuri Andropov.

1983 Kohl's Christian Democrats win German general election. Green Party wins first seats in Bundestag.

Mrs Thatcher re-elected British Prime Minister with increased majority

President Reagan announces Star Wars Initiative (Strategic Defense initiative).

Raul Alfonsin wins general election in Argentina, superceding military junta.

1984 Andropov dies. Succeeded by Chernenko.

Indira Gandhi assassinated

1985 Jacques Delors becomes President of EEC Commission, and driving force behind renewed impetus to European integration.

Chernenko dies. Succeeded by Mikhail Gorbachev.

Helsinki Accords purport to legitimise the territorial status quo in Europe, and to promote respect for human rights.

1986 Chernobyl nuclear disaster.

Spain and Portugal join EEC.

President Marcos flees from Philippines. Succeeded by Corazon Aquino.

Andrei Sakharov released from house arrest.

1987 Chinese suppress Tibet rebellion.

USA and USSR sign treaty to eliminate intermediate range nuclear missiles.

Palestinian *Intifada* against Israel.

Thatcher wins third successive general election.

Single European Act to foster increased economic integration through creating free internal market for all factors of production.

1988 Francois Mitterrand re-elected President of France.

Iran-Iraq war ends.

Soviet army begins withdrawal from Afghanistan.

Chile votes 55% against proposal to renew Pinochet as President.

George Bush elected president of the USA.

1989 Chinese troops massacre pro-democracy demonstrators in Tiananmen Square.

FW de Klerk elected President of South Africa.

Communist rule collapses in Soviet satellites in eastern Europe.

Berlin Wall torn down.

Nicolae Ceausescu and his wife. Elena, executed in Romania.

Vaclav Havel elected President of Czechoslovakia.

1990 Lithuania declares independence.

Nelson Mandela released from prison. Negotiates end of apartheid with FW de Klerk.

Iraqi forces of Saddam Hussein invade Kuwait.

Reunification of Germany

Margaret Thatcher forced to resign as British PM. Succeeded by John Major.

Lech Walesa elected President of Poland.

1991 Gulf War. USA leads alliance to defeat Iraq.

Warsaw Pact dissolved.

Boris Yeltsin elected President of Russia.

Yugoslavia crisis begins with Slovenia and Croatia declaring independence, Serbia attacking Croatia.

Maastricht Treaty launches major steps toward further European integration.

Failed communist coup against Gorbachev.

Gorbachev resigns as President of USSR, and USSR dissolved.

Japanese economic performance begins to deteriorate significantly.

1992 Bosnia-Herzegovina declares independence. Serb regime promotes savage war.

Bill Clinton elected President of USA.

1993 Dissolution of Czechoslovakia into Czech Republic and Slovakia.

Oslo Peace Accords on Israeli-Palestinian conflict.

Maastricht Treaty intended to promote European integration begins to come into effect.

1994 Silvio Berlusconi, TV tycoon, becomes Prime Minister of Italy.

Nelson Mandela elected President of South Africa.

Genocide in Rwanda.

Russia invades Chechnya.

1995 Serbs massacre Muslims at Srbrenica. NATO bombs Serb positions, leading later in year to Dayton Peace Accords.

Jacques Chirac elected President of France in succession to Francois Mitterrand.

Israeli troops begin withdrawal from West Bank.

Assassination of Yitzhak Rabin, conciliatory Prime Minister of Israel, by right wing Jewish fundamentalists.

1996 Benjamin Netanyahu elected Prime Minister of Israel.

1997 Labour under Tony Blair defeats Conservatives under John Major in British General Election to form first Labour Government since 1979.

Death of Deng Xiaoping.

Good Friday peace agreement in Northern Ireland brokered by Sen George Mitchell.

Britain returns Hong Kong to China.

Death of Princess Diana of Britain in car accident inspires popular display of grief for her. Death of Mother Teresa of Calcutta does not.

Hindu Janata Party wins Indian General Election.

South East Asian financial crisis.

Austria, Finland and Sweden join European Union.

1998 General Suharto resigns as President of Indonesia after 33 years in power following riots.

Gerhard Schroeder elected Chancellor of Germany in succession to Helmut Kohl as first Social Democrat Chancellor since 1982, in coalition with Greens.

1999 Common currency for 11 member states of European Union, the Euro, comes into operation.

NATO bombing of Serbia in retaliation against Serbian repression in Kosovo.

Ehud Barak defeats Benjamin Netanyahu to become Prime Minister of Israel.

Further reading

This is a short selection of the books I found useful, or from which I quoted, in composing these essays, augmented by some relevant subsequent publications.

General studies

Blanning, TCW (ed),   *Oxford Illustrated History of Modern Europe* (Oxford, 1996)

Hobsbawn, Eric,   *Age of Extremes. The Short Twentieth Century, 1917-1991* (London, 1994)

Howard, Michael and Louis, W Roger,
      The Oxford History of the Twentieth Century (Oxford, 1998)

Joll, James,   *Europe since 1870* (London, 1990 ed)

Kennedy, Paul,   *The Rise and Fall of the Great Powers* (New York, 1987)

Mazower, Mark,   *Dark Continent: Europe's Twentieth Century* (London, 1998)

Reynolds, David,   *One World Divisible: A Global History since 1945* (London, 2000)

Roberts, John M,   *Twentieth Century: The History of the World, 1901-2000* (London, 1999)

Particular topics

Acheson, Dean,   *Present at the Creation* (New York, 1969)

Alter, Peter,   *The German Question and Europe* (London 2000)

Andrew, Christopher, *The Sword and the Shield. The Mitrokhin Archive and the secret history of the KGB* (London, 1999)

Ash, Timothy Garton, *The Uses of Adversity* (Cambridge, 1989)
In Europe's Name: Germany and the Divided Continent (London, 1993)

Bartov, Omar, *Hitler's Army* (Oxford, 1991)

Bethell, Nicholas, *The War Hitler Won* (London, 1972)

Billington, James H, *Russia Transformed: Breakthrough to Hope: Moscow, August 1991* (New York, 1992)

Blake, Robert and Louis, Wm. Roger (eds),
Churchill (Oxford, 1994)

Bond, Brian, *Britain, France and Belgium, 1939-40* (London, 1990)

Brown, Archie, *The Gorbachev Factor* (Oxford, 1996)

Brown, Judith M, *India. The Origins of an Asian Democracy* (Oxford, 1994)
Gandhi: Prisoner of Hope (London, 1989)

Browning, Christopher, *Ordinary Men: Reserve Police Battalion 101 and the Final Solution in Poland* (New York, 1992)

Bullock, Alan, *Hitler and Stalin: Parallel Lives* (London, 1991)

Bundy, McGeorge, *Danger and Survival: Choices about the Bomb in the first fifty years* (New York, 1988)

Burleigh, Michael, *The Third Reich* (London, 2000)

Chang, Iris, *The Rape of Nanking: the forgotten holocaust of World War II* (New York, 1997)

Charmley, John, *Churchill: The end of glory. A political biography* (London, 1993)

Churchill, Winston S, *Second World War* (London, 1948)

Clarke, Peter, *Hope and Glory: Britain 1900-1990* (London, 1996)

Cowling, Maurice, *The Impact of Hitler: British Politics and British Policy, 1933-1940* (Cambridge, 1975)

De Gaulle, Charles, *War Memoirs* (London, 1955)